Human Service Pr
Through a Social Justice Lens

Human Service Program Planning Through a Social Justice Lens provides a foundation in social justice to students while developing practical skills and knowledge about the steps and tasks involved in planning social programs.

Through the "parallel process" of contextualizing social issues while teaching the process of program planning, students will develop a perspective on the need for social justice planning and its impact on marginalized communities and populations. The textbook explores current concepts and approaches to understanding social issues and involving impacted communities and individuals. These include: Intersectionality, Appreciative Inquiry, Participatory Planning and Visioning, which serve to challenge preconceptions while coupling these with the step-by-step approach to planning using the Logic Model.

Utilizing meaningful examples to demonstrate how social justice planning can be implemented, *Human Service Program Planning Through a Social Justice Lens* is appropriate for students of social work as well as practitioners in human services, public administration and public health.

Irwin Nesoff served as a non profit executive for fifteen years before joining the social work faculty at Kean University in New Jersey. He later joined the faculty at Wheelock College in Boston where he taught social work before becoming the founding chairperson of the Department of Leadership and Policy. He holds a Doctorate in Social Welfare awarded by the City University of New York Graduate Center.

Human Service Program Planning Through a Social Justice Lens

Irwin Nesoff

NEW YORK AND LONDON

Cover image: © Irwin Nesoff

First published 2022
by Routledge
605 Third Avenue, New York, NY 10158

and by Routledge
4 Park Square, Milton Park, Abingdon, Oxon, OX14 4RN

Routledge is an imprint of the Taylor & Francis Group, an informa business

Library of Congress Cataloging-in-Publication Data
A catalog record for this title has been requested

ISBN: 9780367709754 (hbk)
ISBN: 9780367709761 (pbk)
ISBN: 9781003148777 (ebk)

DOI: 10.4324/9781003148777

Typeset in Times New Roman
by codeMantra

Support Material is available for this title at
www.routledge.com/9780367709761

This book is dedicated to

**Paula Nesoff, my life partner, muse and inspiration.
Forever and…**

and

The young activists of the Movement for Black Lives and the Sunrise Movement. You give me hope for a future built on social justice.

Contents

Figures

Introduction

Social work and human service programs are about positive change – changing the conditions of people's lives and changing systems and institutions. Students and practitioners go into this field with the hopes of making an improvement in the world, no matter how small. When human service programs are based in social justice concepts the focus is on social inequities rather than social problems. When we identify an issue as a problem, the door is left open to place the blame, or the locus of the problem, on the individuals or groups experiencing it. However, when these issues are viewed as social inequities, the target of human service interventions is addressing the inequity that manifests as a social problem. This changes the focus from services based on changing and improving individual lives, to one with a dual purpose – addressing policies and conditions contributing to the inequity and services to improve the lives of the individuals disadvantaged by it.

Teaching social work and organizational leadership on the undergraduate and graduate levels for twenty-five years in programs with a focus on social justice, I found students could not define the term, in spite of identifying this as a strongly held belief. Understanding social justice provides a foundation for human service workers to work with people to change the conditions disadvantaging them. While teaching program planning, I reviewed dozens of social work and human services texts designed to teach the mechanics of program planning. However, I was unable to locate any program planning textbooks with a focus on social justice. Even more discouraging, these books contained no mention of social justice. I firmly believe it is not possible to effectively plan and implement human service programs without incorporating social justice into the work.

Based on the foundational belief that human service program planning cannot be separated from an approach incorporating social justice, the intent of this textbook is to fill that void by providing context for addressing social inequities through a social justice perspective. Ella Baker, founder of the Student Nonviolent Coordinating Committee and civil rights activist, summed up the need for a social justice perspective in 1969,

> the system under which we now exist has to be radically changed. This means we have to learn to think in radical terms. I use the

> word radical in its original meaning – getting down to and understanding the root cause. It means facing a system that does not lend itself to your needs and devising means by which you change that system.
>
> (Moses, 2001, p. 3)

Knowledge and understanding of social justice provide a strong foundation for addressing the inequities that disadvantage far too many people in our society. This text serves as a guide to developing the knowledge and understanding of program planning within the context of social justice, with the aim of helping students and practitioners address and challenge inequities through human services program implementation. Nevaeh Johnson, a fifteen-year-old Teen Designer at Artists for Humanity, a social justice-focused program located in Boston, eloquently contextualized the importance of gathering the knowledge needed to effect change when they stated,

> Know your facts, use your facts, and speak your truth. As a society, if we are going to demand change, then you need to know what the change that you demand is. You need to know specifically what you want to change. How do you want to change it and what you want as the results of that change? Otherwise, you're just fighting – which is ineffective to the cause. Arming yourself with knowledge about what's happening, is the most powerful and the most helpful thing you can do for everyone.
>
> (quoted from a verbal source)

If someone so young can have such a deep understanding of the social change process then there is hope that we can change the world. That knowledge Nevaeh speaks of is based upon a foundational understanding of social justice.

Throughout this book the reader will be engaged in examples to illustrate a social justice approach. While presenting these examples, readers will gain insight into the importance of social justice in program planning and the consequences of not building plans upon a foundational understanding of social justice. Through the use of a case example, readers will gain insights into how social justice can be conceptualized and incorporated into program planning.

When human service program planning is not grounded in social justice concepts, planners run the risk of repeating mistakes of the past that helped to create the current conditions, the possibility of further disadvantaging those who have been disadvantaged and privileging the already privileged, and maintaining the status quo. As Osborne (2015) points out, planning scholarship and practice is not only embedded in the individual privilege of the planner, researcher, but in the same systems that created the problems these planners may be seeking to address – it is a product of the society it is called upon to change.

The book is organized into nine chapters, the sequence of which is designed to provide students and practitioners a practical understanding of social justice and how this forms the foundation for effective human services program planning. Building upon this foundation, the specific tools to plan a program, from identifying the issue to the details of planning and implementing the program, are explored.

Chapter 1 examines a new way of thinking about "social problems." A social justice lens is applied to transform thinking, redefining social problems as social inequities. Through an exploration of social justice concepts this chapter explores current thinking on social inequities, developing an understanding that when we look at social problems as unjust or unfortunate the focus is on charity and individual change, rather than true structural change. Exploring the terms social problem, social inequality and social inequity is more than an exercise in semantics. When these terms are scrutinized and their impact understood, we can begin to see issues through a social justice lens. Concepts forming the foundation of social justice planning, including systems thinking and intersectionality, are defined and explored.

Chapter 2 builds on a common mistake planners often make, approaching the planning process believing they know the issue and therefore are prepared to address it. Far too often the issue seems clear and it is defined in simple terms so that it can be addressed. The simpler the definition the easier it is to address, but simple definitions can often be too narrow to lead to lasting and real change. Using a social justice lens to define the issue helps us perform a deeper dive into the causes and understanding of the issue and how it impacts people and communities. The concepts of cultural competence and cultural humility are explored. Additional concepts are introduced to help the reader develop skills to broaden the understanding of the causes and impacts of social inequities, and how to involve people who are impacted. Involving the community as participants in the planning process is discussed through the concept of participatory planning.

Chapter 3 builds on the concepts discussed in Chapter 2, while developing practical skills to determine and define the need to be addressed. Theoretical concepts of need are reviewed, demonstrating how a strengths-based perspective can be used to view communities and populations differently, focusing on social inequities rather than social problems. Building on the concept of participatory planning discussed in Chapter 2, steps used to involve the community or those impacted by the issue are delineated. Practical issues are discussed, including the information and data collection processes to provide an understanding of the contributing factors and impact of the social inequity being addressed. Additional tools are explored, including appreciative inquiry, relational organizing, force field analysis and how these contribute to an understanding of the need.

Building on the needs assessment, Chapter 4 focuses on developing a clear statement of the issue being addressed and creating the intervention hypothesis. The issue statement is then used to create the impact, or larger change that is being sought. The importance of considering cultural differences and an exploration of the concept of "why." This can be drilled down to "why should anyone care?" and "why is this issue important enough to address?" Finally, the theory of change is discussed and how this is used to develop the road map forward.

Chapter 5 explores how planners can move forward from understanding the root causes of social inequities to developing interventions addressing the change being sought and the ultimate impact that is hoped to achieve. Decision making in the planning process is investigated, including planning as a rational process and structured decision making. The impacts of unintended consequences and the value of performing a benefit-cost analysis are discussed as well. This is followed by a discussion of evidence-based practice and evidence-informed practice, and how these can influence the planning process. Finally, building upon the theory of change, this chapter introduces the program logic model as a tool and guide to effective program planning.

Chapter 6 introduces strategy creation and how this guides the development of the program logic model and the determination of long-term goals. The different uses for a theory of change logic model and program logic model are introduced. Focusing on the program logic model, this chapter reviews the logic model components demonstrating how the logic model is developed as a guide to program implementation. The importance of developing SMART objectives and measurable outcomes is presented.

Utilizing a case study based upon a youth program, OurKids After-School, Chapter 7 focuses on developing evidence-informed activities, showing how each activity leads to one or more outcomes. Completing the logic model, outcomes, outputs, activities and inputs are created using the case study example. The GANTT Chart is introduced as a tool for program implementation.

Chapter 8 provides an overview of grant writing, focusing on the program description, using the ongoing case example to illustrate how to present the plan to possible funders. An example of the program description is presented to demonstrate how activities feed into objectives and their connection to the inputs. The importance of language and how to effectively present the program plan is reviewed, as is knowing the audience you are writing for.

Chapter 9 reviews the program evaluation, an important step that can't be overlooked. Without a good evaluation plan, the success or need for modification of the program cannot be known. When the logic model is constructed correctly with measurables built in, it will form the basis of the evaluation plan. The performance measurement feedback loop is illustrated to demonstrate the relationship between the logic model program components and the program evaluation. Data and sources are highlighted for their role in measuring program implementation and the success of the outcomes, focusing on the changes realized as a result of the intervention.

Finally, a note on the use of pronouns. Although pronouns are used sparsely throughout this book, when they are, only nonbinary pronouns will be used. While this may at times seem grammatically incorrect to the reader, it is important that we honor the lives of nonbinary people by recognizing their existence and legitimacy. I grew up with only the male pronoun in general use. Most things, animate and inanimate were referred to as "he." Then that progressed to "he or she" or "s/he," only recognizing two gender choices, assuming that everyone conformed to what was considered the norm. Both of these choices were equally as nongrammatical as the nonbinary pronoun "they," which will be used throughout this text. It would be inconsistent with a social justice approach to use gender specific pronouns, denying the existence of gender nonconforming people

I hope that you find this book and its unique approach useful. I have tried to fill in the void in human services planning texts through the focus on social justice. My hope in writing this text is that students and practitioners will agree with the need to focus on social justice and that these concepts will be incorporated in all future human services program planning. I am aware that one person cannot create a new paradigm of planning for social justice. However, my aspiration in presenting this work is that social workers, human service practitioners and program planners will see the importance of working from a foundation of social justice and help move the needle forward, addressing social inequities and furthering social justice. I look forward to, and welcome feedback on this approach and the effectiveness with which it is presented in this text.

References

Moses, R.P. & Cobb, C.E. (2001) *Radical equations: Civil rights from Mississippi to the Algebra Project*. Boston, MA: Beacon Press

Osborne, N. (2015) Intersectionality and kyriarchy: A framework for approaching power and social justice in planning and climate change adaptation. *Planning Theory*, 14(2), 130–151

1 Social Justice Thinking

Learning objectives

- Articulate the concept of social justice.
- Value the role of social justice in program planning.
- Demonstrate an understanding of systems thinking and how it applies to program planning.
- Articulate the impact of intersectionality on advantaging and disadvantaging people.
- Understand and articulate the differences between social problem, social inequality and social inequity.
- Understand the impact of the status quo in mitigating against change.
- Value the importance of language in planning.

Chapter Overview

Program planning based upon the concepts of social justice is all too often missing where the focus is generally on short-term change. Politicians, once elected, are focused on the short-term goal of reelection; corporate leaders are focused on the next income report. Government funding focuses more on efficiency than effectiveness, and private philanthropies issue grants in single-year or short multi-year horizons, once again based upon showing short-term results. At the same time, planners in the human services, whether focused on the individual, community or geographic levels, specific population groups or agency services, are planning with and for people. Because we are working with people, the results we seek are often long-term. We must name the change and engage in the time-consuming effort to educate about social inequity to ensure that people understand the basis for change and how that will improve the lives of people and communities. Activist and founder of Critical Resistance, Rose Braz, underscored the importance of this in a 2008 interview, "A prerequisite to seeking any social change is in the naming of it. In other words, even though the goal we seek may be far away, unless we name it and fight for it today, it will never come" (Bennett, 2008).

DOI: 10.4324/9781003148777-1

If there is one thing we know about human beings, we are a very diverse lot. We come to the table with differing skills and knowledge, face very different challenges, and have a wide range of abilities to take advantage of programs and resources. In short, there is no one solution or intervention that can meet the needs of diverse people. What works for one person, community or group, may not work for another. Often, the measures and time frames to which human services program planners are beholden do not address the needs of the people, programs or communities that are the focus of their planning. Change takes time and must be built on a foundation of understanding the causes of social inequities and issues, and how to address these rather than merely ameliorating the symptoms. This is the shift in thinking, or paradigm shift, that we must work toward if social inequities are to be diminished.

A Paradigm Shift, Using a Social Justice Lens

Social Justice Thinking

A paradigm shift occurs when the present ways of thinking and viewing the world no longer explain current conditions and a new way of thinking is proposed. Viewing current phenomena through a social justice lens is the paradigm shift that can help address the many serious and seemingly intractable challenges that we are facing today in society. One example of a shifting paradigm is the terminology used to describe people who are currently referred to as homeless. "The word *homeless* has become inseparable from a toxic narrative that blames and demonizes people who are unhoused... The term is increasingly used in a way where it implies someone is dangerous or devious" (Slayton, 2021). Therefore, a less loaded term is more appropriate. In May 2020, the Associated Press Stylebook labeled homeless as a dehumanizing term, suggesting using the terms homeless people or people without housing. Throughout this text, the words *houseless* or *unhoused* will be used instead of homeless.

Social justice is a complex concept with a diversity of definitions and approaches. It is both inspirational and aspirational and requires shifting paradigms. A computer search for the definition of social justice identified 919 million citations. Included in this were a number of articles and references to the "principles" of social justice.

Depending on which reference you choose, there are either four or five, or seven or ten principles. This disparity in the number of social justice principles and what they are highlights the difficulty in developing a definition of social justice that is all encompassing. In *Principles of Social Justice*, Miller (2001) argues that these principles must be understood contextually and that each of these principles exist within human associations, and therefore any theory of social justice must be complex because human societies and interactions are complex as well.

A common mistake that many people make when speaking of social justice is reaching for equality. There will always be income disparity and there will always be people who are more capable than others. Social justice does not seek total equality, rather it seeks equality of opportunity. Some people will make more of opportunities afforded them than others. Some people will be satisfied with a more basic lifestyle while others may seek more comfort and luxuries. Society however should not be a zero-sum game. Those seeking more luxuries or a higher standard of living should not be able to do so at the expense of others. Nor should they be in a position to hold others down, so that they can retain privilege without sharing it. When everyone is equally privileged, the benefits and disadvantages of privilege disappear. And that is a step toward social justice.

Defining Social Justice

While social justice is a widely, and sometime overused, term, there is not complete agreement on its definition. Many writers define social justice in terms of the principles of fairly distributing the goods, services and benefits of society so that all have equality of opportunity. This view of social justice as distributive justice looks at how society or groups allocate resources or products among individuals who may have competing claims (Colton, 2002; Nozick, 1974; Rawls, J 1971; Young, 1990). As far back as ancient Greece, the writings of Plato conflated justice with distributive justice (Greco, 2011). If we only look at the equality of distribution of goods, services and rights as the main tenet of social justice, then we are ignoring the hurdles built into our institutions, and into society itself, that block certain people and groups from exercising that equality.

> Social injustice can be examined not only in terms of the maldistribution of goods and services, but also in regard to the social relations responsible for that maldistribution. These social relations, which can range from centrally oppressive power relations to less central mechanisms of discrimination, determine whether individuals, families, and other groups are excluded from society's important resources and decision-making properties.
>
> (Faegin, 2004, p. 36)

In a socially just society there are no artificial or institutional barriers to achieving full and equal participation.

Another view of social justice is termed procedural justice referring to "the decision-making processes that lead to the decisions about distribution and the relationships between dominant and subordinate groups," such as racial and religious minorities that affect decisions about distribution (Longres & Scanlon, 2001, p. 448) While this view looks at the decisions that cause and perpetuate inequality it is still based upon the distribution of goods, services and rights. The focus on decision making ignores who gets to make those decisions. While it recognizes that the dominant groups make the decisions, others are labeled as "subordinate." Subordinate, by definition, suggests that those who don't have input into the decision-making process are lower in rank or position and are of lesser importance. This begs the question, "in whose eyes?" In order to approach social justice through a lens of procedural justice, must we also accept as true that some people are subordinate in order to attempt to reduce the subordination? Can this also suggest that people who are of lesser importance do not have the abilities to change their subordinate position?

With this in mind, how do we develop a working definition of social justice and a socially just society? A socially just society does not create barriers to participation such as discrimination based upon race, gender, ethnicity, sexual orientation or identity, intellectual or physical abilities or any other identity. A social justice approach then, focuses not on treating the symptoms of societal ills, but rather on finding and uprooting the causes of those ills. As Albert Einstein is credited with saying, "we cannot solve problems with the same thinking that helped to create them."

In the introduction to the paper "Social Justice in an Open World: The Role of the United Nations" (United Nations, 2006), presented as part of the International Forum for Social Development, the authors focus on inequality:

> In the modern context, those concerned with social justice see the general increase in income inequality as unjust, deplorable and alarming. It is argued that poverty reduction and overall improvements in the standard of living are attainable goals that would bring the world closer to social justice. However, there is little indication of any real ongoing commitment to address existing inequalities.

Inequality, however, is a quantitative measure, the result of existing inequities. Inequality cannot be eliminated if the inequities causing the inequality are not addressed. If everyone is equally privileged, meaning there are no longer artificial barriers built into society holding people back, then all people are free to achieve to the best of their abilities. This results in equality of opportunity. Artificial barriers or hurdles that people must overcome would no longer exist. These barriers include all the prejudices that we tolerate in our society, such as racism, homophobia, sexism, ableism, to name just a few. Nor would immigrant or communities of color be marginalized by injustice and unequal treatment.

Social justice is often defined by a list of rights and privileges that are deemed necessary to achieve a just society. For example, the National

Association of Social Workers, lists a series of priorities that includes voters' rights, criminal and juvenile justice, environmental justice, and economic justice (NASW, n.d.). While this list has been crafted with all good intentions, and vetted by committees, no list of rights or privileges can be exhaustive. When we create a list of rights based upon the values of those creating the list, although well-intentioned, some may be left out. We could add to this list a number of priorities or rights such as gender equality, immigrant rights, equal access for people who are disabled, affordable housing, safety, etc. If we view social justice as a concept and an all-encompassing condition to work toward, then it cannot be summarized by listing a set of priorities. Priorities do not inspire, nor are they aspirational. But if we desire a society where all people have equality of opportunity, a society where there are no built-in institutional barriers to achieving self-fulfillment and where all people have the right to self-determination, then we are working toward social justice.

Another view of social justice that all people should be able to relate to is given to us by Michael Dodson (1993), former Social Justice Commissioner for the Commonwealth of Australia:

> Social Justice is what faces you in the morning. It is awakening in a house with an adequate water supply, cooking facilities and sanitation. It is the ability to nourish your children and send them to school where their education not only equips them for employment but reinforces their knowledge and appreciation of their cultural inheritance. It is the prospect of genuine employment and good health: a life of choices and opportunity. A life free from discrimination.

While this very clearly tells us what a socially just world would look like, Dodson does not offer a definition of social justice. Instead, a socially just world is something that should be aspired to. However, a definition can be helpful to guide the work of human services program planning. Adams et al. (2016) offers an aspirational view of what social justice would look like. This is a vision that can be helpful in guiding human services program planning. Adams et al. put forth the goal of social justice as "full and equal participation of all groups in a society that is mutually shaped to meet their needs." They clarify this vision further by writing that social justice

> includes a vision of society in which the distribution of resources is equitable and all members are physically and psychologically safe and secure ... a society in which individuals are both self-determining (able to develop to their full capacities) and interdependent (capable of interacting democratically with others)
>
> (p. 1)

Reisch and Garvin (2016) offer an alternative view of social justice,

> a society in which people individually and in community, can live decent lives and realize their full human potential. This requires us to advocate for the elimination of those policies that diminish people's sense of control over their lives and drain finite resources from basic human needs.
>
> (p. 351)

With these ideas and definitions in mind, the following is a working definition of social justice that will guide the content of this book. This definition is written in the active voice and does not attempt to list rights and privileges but rather provides a goal to be worked toward.

> Social justice is achieved when no one is denied access to the resources and opportunities that are needed to live healthy, productive lives. This is accomplished through equality of opportunity for all members of society through the inclusion of everyone in the full benefits of society and the empowerment of all people to participate fully in the economic, social, political and cultural life of the country.

Dr. Martin Luther King, in his 1957 "Give Us the Ballot" speech at the Lincoln Memorial, stressed the importance of all people participating fully in society. King clearly articulated the importance of including all people, especially African Americans who were denied the ballot, when he said, "Give us the ballot and we will no longer have to worry the federal government about our basic rights." If human services program planners keep social justice in mind as the ultimate impact sought when planning programs and interventions, regardless of the focus of the intervention, every program can help to move the needle in the direction of social justice for the people and communities served.

The Social Justice Approach

Systems Thinking

Systems thinking, as defined by Arnold and Wade (2015) as "a set of synergistic analytic skills used to improve the capability of identifying and understanding systems, predicting their behaviors, and devising modifications to them in order to produce desired effects." Barry Richmond (1994), the originator of the concept, defines systems thinking as, "the art and science of making reliable inferences about behavior by developing an increasingly deep understanding of underlying structure." Engaging in systems thinking is the art of seeing both the "forest and the trees; one eye on each" (Richmond, 1994, p. 139)

There is a difference between understanding systems and systems thinking. Michailakas and Schirme (2014) describe systems theory in this way,

> society consists of a number of differentiated social systems with each fulfilling a function for society. Examples are the systems of politics, economy, science, medicine, religion and law. Each of these function systems provides a solution to a specific societal reference-problem; they observe society from their own, function-specific perspectives, and communicate whatever falls within their scope in a specific way. Function systems can see only what their unique perspective allows them to see. They are blind and indifferent to everything else.
>
> (p. 433)

In contrast, "systems thinking means paying attention to the unpredictable interactions among actors, sectors, disciplines, and determinants [of the problem/challenge]. That thinking results in new ways of approaching, analyzing and solving challenges, which must be applied through policy development, program design, implementation, and research" (USAID, n.d.). A social justice approach utilizes systems thinking by not looking at how one system succeeds or fails at a particular function, but rather how various systems work together to produce the outcomes that lead to inequities. Understanding how systems work together to cause an inequity provides a concrete foundation for understanding how to remedy the condition.

To understand systems thinking let's dissect a car which is made up of a number of interacting systems. For the car to work properly, each system must perform the task that it was designed to do. At the same time, each of these individual systems are dependent upon other systems in the car to work effectively. If the transmission and its component parts are not working, the car would be able to start, but not go anywhere. However, if the battery (part of the electrical system) is not charged, and the transmission is repaired, the car will not start. The mechanic needs to understand the interactions between and purpose of each system in the car to get the car running properly.

Houselessness: An Example of Systems Thinking

Figure 1.1 illustrates a systems thinking approach to houselessness. The larger outer ring represents institutional and societal views and policies that can cause and serve to perpetuate houselessness. These include government policies, the criminal legal system, socio-cultural values, the economy, institutional racism and the media. These systems surround and impact the more direct and personal contributors to houselessness,

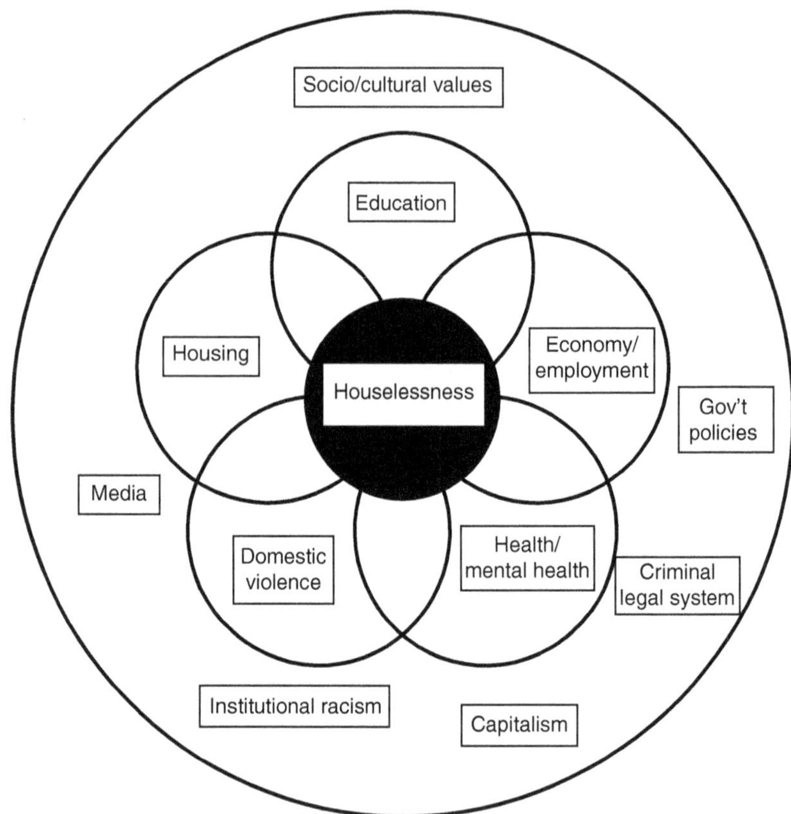

Figure 1.1 Houselessness viewed through systems thinking

and each of these overlap each other converging in the middle demonstrating the multitude of forces coming together to create inequities that contribute to houselessness. These include health and mental health, domestic violence, housing, employment and education, to illustrate some of these forces that weigh on individuals and families.

Examining houselessness, we see there are many interacting systems at play that contribute to individuals and families becoming unhoused. The predominant response to houselessness has been to provide more shelters which serve several purposes. Shelters provide temporary, overnight shelter from the elements and get many people who are houseless off the streets and out of sight. If there were less people living on the streets and visible to the general population, it would appear that the problem was being reduced and the quality of life improved. In reality, this does not reduce houselessness. It merely offers a short-term intervention, addressing one symptom of a larger problem, while a growing number of people are still becoming unhoused. As more people become visibly unhoused, living on city streets, they become an embarrassment, an eyesore and possibly a public health issue. In many cities this becomes a policing issue. These people are breaking the law, dirtying the streets, but mostly reminding us of the failure of our society to ensure that all people are adequately housed. Cities and towns across the country have been issuing ordinances against living on the street and panhandling, criminalizing the very behaviors that people without homes are engaged in merely to survive (Garrow & Bailey, 2021).

If we indeed want to help individuals and families who are experiencing houselessness, we would look to the contributing factors and interacting systems that lead to the loss of a home. For example, cities with the highest rates of houselessness, such as New York City, Seattle, and San Francisco, are the among cities with the highest housing costs in the nation. In addition to being priced out of the rental market, other factors contributing to houselessness include domestic violence, unemployment, mental illness and substance abuse (National Law Center on Homelessness and Poverty, 2015). Sheltering people for a night does not address any of these factors.

To end houselessness, we must think differently and engage in a systems thinking approach to understand why people become unhoused and how best to help them to become permanently and adequately rehoused. That should be the goal, not merely sheltering people, a shelter is clearly not a home. Families and individuals living in shelters are sheltered, but that does not change the reality of their lives, they are still without a home of their own.

We can become overwhelmed if we look at the challenge of houselessness in its entirety, but if we look at it as having its roots in systems then we can begin to deconstruct the inequities and get at the root causes. We begin by asking what are those systems, and how do they interact with each other to maintain or exacerbate the inequity? These system failures include healthcare, education, employment, affordable housing, crime, drugs, mental health and domestic violence to name some of the larger contributors to people becoming unhoused. Each of these represent precursors that become contributing factors. Rather than addressing these, many cities and towns focus on the symptoms by funding homeless shelters and food banks.

By applying a systems thinking approach we would look to the various systems that contribute to the challenge of houselessness and how they interact with each other and with the people whom they impact. It is the failure of the systems noted above that contribute to individuals and families becoming unhoused. Once we begin to understand the complexity of systems contributing to houselessness, we begin to understand the causes of the inequities and no longer look solely to individual failures. We can begin to analyze and understand who the players are that are responsible for these system failures and focus our interventions on them. Houselessness then, is no longer just the responsibility of the local municipality to address, but it becomes an issue that requires a broad-based, holistic approach that addresses the underlying systems. Shelter and food banks, the typical responses of local government without the resources to adequately address houselessness, would no longer be seen as responsible approaches but only as temporary Band-Aids.

Through a systems thinking approach we begin to see that houselessness has its roots in a complicated web of interlocking systems, and that houselessness is the symptom of much deeper issues than just not having a roof over one's head. In order to understand the causes and cures for houselessness we must also take the time to identify these interconnected systems and understand how they work to contribute to individuals and families becoming unhoused.

By addressing the interacting systems and working to help them function in harmony with one another, we can begin to address the causes of houselessness and reduce the number of individuals and families who are impacted. Most current approaches are designed to address individual fault while doing little to prevent more people from experiencing houselessness. A one-to-one approach is doomed to failure since we can never keep pace with the number of people facing houselessness with the limited resources allocated to individual solutions. For example, if we are successful in creating additional units of affordable, permanent housing for people who are unhoused then we may actually increase the problem because families who are doubled and tripled up in housing must make themselves unhoused in order to be eligible (HUD, n.d.).

If we merely look at the most obvious system – housing – we can provide shelter or temporary housing, but this approach does not address the cause, only the most obvious symptom – no home. It is possible to address the immediate need first, help a family or individual find permanent housing and then scaffold services they may need to maintain being housed. One example, the Housing First model, is designed to do this. It is based upon the understanding that the individual or family first needs to be permanently housed before they can begin to address the underlying issues that caused them to become unhoused. According to the National Alliance to End Homelessness (2019),

> Housing First is a philosophy that values flexibility, individualized supports, client choice, and autonomy. It never has been housing only, and it never should be. Supportive services are part of the Housing First model. That might include formal support services, like a doctor, therapist, or social worker. It might involve informal supports, like connecting with family, friends, or faith groups.

While this approach represents a significant step forward in addressing the issue, it still does not change the underlying inequities that cause houselessness.

In the Housing First model for example, the individual or family, once housed, has access to a range of services that they can choose to access. There is no requirement that they participate in these services offered, providing a high level of self-determination. Creating opportunities for people to choose their own path forward is the first step in helping them to regain their footing and to succeed.

By recognizing the interlocking systems at play that contribute to someone becoming unhoused, the wrap-around services offered in this model can begin to address those interlocking systems that serve to keep people unhoused. But this cannot be the only approach to addressing houselessness. While Housing First provides a more socially just approach to helping individuals and families experiencing houselessness, it does not address houselessness as a societal inequity. Human service planners must also become involved in policymaking in order to address serious social inequities, such as houselessness, at their root causes. Everything that human service program planners and service providers do, whether they become involved in social policy or not, is guided by and impacted by policies made by others. The contributing factors enumerated above can only be addressed and ameliorated through policy implementation.

Of course, houselessness is not the only inequity that can be approached through a systems thinking perspective. We saw how inequities built into our laws and attitudes were laid bare during the Covid-19 pandemic of 2020–2022, when these interlocking systems impacted entire communities. As the pandemic spread, it tore away the facade and laid bare many of the inequities that were built into society. According to the Centers for Disease Control (2020):

> Long-standing systemic health and social inequities have put many people from racial and ethnic minority groups at increased risk of getting sick and dying from COVID-19… Inequities in the social determinants of health, such as poverty and healthcare access, affecting these groups are interrelated and influence a wide range of health and quality-of-life outcomes and risks. To achieve health equity, barriers must be removed so that everyone has a fair opportunity to be as healthy as possible.

As the pandemic continued, it impacted communities of color, immigrant and Native American communities in numbers greater than white communities. The systems that came together to envelop these communities included the health inequities above and other systems, including inadequate and overcrowded multigenerational housing, the disproportionate number of members of these communities working in so-called essential and frontline jobs, inadequate health care and access to health care, loss of employment and along with that the loss of health insurance. Further complicating these outcomes for undocumented immigrants was their fear of deportation if they went to a hospital to seek care or to be tested, and the inability to access available government services and relief efforts (Kaiser Family Foundation, 2021).

Intersectionality

Intersectionality is defined as understanding and consideration of "the complex, cumulative ways in which the effects of multiple forms of discrimination (such as racism, sexism, classism) combine, overlap, and intersect especially in the experiences of marginalized groups" (Merriam-Webster, n.d.).

The term "intersectionality" was coined by Kimberlé Crenshaw, in 1989, to describe the experience of Black women facing both racial and gender discrimination. "Because the intersectional experience is greater than the sum of racism and sexism, any analysis that does not take intersectionality into account cannot sufficiently address the particular manner in which Black women are subordinated" (p. 140).

While the theory was first formulated to help understand the challenges faced by Black women resulting from race and gender discrimination, in the three decades since formulating the term, intersectionality has grown to be much broader. Similar to systems thinking, intersectionality theorizes that we must look at the multiple identities of people and how these interact with each other and with the person, in order to understand their life situation. Intersectionality can help us to understand the intersections of privilege as well as the intersections of discrimination. An intersectional lens moves human service planners and policy makers away from "single-axis thinking," so that rather than seeing identities as mutually exclusive categories we begin to see people as complex organisms with multiple identities that can be synergistic in privileging or disadvantaging them.

Intersectionality is a conceptual framework through which we can examine the interconnections and interdependencies between systems and the social categories that make us who we are. This perspective provides theoretical explanations of the ways in which individual members of specific groups experience interactions differently based upon their individual identities, such as ethnicity, sexual orientation, class and other social positions. For example, an African American woman may experience interactions differently in her workplace than a white woman in the same workplace. Just as an LGBTQ+ woman may experience interactions differently than other women co-located in the same community, organization or workplace. They all share the experience that is unique to women in the workplace and in the world, but overlaying that common identity is their identity of race or sexual orientation. As a result, their experience can be significantly different than that of white, straight or cis gender women in the same workplace. "Sensitivity to such differences enhances insight into issues of social justice and inequality in organizations and other institutions, thus maximizing the chance of social change" (Atewologun, 2018).

The United Nations defines intersectionality as:

> the structural and dynamic consequences of the interaction between two or more forms of discrimination or systems of subordination. (Intersectionality) specifically addresses the manner in which racism, patriarchy, economic disadvantages and other discriminatory systems contribute to create layers of inequality that structure the relative positions of women and men, races and other groups.
>
> (2000)

Figure 1.2 illustrates intersectionality by showing some of the various overlapping identities that an individual can have. These include

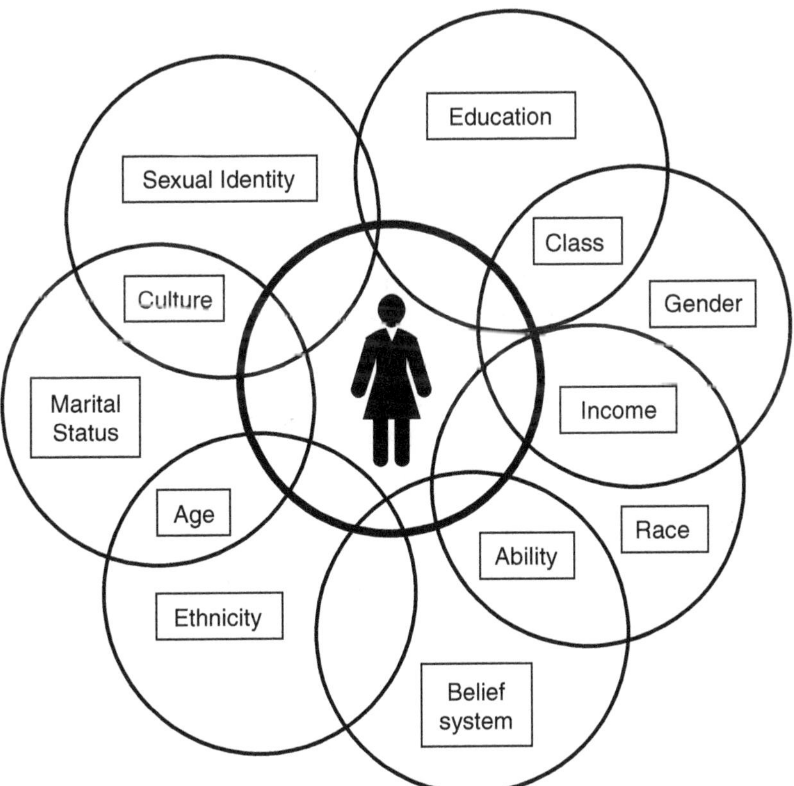

Figure 1.2 Intersectionality

education, socioeconomic class, gender, income, race, level of ability, belief system, ethnicity, age, marital status, culture, and sexual and gender identity.

Understanding the impact of intersectionality, similar to approaching issues through systems thinking, is crucial to understanding and analyzing the inequities faced by individuals, groups, organizations and communities. Understanding these multiple identities and how they interact to advance or hold people back is essential to planning appropriately to address underlying inequities. For example, an African American female faculty member may be advantaged because she holds a post-graduate degree, but can also be disadvantaged by her gender and racial identity. As a result, she may find that she does not have access to the same advantages as her white, male counterparts. This may result in a lower salary, reduced research opportunities and denial of tenure. We can also see this in communities where the intersection of race and class can serve to deny communities municipal services and economic opportunity.

Moving from Independence to Interdependence

American ethos teaches us from an early age that the worst position to be in is one of dependence. The opposite of dependence is independence, which we are taught to strive for. The heroes in our literature and movies are independent, they don't wait for anyone else to act, they take charge and go forward on their own. There is however a greater goal that brings society together – interdependence. We are all interdependent upon each other for society to function at its fullest.

For example, we depend on the building maintenance crew to ensure that the elevator is working when we need to get to the upper floors, just as we depend on EMS workers to respond when we call for an ambulance. If no one came to the building to use the elevator, the elevator maintenance crew would be out of work. We pay taxes so that there will be an ambulance crew and roads for them to drive upon. Without this interdependence, society ceases to function, yet we do not value this as much as we do independence.

The African concept of Ubuntu offers us insight into interdependence. This is a belief in a communal approach to society. However, practicing such an approach does not subordinate the goals of the individual, nor do they pursue communalism at the expense of their own good. Ubuntu teaches the pursuit of one's own good through the pursuit of the common good (Lutz 2009). Ubuntu further stresses that only through promoting the good of others, can people find their own good. Turaki sums this up succinctly, "People are not individuals living in a state of independence, but part of a community, living in a relationship and interdependence" (2006, p. 36).

New Beginnings Reentry Services

An Intersectional Approach

Founded by a formerly incarcerated woman in Boston, New Beginnings Reentry Services (NBRS) recognizes that there are many issues that women who are incarcerated share in common, and that the whole person must be addressed to avoid reincarceration. While the women were incarcerated for crimes, the focus is on the underlying issues that contributed to their incarceration. These issues include trauma, abuse, poverty, substance use, mental health issues and discrimination. Research has shown that women who are incarcerated report greater incidence of mental health problems and serious mental illness than their male counterparts. Additionally, incarcerated women report higher rates of substance dependence, past physical and sexual abuse, interpersonal trauma, and post-traumatic stress disorder (Green et al., 2005; James & Glaze, 2006; Lynch et al., 2014; Steadman et al., 2009).

Staff and board of NBRS work in partnership with community agencies to empower and provide supportive services to formerly incarcerated women to successfully rejoin their communities. NBRS addresses the critical issues of education, physical and mental health, as well as personal development through trauma-informed programs and services. Services include drug and alcohol counseling, expressive and dramatic arts, allyship with LGBTQ+ women and housing services. Addressing the many challenges the women still face after incarceration, such as successfully reintegrating in their communities, services also include a residence where the women can live safely while working on getting their lives back on track.

Racial and gender discrimination are also contributing factors that are part of the approach. From 1980 to 2019 the number of women incarcerated in the United States increased by over 700%, with 83 African American women per 100,000 and 48 Latinx women, versus 63 white women incarcerated (The Sentencing Project, 2020). New Beginnings combines both intersectionality and systems thinking into their services. While the approach to individual clients addresses the many challenges that led to incarceration, the program also focuses on the larger systems and their interconnections that contribute to the tremendous growth in the incarceration of women. New Beginnings works in coalition with other programs on issues that include prison abolition, affordable housing, women's crisis intervention, domestic violence, drug abuse and poverty.

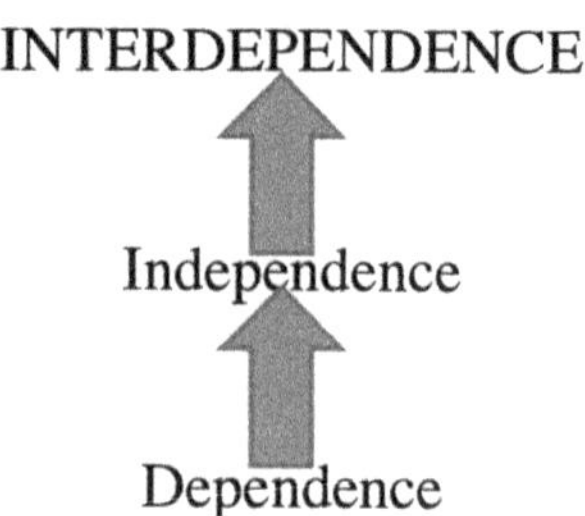

Figure 1.3 Moving from dependence to interdependence

Interdependence represents the combination of embracing systems thinking and intersectionality. No one stands alone when it comes to community and society; we are all in this together. Human service program planners are interdependent with the communities and people for whom they are working. Social justice planners plan with people and communities rather than for them. To develop and implement successful programs and interventions, the community relies on the professional expertise and training of program planners, and in turn, to be successful, planners must rely on the knowledge, experience and input of the community.

Applying the Social Justice Lens

Reviewing the definitions and components of social justice enumerated above we can see the essential human services program ingredients that will help to move us in the direction of social justice. These can include:

- Full participation of people and communities that will be impacted by the program intervention in the planning and evaluation of the program;
- A broader component that addresses policies that perpetuate the inequities to be addressed;
- Capacity building components for individuals, groups and/or the community;
- Fostering interdependence through meaningful interactions;
- Opportunities for self-determination where participants can make choices on their own behalf;
- Opportunities to participate in actions and activities that work toward improving social and economic conditions in the community;
- Ongoing evaluations that determine the efficacy of the program interventions;
- Sharing information on what works for possible duplication.

ACT UP

A Social Justice Approach in Action

In the early 1980s, when HIV/AIDS was just identified in the gay community, it was referred to as the "gay plague" (Curran & Jaffe, 2011). Once HIV/AIDS was labeled in this way, society was absolved of any responsibility to address the disease in its earliest stages, when significant progress could have been made. The cure was simple and straightforward, if gay men did not want to contract this disease all they had to do was stop their "perverted lifestyle" and stop having sex with men. If gay men were not willing to do this then it was a personal choice and there was no societal responsibility. While the epidemic ravaged the gay community, President Ronald Reagan did not address AIDS until almost eight years into the growing pandemic, in a speech in 1987 at the Philadelphia College of Physicians. By that time more than 20,000 Americans had died from the disease. Dr. C. Everett Koop, Reagan's Surgeon General, who was cut out of any response to the crisis, explained the administration's policy of willful ignorance, "because transmission of AIDS was understood to be primarily in the homosexual population and in those who abused intravenous drugs" the president's advisors "took the stand they are getting what they deserve" (White, 2004).

Although there were many challenges to overcome, a social justice approach helped pave the way for lasting, meaningful and life-saving change. This social justice approach was enacted by the radical, gay and lesbian led organization ACT UP (AIDS Coalition to Unleash Power), employing direct action and mass protest to bring attention to the issue that was being ignored by mainstream society. Looking back on the work of ACT UP, David France (2020) wrote in the *New York Times*:

> In the face of frustration, ACT UP pivoted brilliantly. Instead of demanding action from others, they took on the work themselves. Breaking down the myriad problems inhibiting the response to AIDS, the group spun off into committees to address them one by one: a women's committee, because women were excluded from drug trials and disease statistics; a needle-exchange committee, because no one else was trying to prevent the spread of disease among IV-drug users; a committee concentrated on minorities, because cases were growing in those

communities; a housing committee, because so many lost their homes after lengthy hospitalizations; even a science committee, because the labyrinthine research institutions lacked a cogent agenda.

This multi-pronged approach by ACT UP followed a true social justice model. Through a systems thinking approach, the activists addressed the overlapping systems that were working to keep the AIDS crisis under wraps at the same time that it was pushing LGBTQ people deeper into the closet. Following the model of civil protest of the Civil Rights movement, ACT UP showed what could be done when people challenge the status quo and bring activism to the streets. Fighting AIDS through an approach based upon social justice, systems thinking and direct action, ACT UP established itself as the vanguard of civil rights for LGBTQ people.

Sarah Schulman (2021) writes that through the process termed "direct action to end the AIDS crisis," ACT UP addressed the inequities that were underlying the crisis. ACT UP did not just demonstrate against, they provided alternative solutions that they agitated for, resulting in a number of progressive changes including:

- A fast-track system for sick people to access an unapproved experimental drug, then forcing the FDA to adapt it;
- Changes in the U.S. Centers for Disease Control's definition of AIDS so that women could access benefits including experimental drugs;
- Needle exchanges becoming legal in New York City;
- Ending insurance exclusion for people with AIDS.

(p. 9)

Figure 1.4 illustrates the concept of paradigm shift focusing on the AIDS crisis as an example. The left side demonstrates how AIDS was first viewed when it was thought to only affect the gay community. The dominant view blamed the people impacted by the disease, resulting in a path of nonintervention to fight the disease. The right side illustrates the result of a paradigm shift once it was determined that it was a serious medical condition that was not limited solely to the gay community and intravenous drug users. This paradigm shift, or change in thinking, resulted in government and private efforts to fight the disease.

Figure 1.4 Paradigm shift

Social Inequity, Inequality or Social Problem

Throughout this book you will see the term *social inequity* instead of *social problem* or *inequality*. Unpacking the difference between these labels will illustrate why it is important to make these distinctions and will illuminate the impact of focusing on social inequities rather than merely addressing social inequalities or problems. Exploring the differences in these concepts and the implications of each will help to understand the importance of viewing social problems as social inequities, and inequality as the result. Through this understanding, and by developing a more analytic conceptualization, we begin to see the issues through a social justice lens. Each of these terms, social problem, social inequality and social equity, provide a different perspective through which societal conditions impacting people negatively can be understood.

Defining the Terms

- **Social problem** is a statement of an existing condition that does not provide insight into how that condition was created or why it still exists. When used to identify a specific social condition it can provide the space to place the onus of problems that are faced by individuals or population groups upon those affected. "A social problem is any condition or behavior that has negative consequences for large numbers of people and that is generally recognized as a condition or behavior that needs to be addressed" (Libretexts.org, 2020).
- **Social inequality** is a quantitative statement of fact that there is an inequality that can be measured, but like the term social problem, it does not provide any insight into how the inequality was created or why it still exists.[1]
- **Social inequity**, as a qualitative measure, states that there is an unfairness underlying the issue that must be dealt with if the issue or challenge

> is to be alleviated. A social inequity suggests that there is a dominant group that holds power or is privileged more than another group.[2]

Figure 1.5 describes the disparity in wealth in the United States, where the top 10% own almost 78% of all of the wealth (Stone et al., 2020, p. 14). Wealth and income are different measures. Income is a measure of what a person earns annually, while wealth is the total value of all of their resources and possessions. Wealth, in a sense, is a measure of how secure a person is. If you have sufficient wealth you can cover the costs of unexpected circumstances, enjoy a certain level of luxuries, send your kids to the best schools, etc. When 90% of the people only control 22% of the wealth that translates to not having sufficient resources to cover basic necessities including decent housing, quality healthcare and a good education for your children, resulting in a diminished quality of life. The inequality, or the social problem defined as the wealth gap is a quantitative measure of the unequal distribution of wealth. The inequity underlying this however are the societal rules that allow and encourage this wealth disparity, even in the face of knowledge about how it impacts the majority of the population.

Language Affects Planning

Stating something as an inequality does not get to the root causes of the inequality, instead it serves as a statement of a particular condition that is

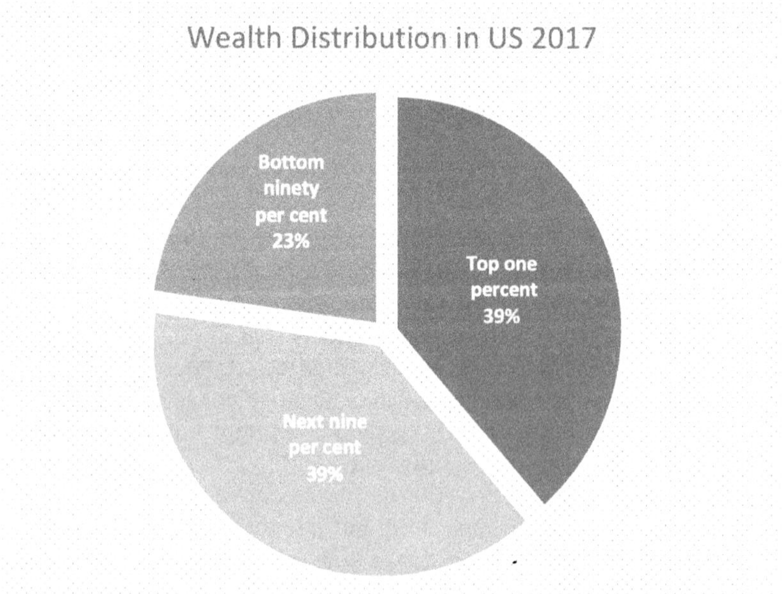

Figure 1.5 Wealth disparity in the U.S.

measurable. For example, the average white family in the U.S. has accumulated almost seven times as much wealth as the average Black family (Urban Institute, 2017). Simply stated as an inequality in wealth, there can be many reasons for this disparity that do not get to the cause, but can be seen as possible explanations. For example, one perspective blames Black families for this disparity, claiming they do not know how to manage their money as well as white families, thereby preventing them from accumulating wealth. The many negative stereotypes of African Americans can also play into a societal explanation for this wealth gap. If we state that there is an inequity in wealth accumulation in the United States resulting in white families having seven times the amount of wealth as the average Black family, we have a wealth gap. While the wealth gap stated in numeric terms is merely a quantitative measure of this social reality, stating the same condition as an "inequity" provides a qualitative measure that should lead us to seek a deeper understanding of its causes and the reasons it continues.

Figure 1.6 illustrates the persistence of the wealth gap between whites and Blacks and how it continues to grow over time. Also note that there is no consistent direct relationship between growth or decline in wealth among whites and Blacks. For example, in both 2007 and 2017 white wealth increased while Black wealth decreased. It's only in 1992 when Black wealth increased while white wealth decreased. In 2004, white wealth increased and Black wealth remained steady. Over the three decades illustrated, Black wealth, while still a fraction of white wealth, increased 100% while white wealth increased by 22%. Some may point to this as proof that the economic stability of Black Americans is increasing and a sign that their lives are improving as well. However, the fact that in 1989 median Black wealth was a mere 6% of the median wealth of whites, and three decades later it has grown to 10% of whites is not a sign of significant progress.

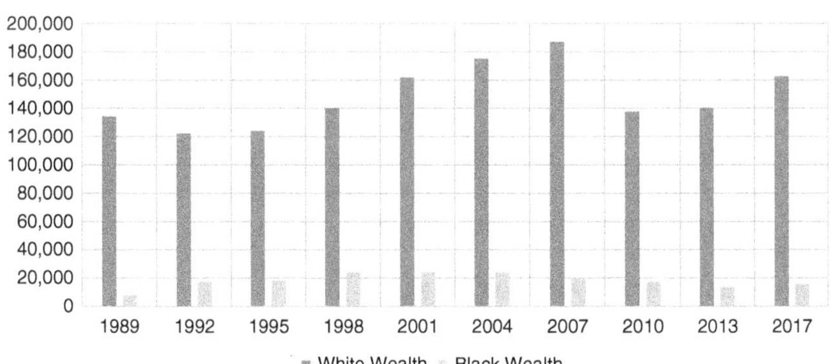

Figure 1.6 White vs. Black wealth

Source: Survey of Consumer Finances, Federal Reserve Board (2019)

Beginning the planning process by defining a "social problem" as our starting point may lead us to look more closely at the individual qualities and characteristics of those who are impoverished. From a planning perspective, this approach could lead to developing programs aimed at helping improve those individuals who are experiencing poverty such as money management classes or job training programs. However, when we begin from a starting point of social inequities, we can look into the institutional factors that have created and maintain poverty and the wealth gap. These include many contributing factors such as government policies like redlining, where red lines were drawn on maps around low-income and minority neighborhoods denying them bank mortgages. Other factors include housing and job discrimination, unequal pay, mass incarceration and other historical factors that robbed Black families of the opportunity to amass wealth. This can also lead to an historical understanding of the institutional and societal factors that prevented and limited Back Americans from amassing generational wealth.

Moving away from a problem focus and approaching issues through a social justice focus opens the possibility of examining the many contributing factors that are built into the foundations of our society. Once we look at these institutional causes, we then become obligated to do something to correct them.

Being more precise with language and how we define social justice and inequities that pervade society is an important and necessary first step. An understanding of these issues obligates social justice planners to take action in the face of society's inclination to maintain stasis leading to inertia. Enacting a social justice approach requires changing the way society thinks and acts. To do this requires challenging the status quo.

The Status Quo

Simply put, the status quo is the way that things are, or the existing state of affairs. Changes to the status quo are often seen as a threat to those that are comfortable with or benefit from the way that society is currently organized and functions. Change is often resisted when it is seen as a threat to the status quo. Organizations and society tend to gravitate to a state of homeostasis, or the tendency to maintain an internal stability in the face of change. This tendency toward homeostasis, or stasis which is a state of equilibrium or balance, mitigates against change that may bring people into the unknown or to a place where the majority or those with power and influence are uncomfortable.

Maintaining the Status Quo

While human service planners are focused on social justice and how to make our society more just and equitable, there is often a sense that they are swimming against the current. Our politics tend to drift toward the status quo, while making small changes that all too often favor one group over another. Human service organizations seeking to improve the lives of their constituents are dependent upon government funding and grants from foundations and corporations. Government priorities change with each election and new occupants in the seat of power. Many foundations are funded by the bequests of wealthy and powerful people who determine the mission of the foundation, often based upon their own interests and not necessarily on the most pressing needs that should be addressed. This places an additional burden on social justice planners to show that it is the institutions perpetuating inequality that must be addressed.

Figure 1.7 illustrates examples of the social forces that work to maintain the status quo. Program planners often run into these challenges that tend to mitigate against change. People are often afraid or reticent about change because they have grown familiar with the current situation. Change can cause fear because it often asks people to venture into

Figure 1.7 Maintaining the status quo

the unknown. While people may be unhappy or question current conditions, they may be more fearful stepping out of their comfort zone or of failure, choosing to stay with the familiar instead of seeking needed change.

When the government does not provide the resources needed at the local and national level to fight poverty, discrimination, substance abuse, racism or to address mental health issues, domestic violence or other challenges that so many people face in society today, the human services are forced to look to the private sector to fund initiatives. This gives wealthy individuals the option to choose the issues they will address through their philanthropy and private foundations. The National Committee for Responsive Philanthropy (n.d.) calls on philanthropies to provide "at least 25 percent of its grant dollars for advocacy, organizing and civic engagement to promote equity, opportunity and justice in our society." If this call must be made to motivate foundations to focus on social justice issues it is clear that this is not happening. Additionally, with a target of only 25%, the bulk of foundation philanthropy would still be focused on programs and interventions that address a need but still may be a part of maintaining the status quo.

To understand human services planning and funding we must ask the question "who benefits, who pays" (Abramovitz, 2001). If the beneficiaries of a proposed program are not perceived as the ones who also pay for it, then the human service planners are placed in a more challenging position to gain sufficient funding. Far too often the human services are faced with the response "I work hard, why should I pay for people who are unwilling to work?" When posed this way, this seems a reasonable question to ask. Why should hard working people be asked or even forced to pay for services and benefits for people who they believe to be "unwilling to work?" We have a long history in the U.S. of placing blame for poverty, houselessness, substance abuse and other societal inequalities on the people who are experiencing them.

Challenging the Status Quo

A social justice perspective challenges the status quo by moving us beyond the way things have always been to a new paradigm encouraging us to think differently. In other words, it takes us out of our comfort zone and opens up other possibilities beyond what we know and how we are used to doing things. And therein lies the challenge. People are used to things the way that they are, even if they may disagree with current conditions. To put it simply, the familiar is the enemy of change. People grow comfortable with what they know and what they have experienced, even if they know there might be something better out there. We've all heard the phrase "better the devil that you know than the one you don't." This mindset is what helps get ineffective leaders and politicians elected and reelected, and helps to keep us mired in the old ways of doing things. This is where a social justice perspective comes in. It is incumbent upon human service planners to develop a better way. This can be done by demonstrating that another way of organizing society exists and how it will benefit all people, not just those affected by social inequities. In the book *The Sum of Us*, Heather McGhee (2021) interrogates this idea, demonstrating how racism has costs for white people as well, and how the belief in a zero-sum society hurts all members of society when any one group is held back.

To build a society based upon a belief in social justice we must work to break down the myths of poverty and other conditions that cause people to depend upon government welfare programs to address their unmet needs. A social justice approach requires examining the causes of poverty and other issues affecting families and individuals through a structural lens. Rank (2005) points out that at some point in their lives as many as 50% of Americans will experience poverty. The author goes on to explain that it cannot be an individual failing but rather it is a societal, or institutional failing when that many people experience poverty at least once in their lives. Weissman (2013) updated Rank's work:

> more adults than you might expect – 44.8 percent by age 60 – end up relying on safety-net programs such as food stamps and TANF. But only a relatively small portion of the country uses these services for more than a handful of years.

Figure 1.8 illustrates some of the structural conditions that contribute to poverty. As of this writing, the federal minimum wage is just $7.25 an hour, barely enough to raise a full-time employee above the federal poverty level for an individual, but well below the federal poverty level for a family of two or more. This is just one of many structural barriers that keep so many

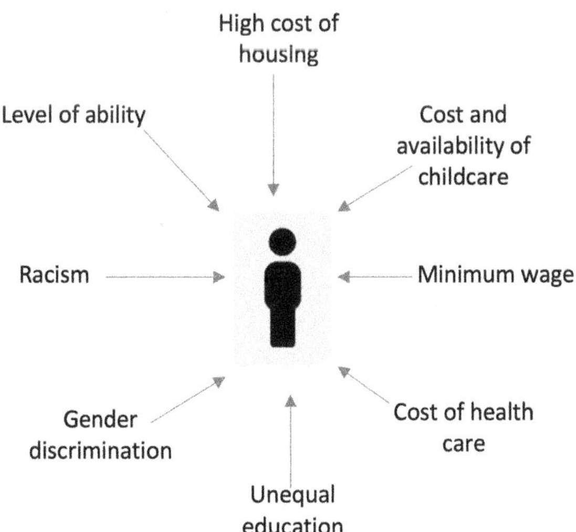

Figure 1.8 Structural poverty

Americans trapped in poverty. Other factors include the unaffordability and lack of available childcare, the high cost of health care, discrimination and the paucity of affordable housing. These structural barriers in the United States, with a poverty rate of 17.8%, mean that the country has one of the highest poverty levels of any industrialized nation (World Population Review, 2020). There are many grassroots and national efforts working to change these structural barriers, but they are met with significant resistance. After the 2020 presidential election, there was a significant effort to raise the minimum wage to $15 an hour, based on the belief that no one should be forced to work full-time and still live in poverty. But that argument was not enough to change the minds of legislators.

An Approach to Youth Crime

Challenging the Status Quo

According to statistics compiled by the Annie E. Casey Foundation (n.d.) the United States leads the industrialized world in the number and percentage of incarcerated young people. The most recent statistics show that more than 60,000 young people are held in juvenile detention centers. A study conducted by Human Rights Watch and the American Civil Liberties Union found that in 2011 more than 95,000 youth were incarcerated in adult prisons (2016). The fact that the U.S. singularly, among all industrialized nations, incarcerates a higher percentage of its young people points to a systemic inequity rather than a problem with young people. Youth incarceration is so pernicious in this country that it has been given a name, the "School to Prison Pipeline."

Research by the U.S. Department of Education (n.d.) demonstrates how the school to prison pipeline operates. In 2016, nearly one quarter of all African American school-age children were punished with suspension or expulsion from school, while only 8% of white school-age children received the same punishment.

> Black students are more likely to get in trouble in school and to end up suspended, compared to white students. This racial disparity in school discipline is both a cause and consequence of enduring racial inequality in America. And it is important because it means that black students, especially black boys, are more likely to end up on the wrong track: getting less schooling, heading towards trouble with the criminal justice system, and, later in life, having fewer opportunities in the labor force.
>
> (Zill & Wilcox, 2019)

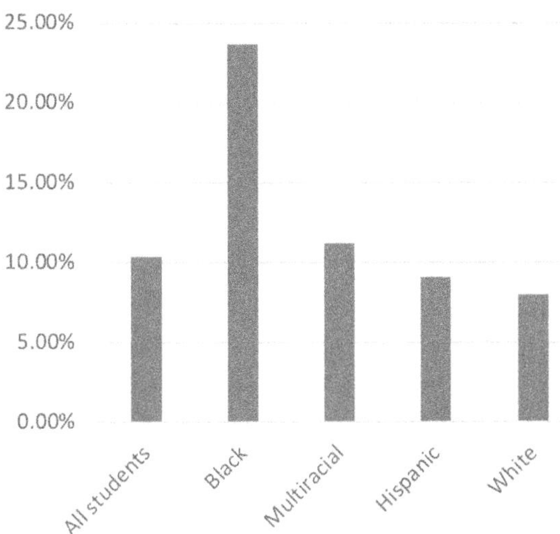

Figure 1.9 School suspensions and expulsions, 2016
Source: National Household Education Surveys

The crime and high school dropout statistics suggest that we are losing many of our young people to violence and to the criminal legal system. According to the Centers for Disease Control (CDC), homicide is the third leading cause of death for young people between the ages of ten and twenty-four, but it is the leading cause of death for young African Americans in that age group. The CDC further reports that young people under the age of eighteen represent 10% of all arrests for violent crimes and that 20% of young people report being bullied in school (CDC, 2020).

Can a social justice approach to youth and adolescents who are deemed at-risk or in violation of some societal norms help reduce the harm that is being done by the current approach? Currently there are developing approaches that incorporate a social justice response and help young people to get back on track to creating a better future for themselves, their families and communities. These social justice approaches are Restorative Justice and Positive Youth Development.

> Positive Youth Development is a holistic approach that focuses on creating a developmentally appropriate learning setting for young people. Positive youth development strategies focus on forging positive relationships; strengthening academic, soft and technical skills; cultivating trustworthy, safe

> spaces; and offering youth opportunities to succeed in meaningful ways. Another defining characteristic of Positive Youth Development is that youth are treated as equal partners and engage with their communities, schools, organizations, peer groups and families in ways that are both constructive and productive.
>
> (Barton and Butts, 2008)

Restorative Justice, providing a social justice approach to crime, includes both perpetrator and victim, by

> acknowledging that crime causes injury to people and communities, it insists that justice repair those injuries and that the parties be permitted to participate in that process. Restorative justice programs, therefore, enable the victim, the offender and affected members of the community to be directly involved in responding to the crime. They become central to the criminal justice process, with governmental and legal professionals serving as facilitators of a system that aims at offender accountability, reparation to the victim and full participation by the victim, offender and community.
>
> (Center for Justice and Reconciliation at Prison Fellowship International, 2005)

Restorative justice is an approach to justice emphasizing repairing the harm caused by crime. It also focuses on addressing the harms revealed by criminal behavior, recognizing that crime can also be a byproduct of inequities faced in everyday life.

> The premise behind restorative justice is to shift attention from determining what law was broken, who we should punish for breaking that law and how we should punish them, to determining what harm has been done, and to whom and how we can best address the concerns of those affected by the harm.
>
> (Gordon, 2020)

Summarizing this approach, van Wormer (2003) writes,

> restorative justice suggests that the most important fact about crime is that it causes harm to individuals, their families and communities... Instead of focusing on a past wrong, what is needed is a form of justice that helps orient offenders toward the present and future state of affairs, toward membership in

the community rather than removal from it. What is needed is a three-pronged system of justice: justice for the individual offender, the victim, and the community.

(p. 442)

Challenging Implicit Bias and Victim Blaming

Challenging the status quo also requires social justice planners to both understand and challenge implicit bias and victim blaming. Looking at social issues through a lens of social inequity goes beyond blaming the individual by examining the causes of inequality and the structures and beliefs that perpetuate it. It moves us away from "blaming the victims," toward an understanding of why certain people are impacted by challenges while others are not. Casting societal challenges as social problems caused by some inadequacy of those impacted by these problems allows society to absolve and insulate itself by blaming the victim through finding fault with those experiencing these challenges.

For example, implicit bias on the part of many white Americans supports the belief that Black men are overrepresented in the criminal legal system due to their own lack of self-control and criminal tendencies.

> Implicit bias tests have shown that the general public holds negative associations of Blacks and Latinos and suspects them of criminality. These biases have also been documented among police officers and judges and are believed to reach all corners of the criminal justice system.
>
> (Ghandnoosh, 2014)

These attitudes and stereotypes demonstrate how a victim can be seen as a perpetrator or responsible for the challenges they face due to implicit bias on the part of those with power and authority. By blaming the victim, society lessens the exposure of its institutions and places the cause of the problem within the affected individuals or groups. As Ibram X. Kendi (2016) points out, racist ideas about the inferiority of Africans were used to justify the transatlantic slave trade. These same racist ideas and attributes that were developed to justify slavery have been used since emancipation to justify the social inequities that result today.

In the article "Why do people blame the victim?" Feldman (2018) places victim blaming in a different context:

> we psychologically separate ourselves from the victim. We wonder if he or she had done something to invite the tragedy … we tell ourselves, then it won't happen to me. After all, the world is a just place. So, our tendency to blame the victim is ultimately self-protective.

Implicit Bias and Policing

In the summer of 2020, the protests under the banner of "Black Lives Matter" coalesced over police shootings of unarmed Black men who were often described as threatening to the police. One example of how implicit bias plays out in policing of Black men can be seen in the comments of Police Officer Darren Wilson after he shot and killed an unarmed Black man, eighteen-year-old Michael Brown. In his grand jury testimony, Wilson described Brown as

> just staring at me, almost like to intimidate me or to overpower me, he looked up at me and had the most intense aggressive face. The only way I can describe it, it looks like a demon, that's how angry he looked.
>
> (Sanburn, 2014)

Darren Wilson was a trained police officer who stood 6' 4" and weighed 210 pounds, using as his defense the fact that he was afraid of an unarmed eighteen-year-old youth. Because Brown was physically large as well, and Wilson felt intimidated by this large, unarmed Black man, the grand jury did not indict Wilson for murder, one more example of how pervasive implicit bias is in our society.

Social Capital

Social capital offers program planners another intervention to help challenge the status quo. Social capital refers to the productive value of social connections and how these contribute to improving the quality of life and one's chances of succeeding in life.

Social capital helps to explain how power relations and hierarchies are maintained in an unequal society and can help explain how these imbalances exist beyond mere economic explanations. Social capital consists of three major components: bonds, bridges and linkages. Bonds are links to people who share a common identity. Social bonds help in a number of ways, providing support – emotionally, socially and economically. These can include family, close friends and others who share a culture or identity. Bridges extend beyond this shared identity to friends, colleagues and associates who help to enlarge one's social and professional network. Finally, linkages further extend one's circle to people who command more social capital than they do (Scrivens & Smith, 2013). When designing a program intervention to help individuals, families or communities to rise out of poverty or to improve their quality of life, program planners can increase the chances of success if they include a component to raise the social capital of the community and/or program participants.

Figure 1.10 illustrates the range of components of social capital that create value for individuals. These include:

- family connections; family, business and personal networks;
- reciprocity, which includes favors and help done by and for people;
- social norms that determine what is and is not acceptable;
- personal and collective efficacy which is the belief in one's ability, or those of the group to which one belongs, to perform behaviors that will lead to success;
- sense of belonging determines if a person feels that they belong to a group or institution that can help them to succeed;
- trust, the basic sense that you feel can trust others;
- networks are the connections that you have that can help you to pursue your goals.

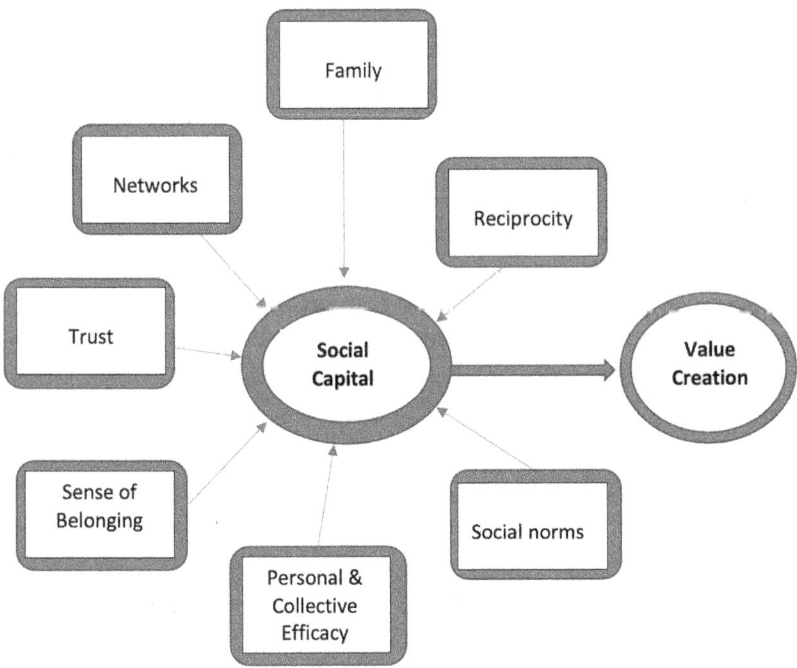

Figure 1.10 Social capital

Most middle-class people know the value of social capital. We see this when a young person gets an internship in their chosen field because a parent, relative or family friend have connections. A prime example of social capital is "legacy" admissions to elite colleges and universities. If an applicant has a parent or grandparent that attended the school, that can improve a student's chances of being accepted. At the selective institutions, 10 to 15% of students have a parent who also attended (Pinsker, 2019).

An example of how lack of social capital can impact individuals and communities can be seen in the Covid-19 pandemic of 2020–2021. When schools closed in-person classes and resorted to virtual classrooms, many low-income and rural students were essentially left behind. Students without available computers or access to reliable internet were unable to participate in the learning process at the same level of their more privileged classmates.

> Closing schools and transitioning to online learning is critical to stymying the spread of the virus, but experts agree that the transition won't be easy. Among the many challenges – from providing meals for low-income students to finding childcare for essential workers – relying on remote learning and online classes also exposes the country's deep digital divides. Simply put, too many American children live without essential internet services.
>
> (Fishbane & Tomer, 2020)

In an attempt to offset the negative impacts of closing schools for in-person learning, middle and upper-class families with resources resorted to creating so-called "learning pods." According to the *New York Times*,

> these pods consisted of small groups of students who come together outside of the classroom, often with a paid online tutor engaging students in their school's curriculum. The high cost of participating in these pods exacerbate inequalities between those who have the time and resources to network with potential pod-mates or hire private tutors and those who can't.
>
> (Blum & Miller, 2020)

Learning pods helped to further the social capital of participants while leaving behind many low-income students forced to struggle on their own without computers, internet access or tutors to help them engage in the material.

When Good Intentions Are Not Enough

As the late John Lewis, civil rights icon and Congressperson from Georgia, has said, "make good trouble." We may have the best of intentions, but if we do not make "good trouble," change does not happen. The fight for social justice is not an easy one. The forces mitigating against it are strong and our societal institutions are firmly rooted. Good intentions alone are not enough to overcome this. Understanding the social inequities built into our societal institutions builds a strong foundation to fight that good fight and get into "good trouble."

The words inscribed on the Martin Luther King, Jr. memorial in Washington DC – *The arc of the moral universe is long, but it bends toward justice* – encapsulate the long, hard work needed to achieve true social justice. Good intentions are merely the first step in this long march toward justice.

Good intentions can also lead to unintended consequences. This phenomenon was first identified by the sociologist Robert Merton in 1936 and is still relevant today. Merton first identified the detrimental outcomes that result from actions taken for good purposes. Unintended consequences are outcomes that would not have happened if the action, based on good intentions, had not occurred. In order to avoid unintended consequences, human service program planners must uncover the variables that can have an impact on the outcome. However, it is not possible to identify and understand all variables before taking action. The need to move forward before all information is known and understood can lead to a discrepancy between what is anticipated and the actual outcomes.

Merton (1936) highlights a number of ways in which good intentions can lead to unintended consequences. These can include incomplete knowledge, faulty assumptions, ignoring or not considering some issues, ignoring contrary facts and information, and the impact of values held by the planners who are often under pressure to respond in a timely manner to issues that are identified. This pressure to move quickly, whether to meet demands of a funder or to address issues that have moved into the public consciousness, can subvert good intentions through unintended consequences. Pressure to move quickly or to meet a funder's requirements or priorities can cause planners to move forward before enough is known about the issue in order to develop an understanding of how best to address it.

Moving forward with good intentions can often hit roadblocks that compound the planning effort. Even though planners may have the best of intentions and develop an intervention that will effectively address the issues, there are external concerns that can undermine these efforts. Moving forward with the belief that you are doing the right thing and correcting a wrong can be subverted by the fact that there can be differing values between individuals and groups and these values may be conflicting. A condition that presents itself as a need to be addressed may not be viewed as such by others who do not see how the issue impacts them. It can be difficult to define the issue you are addressing because others may not agree on the issue. Often, the conflicting costs and values cannot be enumerated, compared and weighed to determine the best course of action. Finally, it can be difficult to predict the costs and impact of various alternatives, making it difficult to choose the best path forward.

Good intentions must be balanced with and weighed against how best to move forward. While it is never possible to gather all of the information or explore all possible outcomes, there is a point when program planners determine that enough information has been gathered and unintended consequences and outcomes have been sufficiently explored so that a determination can be made of the best path forward. It is not possible to investigate all possible outcomes and enumerate all related costs. The need to move forward to correct inequities must be tempered through a plan informed by the best available information. Exploring the limitations to an effective intervention plan can also include investigating

The Intersection of Program Planning and Social Policy

Human service professionals are impacted by social policies, legislation and funding in every aspect of our work. These often limit the breadth of interventions that can be successfully developed. A program plan that does not address or solve the inequities or prevent others from experiencing the same inequities can still provide relief and much needed assistance to people who are impacted. Perhaps the best metaphor to illustrate this is told in a story that has been attributed to many authors over the years. In this story a person is walking on the beach and sees a dancing woman in the distance. They also notice thousands of starfish that were stranded by the receding tide. As they approach the dancing woman, they see that the woman is tossing starfish back into the sea one at a time. They question what difference can the woman make when there are so many starfish on the beach? In response the woman picks up and tosses one more starfish into the sea and turns and says, "I just made a difference for that one."

Policy advocacy is the tool that human service planners can use to broaden their impact. While developing programs and interventions that provide direct support and services, program planners can also become involved in policy advocacy to address the causes and implications of the social inequities that are being addressed in program planning. As we help each starfish, we can also advocate to help the many starfish for whom we cannot intervene and for an intervention that will help prevent many more from becoming stranded by the receding tide. Another way of looking at this is that individual interventions address the inequity downstream, while impacting the policies that cause the inequity would address the problem upstream.

the policies and regulations that may limit the effectiveness or breadth of a planned intervention.

Chapter Summary

Main Points

1. Social justice is achieved when no one is denied access to the resources and opportunities that are needed to live healthy, productive lives. This is accomplished as a result of equality of opportunity for all members of society through the inclusion of everyone in the full benefits of society and the empowerment of all people to participate fully in the economic, social, political and cultural life of the country.
2. Systems thinking examines issues through an understanding of the various systems in society and how they interact to produce the outcomes that lead to inequality.
3. Intersectionality requires looking at the multiple identities and how these interact with the person in order to understand their life situation.
4. The program components that further social justice include full participation of the people and communities served in the planning and evaluation of the program, addressing policies that impact the inequities being addressed, capacity building for participants and the community, self-determination for participants, a focus on improving social and economic conditions, ongoing evaluation, and sharing information on what works.
5. *Social problem* and *inequality* are common terms that do not give insight into the causes of an issue. *Social inequality* suggests that there is an underlying unfairness that is causing the problem or inequality. Looking at something solely as an inequality or a problem can lead to victim blaming.
6. *Social capital* is the benefits enjoyed by people provided by family, friends or others that share a cultural identity. It also includes friends, colleagues, associates and networks that can help an individual improve their quality of life and chances of succeeding.
7. Policy advocacy is an important tool for social justice program planners to become involved in to broaden impact and make larger social change.

Key Terms

Social justice
Systems thinking
Intersectionality
Social inequity
Implicit bias
Status quo
Paradigm shift
Interdependence
Social capital

Discussion Questions

1. Choose a current social issue that impacts a particular population group negatively and discuss it through the perspective of social problem, social inequality and social inequity.
2. How does social capital compare to economic capital? How are each accrued and how do they help a person to advance or overcome barriers and challenges?
3. What do you think Einstein meant by the quote commonly attributed to him that "we cannot solve problems with the same thinking that helped to create them"? Apply this to a current social program; how does the design or goal of the intervention reflect this?
4. If you were designing a program for a family that is unhoused, how would knowledge of intersectionality help you to understand the challenges that the family is facing?
5. Is it a fair expectation that human service program planners and providers should also become policy advocates, or should this reasonably be left to others?

Notes

1 A review of professional journal articles focusing on inequality did not produce a definition of "social inequality." When the term is used, it appears that authors assume a common understanding on the part of the reader.

2 This author reviewed professional journal articles with "social inequity" or "social inequities" in the title and all assumed a common understanding of the term as none included a definition.

References

Abramovitz, M (2001) Everyone is still on welfare: The role of redistribution in social policy. *Social Work*, October 2001, 46(4), 297–308

Adams, M., Bell, L. A. & Griffin, P. (2016). Teaching for diversity and social justice (3rd ed.). New York: Routledge

Annie E. Casey Foundation (n.d.a) Positive youth development, https://www.aecf.org/topics/positive-youth-development/?gclid=Cj0KCQjw0oCDBhCPARIsAII3C_EPK53dzCHi5Okkw9hYPBs65oF7QxBQc0bhbnltMU2SzvCncY3KWroaAvJfEALw_wcB, retrieved 3/29/21

Annie E. Casey Foundation (n.d.b) Youth residing in juvenile detention, correctional and/or residential facilities in the United States, https://datacenter.kidscount.org/data/tables/42-youth-residing-in-juvenile-detention-correctional-and-or-residential-facilities?loc=1&loct=2&gclid=Cj0KCQjw0oCDBhCPARIsAII3C_EYYN8C-ytGx7Oupt6rDKo75iC2XPPgElVrt6pTEmDG8uiKJ0gT7bQaAoCzEALw_wcB#detailed /2/2-52/false/871,573,36,867,133,18,17,14,12,10/any/319,17599, retrieved 3/26/21

Arnold, R.D. & Wade, J.P. (2015) A definition of systems thinking approach. *Procedia Computer Science*, 44, 669–678

Atewologun, D. (2018) Intersectionality theory and practice, human resource management, organizational behavior, research methods, *Social Issues Online*, https://oxfordre.com/business/view/10.1093/acrefore/9780190224851.001.0001/acrefore-9780190224851-e-48, retrieved 11/30/20

Associated Press (2020) *Stylebook*, 55th ed. New York, NY: Associated Press

Barton, W.H. & Butts, J.A. (2008) Building on strengths: Positive youth development in juvenile justice programs. *Chapin Hill Center for Children at the University of Chicago*, https://assets.aecf.org/m/resourcedoc/aecf-BuildingOnStrengthPositiveYouthDevelopment-2008.pdf, retrieved 4/10/21

Bennett, H. (2008) Organizing to abolish the prison-industrial complex. *Dissident Voice*, 7/11/2008, https://dissidentvoice.org/2008/07/organizing-to-abolish-the-prison-industrial-complex/, retrieved 11/30/19.

Blum, D. & Miller, F. (2020) What parents need to know about learning pods, *New York Times*, 8/18/20

Center for Justice and Reconciliation at Prison Fellowship International (2005) What is restorative justice? https://www.d.umn.edu/~jmaahs/Correctional%20Assessment/rj%20brief.pdf, retrieved 3/29/21

Centers for Disease Control (2020) Health equity considerations and racial and ethnic minority groups, https://www.cdc.gov/coronavirus/2019-ncov/community/health-equity/raceethnicity.html?CDC_AA_refVal=https%3A%2F%2Fwww.cdc.gov%2Fcoronavirus%2F2019-ncov%2Fneed-extra-precautions%2Fracial-ethnic-minorities.html, retrieved 7/24/20

Colton, M. (2002) Special issue editorial. *British Journal of Social Work*, 32, 643–663

Crenshaw, K. (1989) Demarginalizing the intersection of race and sex: A black feminist critique of antidiscrimination doctrine, feminist theory and antiracist politics, *University of Chicago Legal Forum*, 1, Article 8, retrieved 110/15/20

Curran, J.W. & Jaffe, H.W. (2011) AIDS: The early years and CDC's response, https://www.cdc.gov/mmwr/preview/mmwrhtml/su6004a11.htm, retrieved 6//30/21

Dodson, M. (1993) Human rights in Australia, Australian Human Rights Commission, https://humanrights.gov.au/our-work/education/human-rights-australia, retrieved 3/2/21

Faegin, J.R. (2004) Social justice and sociology: Agendas for the twenty-first century. In W.K. Carroll (ed.) *Critical strategies for social research*. Canadian Scholars Press

Federal Reserve Board (2019) Survey of consumer finance, https://www.federalreserve.gov/econres/scfindex.htm, retrieved 7/9/21

Feldman, D.B. (2018) Why do people blame the victim? *Psychology Today*, 3/2/18, https://www.psychologytoday.com/us/blog/supersurvivors/201803/why-do-people-blame-the-victim, retrieved 10/1/20

Fishbane, L. & Tomer, A. (2020) As classes move online during COVID-19, what are disconnected students to do?, Brookings Institution, https://www.brookings.edu/blog/the-avenue/2020/03/20/as-classes-move-online- during- covid-19-what-are-disconnected-students-to-do/, retrieved 9/30/20

France, D. (2020) The activists, How ACT UP – The coalition that fought against AIDS stigma and won medications that slowed the plague – Forever changed patients' rights, protests and American political organizing as it's practiced today. *The New York Times*, 4/13/20

Garrow, E. & Bailey, T. (2021) Banished and abandoned, https://www.aclusocal.org/sites/default/files/banished_and_abandoned_in_lancaster_-_aclu_socal_report_-_feb_2021.pdf, retrieved 7/9/21

Ghandnoosh, N. (2014) Race and punishment: Racial perceptions of crime and support for punitive policies, Sentencing Project, https://www.sentencingproject.org/publications/race-and-punishment-racial-perceptions-of-crime-and-support-for-punitive-policies/#B.%20Implicit%20Biases%20About%20People%20of%20Color, retrieved 10/1/20

Gordon, N. (2020) Understanding what restorative justice is and isn't, *Law 360*, https://www.law360.com/articles/1228012/understanding-what-restorative-justice-is-and-isn-t, retrieved 3/29/21

Greco, A. (2011) "Having one's own" and distributive justice in Plato's Republic. *History of Political Thought*, 32(2), July, 185–214

Green, B.L., Miranda, J., Daroowalla, A. & Siddique, J. (2005). Trauma exposure, mental health functioning and program needs of women in jail. *Crime and Delinquency*, 51, 133–151

HUD, n.d., https://files.hudexchange.info/resources/documents/HomelessDefinition_Recordkeeping RequirementsandCriteria.pdf, retrieved 10/15/20

Human Rights Watch (2016) Children behind bars: The global overuse of detention of children, https://www.hrw.org/world-report/2016/country-chapters/africa-americas-asia-europe/central-asia-middle-east/north#, retrieved 3/26/21

Kaiser Family Foundation (2021) Health coverage of immigrants, https://www.kff.org/racial-equity-and-health-policy/fact-sheet/health-coverage-of-immigrants/, retrieved 8/10/21

Kendi, I.X. (2016) *Stamped from the beginning.* Bold Type Books

James, D. & Glaze, L. (2006). *Mental health problems of prison and jail inmates: Special report.* Washington, DC: U.S. Department of Justice, Bureau of Justice Statistics

Libretexts.org (2020) What is a social problem?, 11/14/2020, https://socialsci.libretexts.org/Bookshelves/Social_Work_and_Human_Services/Social_Problems_Continuity_and_Change/01%3A_Understanding_Social_Problems/1.01%3A_What_Is_a_Social_Problem, retrieved 6/29/21

Longres, J. & Scanlon, E. (2001) Social justice and the research curriculum, *Journal of Social Work Education*, 37, 447–463

Lutz, D.W. (2009) African Ubuntu philosophy and global management. *Journal of Business Ethics*, 84(S3), 313–328

Lynch, S.M., DeHart, D.D., Belknap, J.E., Green, B.L., Dass-Brailsford, P., Johnson, K.A., & Whalley, E. (2014). A multisite study of the prevalence of serious mental illness, PTSD, and substance use disorders of women in jail. *Psychiatric Services in Advance*, 3, 1–5

McGhee, H. (2021) *The sum of us.* New York, NY: One World

Merrian-Webster (n.d.) Intersectionality, https://www.merriam-webster.com/dictionary/intersectionality, retrieved 7/6/21

Merton, R.K. (1936) The unintended consequences of purposive social action, *American Sociological Review*, I, 894–904

Michailakas, D. & Schirme, W. (2014) Social work and social problems: A contribution from systems theory and constructionism, *International Journal of Social Welfare*, 23(4)

Miller, D. (2001) *Principles of social justice.* Cambridge, MA: Harvard University Press

NASW (n.d.) Social justice priorities, https://www.socialworkers.org/Advocacy/Social-Justice/Social-Justice-Priorities, retrieved 10/01/20

National Alliance to End Homelessness (2019) What housing first really means, https://endhomelessness.org/what-housing-first-really-means/, retrieved 10/01/20

National Committee for Responsive Philanthropy (n.d.) Philanthropy at its best, https://www.ncrp.org/about-us/philanthropy-at-its-best, retrieved 10/15/20

National Law Center for Homelessness and Poverty (2015) Homelessness in America: Overview of data and Causes, January 2015, https://nlchp.org/wp.content/uploads/2018/10/Homeless_Stats_Fact_Sheet.pdf, retrieved 10/15/20

Nozick, R. (1974) *Anarchy, state and utopia.* New York, NY: Basic Books

Pinsker, J. (2019) The real reasons legacy preferences exist, *The Atlantic*, 4/4/2019, https://www.theatlantic.com/education/archive/2019/04/legacy-admissions-preferences-ivy/586465/, retrieved 10/10/20

Rank M.R. (2005) *One nation, underprivileged.* Oxford University Press

Rawls, J. (1971) *A theory of justice.* Harvard University Press

Reisch, M. & Garvin, C.D. (2016) *Social work and social justice: Concepts, challenges and strategies.* New York, NY: Oxford University Press

Richmond, B. (1994) Systems thinking/Systems dynamics: Let's just get on with it. *Systems Dynamics Review*, 4(2–3), Summer/Fall, 135–157

Sanburn, J. (2014) All the ways Darren Wilson described being afraid of Michael Brown, *Time*, 11/25/2014

Schulman, S. (2021) *Let the record show.* New York, NY: Farrar, Straus and Giroux

Scrivens, K. & Smith, C. (2013) *Four interpretations of social capital: An agenda for measurement*, OECD Statistics Working papers, No. 2013/06. Paris: OECD Publishing, Paris, https://doi.org/10.1787/5jzbcx010wmt-en, retrieved 6/2/20

TheSentencingProject(2020)Incarceratedwomenandgirls,https://www.sentencingproject.org/publications/incarcerated-women-and-girls/, retrieved 6/29/21

Slayton, N. (2021) Time to retire the word "homeless" and opt for "houseless" or "unhoused" instead, 5/21/21 https://www.architecturaldigest.com/story/homeless-unhoused, retrieved 7/8/21

Steadman, H.J., Osher, C., Clark Robins, P., Case, B. & Samuels, S. (2009) Prevalence of serious mental illness among jail inmates. *Psychiatric Services*, 6(6), June, 761–765

Stone, C., Danilo, T., Sherman, A. & Taylor, R. (2020). *A guide to statistics on historical trends in income inequality.* Washington, DC: Center on Budget and Policy Priorities. https://www.cbpp.org/research/poverty-and-inequality/a-guide-to-statistics-on-historical-trends-in-income-inequality, retrieved 2/24/21

Turaki, Y. (2006) *Foundations of African traditional religion and worldview.* Nairobi, Kenya: World Alive

United Nations (2000) Gender and racial discrimination, report of the expert group meeting, Zagreb, Croatia, November 21–24, 2000, https://www.un.org/womenwatch/daw/csw/genrac/index.html, retrieved 9/15/20

United Nations (2006) Social justice in an open world: The role of the United Nations, The International Forum for Social Development, https://www.un.org/esa/socdev/documents/ifsd/SocialJustice.pdf, retrieved 9/15/20

Urban Institute (2017) Nine charts about wealth inequality in America (updated), https://apps.urban.org/features/wealth-inequality-charts/, retrieved 9/15/20

USAID (n.d.), Systems thinking and action for nutrition, https://www.spring-nutrition.org/publications/briefs/systems-thinking-and-action-nutrition, retrieved 9/15/20

Van Wormer, K. (2003) Restorative justice: A model for social work practice with families. *Families and Society: The Journal of Contemporary Human Services*, 84(3), 441–448

Weissman, J. (2013) A shockingly high number of Americans experience poverty, *The Atlantic*, 11/6/2013, https://www.theatlantic.com/business/archive/2013/11/a-shockingly-high-number-of-americans-experience-poverty/281172/, retrieved 10/1/20

White, A. (2004) Reagan's AIDS Legacy/Silence Equals Death, SF GATE, https://abcnews.go.com/Health/video/president-reagan-delivers-major-speech-aids-epidemic-1987-46492956, retrieved 10/1/20

World Population Review (2020) https://worldpopulationreview.com/country-rankings/poverty-rate-by-country, retrieved 7/11/21

Young, I. (1990) *Justice and the politics of difference*. Princeton, NJ: Princeton University Press

Zill, N. & Wilcox, W.B. (2019) The Black-white divide in suspensions: What is the role of family? *Institute for Family Studies*, https://ifstudies.org/blog/the-black-white-divide-in-suspensions-what-is-the-role-of-family, retrieved 7/10/21

2 Working with the Community to Define the Issue

Learning Objectives

1. Understand the importance of clearly defining the issue to be addressed.
2. Articulate the difference between cultural competence and cultural humility.
3. Understand the framework for engaging underserved populations.
4. Value the importance of participatory planning.
5. Articulate how an understanding of Maslow's Hierarchy of Needs can be used to inform program planning.
6. Understand the value of "why" and how that understanding can be used to help motivate people.

Chapter Overview

This chapter explores the importance of community participation in program planning and reviews concepts and ideas to foster this participation.

The first step for human service program planners is to establish trust with the community as a preface to developing a working partnership. Then the planner can work with the community to define the issue or change to be addressed. The way in which the issue is defined, sets up the intervention and the outcomes that will be sought. Accomplishing this requires focusing on how to communicate effectively with community members and understanding how to work with marginalized populations. Cultural competence and cultural humility are discussed as a foundation for developing trust and open communication. Concepts including participatory planning and the importance of understanding Maslow's Hierarchy of Needs, and its impact on determining where planners begin the intervention, are explored. Finally, the chapter concludes with a discussion of the importance of "why." Why it is important to address the inequity and why should anyone care enough to get involved in changing the inequities for the better.

Lilla Watson, Australian aboriginal elder, activist and educator expressed the importance of working with the community rather than for

DOI: 10.4324/9781003148777-2

the community: "If you have come here to help me, you are wasting your time. But if you have come because your liberation is bound up with mine, then let us work together."

The Definition Defines the Impact

As discussed in Chapter 1, language matters. How we define the issue determines how we will address it. For example, if we are addressing food insecurity as the problem, defined as some people with lack of food, then we have implicitly determined that the solution is to provide food. Simply stated any food will do and any program that provides food is addressing the issue successfully. But do they? Food banks, our front-line defense against food insecurity, do not address the issue of why – why in the world's richest country do millions of families experience food insecurity at least once?

According to the USDA (n.d.), in 2018 "11.1 per cent of U.S. Households were food insecure at least once during the year," including 5.6 million households that experienced "very low food security." The report further found that "Rates of food insecurity were substantially higher than the national average for single-parent households, and for Black and Hispanic households." These statistics point to an institutional cause that cannot be solved solely through local and regional food banks. Merely providing these families with food does not address the fact that food insecurity, poverty, discrimination, unemployment, and underemployment are all part of the problem. During the pandemic of 2020–2022 another factor affecting millions of people was added to the equation – job loss. As the pandemic continued to ravage communities and businesses were forced to close or reduce their workforce, food banks across the country reported more than a 64% increase in demand (Reily, 2020).

The Problem with Problematic Language

This brings us to the challenge many human service program planners face in defining the issue(s) to be addressed. Once the problem is defined as "lack of" something, then the solution is defined as providing that which is lacking. While in the above example the problem is defined as "lack of food," this is merely a symptom of a larger problem. Yet so many human service and government planners fall back on this simple definition and miss the opportunities to address social inequities at their core.

Therefore, social justice planners must begin by taking the term "lack of" out of their nomenclature. Simple solutions to widespread social inequities rarely work. If the solutions were simple, or as straightforward as "lack of," then they would have been solved long ago. There are many ways to say "lack of" without actually using those two words. A cautionary note here, no matter how you state lack of, it merely simplifies the

Figure 2.1 Do not use "lack of"

problem to "if only we had x then we could solve y." Simplistic at its base, and a nice thought, but a woefully inadequate analysis of the challenge to address the issues involved.

For example, defining food insecurity as a social inequity begins the planning at a more defined and actionable point. We are in a better position to explore the *why*. Why do so many people in the United states suffer from food insecurity, while others do not? Why do millions of people suffer food insecurity during the course of their lives, while others never do?

In order to address complex issues, program planners need a broader and deeper understanding of the challenges and inequities to be faced. To begin exploring this social inequity we must conduct a needs assessment. This will be addressed in detail in Chapter 3. But for now, let's continue to build the case for first understanding the real issues that need to be addressed to reduce the impact of social inequities on people. We are not only addressing inequities, but more importantly we are addressing how these social inequities impact people.

How different would the approach to food insecurity be if program planners and policy experts took the time to understand the inequities more deeply and as a result the definition of the problem changed to something such as: *too many people in the U.S. experience food insecurity due to poverty, unemployment, discrimination and limited access to affordable, nutritional food*? With this definition of the inequity, we begin to see food insecurity through a systems thinking approach, which leads us to the causes of food insecurity. Now we are looking at a broader approach that tackles issues such as the limited availability of fresh vegetables and nutritious food choices and higher prices in low-income communities and communities of color, many of which have been classified as *food deserts*. There are more than 6,500 such areas in the U.S. These so-called food deserts tend to be low-income areas with high rates of abandoned or vacant property, low rates of education, and high unemployment (Dutko et al., 2012). In this description we see the overlapping systems of poverty and racism that contribute to limiting the fresh and nutritious foods available to residents of low-income and communities of color. With this information, we see the direct connection between poverty and income as barriers to the availability of and to people's ability to afford nutritious foods.

Figure 2.2 illustrates some of the major causes of food insecurity and how this inequity can become a vicious cycle feeding upon itself. The inner ring represents some of the major causes of food insecurity. These are surrounded by the impacts of food insecurity on individuals and families. The diagram represents how food insecurity exacerbates the causes, making these inequities even greater and more difficult to overcome.

Without looking at the problem through a systems thinking approach, we can see the issue as the individual fault of people who cannot manage their money to purchase the food needed or worse yet, spending their money on things other than food. This leads to individual approaches to the issue, such as giving away food at a food pantry, offering budgeting workshops for low-income people or nutrition and cooking classes. All of these approaches focus on the individual as the locus of the inequity.

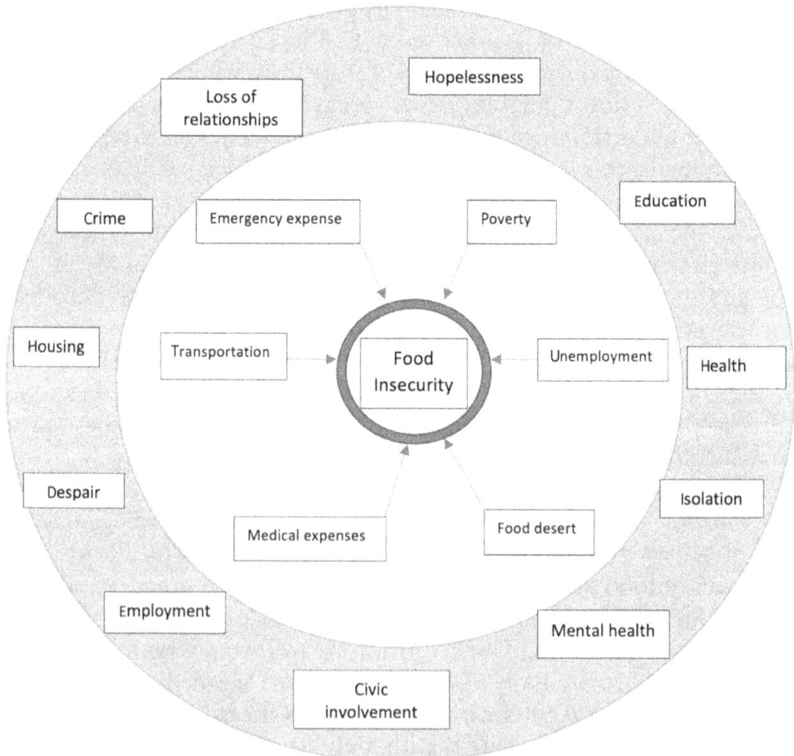

Figure 2.2 Food insecurity contributing factors

Food insecurity is one example of how resources are not fairly or equitably distributed and of our failure, as a society, to address issues that we have come to see as intractable and resulting from personal failings.

Whoever defines the issue and how it is defined sets up the intervention. If we are to address social issues from a social justice perspective, we must first understand the issue and why it remains a challenge. The more narrowly the definition of the problem is focused, the less success we will have in addressing its root cause and its manifestation. When poverty is seen as the core of the issue, rather than food insecurity, we challenge the very foundations of our society. Why are there so many people living in poverty or at risk of poverty and food insecurity in the richest nation in the world. Why do we find this acceptable? A systems thinking and social justice approach does not look to blame the individual but looks into the very systems that not only contribute to or create the problem, but allow it to continue to exist.

Moving from Cultural Competence to Cultural Humility

Cultural competence and cultural humility are significant concepts to understand when working with people and communities who have been marginalized or are culturally or ethnically different than the practitioner. These concepts were first developed in health care settings and later migrated to the human services fields. Each focuses on working across cultural differences, but with different paths forward to successfully arrive at a point of practitioner comfort and effectiveness. While well intentioned, many of these definitions ultimately prove inadequate.

Examining Definitions of Cultural Competence

Betancourt et al. (2003) define cultural competence in health care as

> understanding the importance of social and cultural influences on patients' health beliefs and behaviors; considering how these factors interact at multiple levels of the healthcare delivery system... and, finally, devising interventions that take these issues into account to assure quality health care delivery to diverse patient populations.
> (p. 297)

While this definition is directed toward health care practitioners and institutions, it is also applicable to the human services. The National Association of Social Workers defines cultural competence in the human services as

> the process by which individuals and systems respond respectfully and effectively to people of all cultures, languages, classes, races,

> ethnic backgrounds, religions, spiritual traditions, immigration status, and other diversity factors in a manner that recognizes, affirms, and values the worth of individuals, families, and communities and protects and preserves the dignity of each.
>
> (NASW, 2015, p. 13)

Sue (2006) offers the following working definition of cultural competence:

> Cultural competence is the ability to engage in actions to create conditions that maximize the optimal development of client and client systems. Culturally competent social work practice is defined as the service provider's acquisition of awareness, knowledge, and skills needed to function in a pluralistic democratic society (ability to communicate, interact, negotiate and intervene on behalf of clients from diverse backgrounds), and on an organizational/societal level, advocating effectively to develop new theories, practices, policies, and organizational structures that are more responsive to all groups.
>
> (p. 29)

Implied "Otherness"

These and other definitions of cultural competence rely on a knowledgeable practitioner utilizing this knowledge to help others, thereby placing the practitioner above the receiver of their service or knowledge. They do not address the existence of a power differential between the practitioner and the people with whom they are working.

Fisher-Borne et al. (2015) critique cultural competence when they write that it

> suggests that knowing broad descriptions of various group identities can translate into knowing the life experiences of an individual client. This 'other' focus also assumes that the 'locus' of normalcy is White, Western culture while the 'other' is defined as 'nonwhite, non-Western, non-heterosexual, non-English-speaking, and non-Christian.' With this orientation, the only barriers between provider and client are 'understanding' and 'awareness,' not systemic inequalities.
>
> (p. 170)

Important to note here is that the authors point out the "other" focus, as if the recipient of services and not the practitioner is the other. The practitioner is assumed to be a member of the dominant culture who must learn to interact with the "other." It is this assignment of "otherness" to the recipient of the service that helps to solidify the power differential. The act of "othering" people can lead to maintaining "positions of superiority, dominant groups may deploy processes of 'othering' anyone deemed to be different, creating 'them–us' divisions which label 'others' as inferior and legitimate the exercise of power over them" (Dominelli, 2002, p. 18).

Fisher-Borne et al. (2015) further critique cultural competence, stating,

> Dominant groups (e.g., White people) learn about non-dominant groups (often people of color) to characterize behavior in the name of understanding. With this orientation, learning a group's history is seen as sufficient, with little need to strive for social justice to eliminate oppression.
>
> (p. 170)

Betancourt et al. (2003) critique their own definition of cultural competence offered above, when they write the following:

> ... with the huge array of cultures in the U.S. and the many powerful influences such as acculturation and socioeconomic status leading to intra-group variability, it is difficult to learn a set of facts about any particular culture and hope to be effective.
>
> (p. 118)

In other words, all people are different and unique. Because a person belongs to or identifies with a particular racial, ethnic or cultural group does not suggest that all of the behaviors and beliefs attributed to that group exist within the individual. Chavez (2018) critiques cultural competence as too binary a construct, suggesting that if a practitioner is not culturally competent, they are culturally incompetent, and therefore not prepared to interact with members of groups other than their own.

The term cultural competence can be seen as suggesting there is an end point where one becomes culturally competent and they have done their work. Can such a point ever be reached when there are so many ways that individuals and groups reflect and live their cultural identities?

Striving for Cultural Humility

Cultural humility has emerged as an alternate approach that addresses these critiques. The term humility suggests that the practitioner is humble enough to not believe that they can get to a point where it is possible to know enough about cultures, races, ethnicities and identities that are different than their own. Cultural humility is a journey and not a destination. It is an ongoing process with the recognition that culture is complex and personal and there is always more to know about each other and their lived experiences. It also recognizes that culture and identity are dynamic and evolve over time and with new experiences and perspectives.

CULTURAL COMPETENCE	CULTURAL HUMILITY
• Focuses on knowledge and training • Challenges stereotypes • One can develop competence in a culture that is not their own • Acknowledges the complexity of identity and intersectionality • Identifies the issue as a lack of knowledge • Stresses development of skills to work across difference • Stresses knowledge, skills and behaviors • Can lead to stereotyping the "other" • Focus is on acquisition of knowledge • Suggests the existence of clear, delineated steps to follow • Academic knowledge • There is an endpoint to be achieved	• Understanding cultural difference is a lifetime pursuit with no end goal but with an appreciation of the journey • Acknowledges the complexity of identity and intersectionality • Stresses understanding of self and others • Focuses on developing an understanding of communities, institutions and societal norms • Recognizes the power imbalance in the relationship between planners and the community • Challenges those power imbalances • Requires ongoing self-reflection as a lifelong pursuit • Introspection and co-learning with community members • Challenges power dynamics

Figure 2.3 Cultural competence and cultural humility compared

The National Association of Social Workers in its *Standards and Indicators for Cultural Competence in Social Work Practice* relies on Trevalon and Murray-Garcia (1998) for its definition of cultural humility, in spite of the fact that the authors approach this through a medical lens.

> Cultural humility incorporates a lifelong commitment to self-evaluation and self-critique, to redressing the power imbalances in the patient–physician dynamic, and to developing mutually beneficial and nonpaternalistic clinical and advocacy partnerships with communities on behalf of individuals and defined populations.
>
> (NASW, 2015, p. 16; Trevalon & Murray-Garcia, 1998, p. 123)

Engaging Marginalized Populations and Overcoming Cultural Differences

"Marginalization is both a condition and a process that prevents individuals and groups from full participation in social, economic, and political life enjoyed by the wider society" (Alakhunova et al., 2015). With the knowledge that this lack of participation can be caused by factors beyond the individual or group's ability to control, planners should not assume that people have not been able to improve the conditions of their own lives or communities because they do not have the interest or capacity to participate in the planning process.

Framework for Engaging Underserved Populations

1. Earn trust through partnership,
2. Identify gatekeepers or community leaders,
3. Be multilingual and inclusive,
4. Communicate for understanding,
5. Respect schedules, and
6. Offer something useful.

It is important that planners have a plan for engaging underserved populations, as well as maintaining engagement over time. Stonewall et al. (2017) propose a framework for accomplishing these goals.

Exploring this framework can serve as a guide to engaging marginalized populations and to working within cultural differences.

Earning Trust

Earning trust through partnership is the bedrock foundation of working with any population, but especially with populations that have been marginalized and as a result may not trust planners who represent a formal organization or are from outside of their community. Trust can be seen as both a process and an outcome. As process, trust can be achieved through continuous learning and self-reflection. This can be accomplished through sharing stories and personal and community histories while maintaining an awareness of the existence and impact of power relationships. Trust takes time and consistency and can only be earned through actions that demonstrate a commitment to collaboration. The planner must actively engage in listening to understand the lived experiences and histories of marginalized people that form shared meaning for them (Prusia, 2019).

When community people are invited to be a part of the planning process, room must be made for them as full participants. "Engagement must be a meaningful two-way conversation that accounts for a community's individual and collective history, perceptions, opinions, and successes and failures" (Toor et al., 2014). If the planner invites community members into the process only for the purpose of informing them of the ideas and information that have been gathered and the plans that have already been made that would be a violation of trust. This can result in a wall being built between human service planners and the people for whom they are planning. When the population to be served is not at the table from the beginning, this can be interpreted to mean their input is not important, and their compliant consent is all that is being sought.

In contrast to this negative message, early "participation provides the opportunity for often-disenfranchised groups to be heard and teach the community that they have important things to say" (Community Tool Box, n.d.). Trust is only established when there are real opportunities for meaningful engagement in the planning process.

Identify Community Leaders

Grassroots community leaders are not necessarily people with formal leadership roles or organizations behind them. Often, they can be residents whom others have come to trust and look up to.

> These leaders begin with higher levels of trust and confidence from community members than externally-based, formally named, leaders – often because they operate from real, rather than projected, accountability to community needs. These people are critical to resident participation.
>
> (W.K. Kellogg Foundation, n.d., p. 16)

Keys to Building Trust

- **Effective communication**. Ensures the constituency you are working with will understand the process, goals and outcomes and the information needed to make informed decisions. Stay away from jargon, abbreviations and use clear language that respects the intelligence of the people you are working with.
- **Respect**. The tone, content, and facilitation of all your interactions with the community genuinely respects the input of all participants, even if it's sometimes difficult.
- **Transparency of processes**. All efforts should be clear and well-understood by all stakeholders, with no hidden or alternative agendas. This includes clarity about the role and influence of participants in the decision-making and implementation.
- **Sharing information widely**. Effective engagement and trust requires that everyone involved is working from a common understanding of the issue and each other's perspectives. Participants must feel that information is shared and does justice to all perspectives on the issue.
- **Engaging stakeholders in meaningful ways**. Welcome and encourage the perspectives, contributions, and skills of participants in a manner that they feel is consistent with their perspectives and attributes.

Penn State College of Agricultural Sciences (n.d.)

Take the time to learn who these grassroots leaders are and reach out to them. Listen to their stories and respect their positions. These may be people in your own organization that have special ties to the community; they may also be consumers of the services offered by your organization. Whoever they are, whatever their position in the community or organization, others may hold back their participation or engagement, waiting to see how these leaders and gatekeepers respond.

In order to locate the community leaders who can help move a planning effort forward, planners should look for those people who have demonstrated the desire or ability to work toward positive community change. These are the community members who have a track record of working collaboratively with others on behalf of the community. Four keys to identifying community leaders have been suggested. These include:

- *Positional method:* This includes individuals in key authority positions in organizations within the community.
- *Reputation:* These are people who enjoy a level of agreement by others in the community that they are respected and looked up to.
- *Event analysis:* The people who actively involve themselves in decisions and efforts that positively impact the community.
- *Social participation:* The people who hold positions of authority in a number of community-based organizations. This can include block or tenant associations, religious organizations, scouting, organized sports, youth activities, etc.

(USDA, 2005)

Be Multilingual and Inclusive

Prior to beginning work within any community, it is important to identify the languages that are spoken in that community. Entering a community with a significant immigrant population, which may have a large number of adults who are not bilingual or fluent in English, requires sensitivity to language as a possible barrier to community participation. While program planners may not be multilingual or proficient in the variety of primary languages spoken in any given community, there are methods for planners to help overcome barriers of language and to be inclusive of the different populations in the community.

The first step is to identify the language composition of the community. This includes the languages that are spoken, the level of multilingualism, and the preferences of the residents. Once these have been identified then the planner must develop a plan to address language in an inclusive manner. There are a number of steps that can be taken to ensure that the work is linguistically inclusive, these include:

- Locating trusted people in the community who are supportive of the planning effort and can serve as translators;

- Ensuring that all written materials are multilingual and in appropriate languages;
- Making arrangements to have translators at all public meetings;
- Finally, if children act as translators, trying to have a way to cross check their translations.

(Stonewall et al., 2017)

Whenever possible, the use of children as translators should be minimized. Depending on the subject of the discussion, children can have a difficult time translating thoughts and emotions. Weisskirch and Alva (2002) have found that when children translate these issues for their parents, it can introduce acculturative stress, discomfort or bias, as the children try to understand the thinking and emotions being expressed by their parents.

> Two components of communication particularly relevant to engaging marginalized populations are images and similarity. Images are often used to convey ideas across language barriers while perceived similarity between two communicators leads to more effective communication.
>
> (Stonewall at al., 2017, p. 131)

When utilizing printed information, such as posters and flyers, the use of images can help to represent complex information and overcome language barriers. Images can help to communicate complex information and require less translation than text-based documents. Another benefit of using images to replace text, when practical, can be the reduction of incidences of incorrect translations (Horton, 1993; Otten et al., 2015).

The perceived dissimilarity between the planner and community members can create a barrier to effective communication (Rogers & Bhowmik, 1971). Therefore, when trying to build similarity it is helpful to use speech that is informal, accessible and familiar to the recipients. Accessible communication means staying away from professional jargon and abbreviations. These only serve to separate you from the people who may not be knowledgeable about the terms and language being used. Professional jargon can also contribute to the power differential that may exist.

When program planners use terms that are not easily understood by their audience, they are setting themselves up as the experts with more knowledge than the people for whom they are planning. The planner may have different knowledge, but that does not make it more important to the process. Also, the converse is true. If you do not understand terms used by your audience, don't be afraid to ask. If you do not ask, you may be missing important information at best and at worst you may demonstrate that you are not truly interested in their input. Some people may be concerned that if they ask too many questions about language, slang or terms used then they will not earn the respect of the people they are there to serve. Asking questions can demonstrate that you are indeed interested and want to hear and understand what is being communicated.

Communicate for Understanding

Another skill for effective communication is listening for understanding. While we may think we do this whenever we are listening to someone else, that is not always the case. When engaging with people in the planning process it is important to use active listening skills. Listening to understand means taking the time and effort to actually hear what the person is saying and not thinking about your response or next question.

Listening to understand involves asking clarifying questions. Don't assume that you understand what the person is expressing and don't be afraid to ask to clarify language or ideas. Asking these types of questions signals that you truly want to engage with the people and understand their ideas and issues. If you try to give the impression that you are listening, but do not ask clarifying questions, you may be hearing something different than what the person was trying to communicate to you. Clarifying questions help to check out your perceptions of what is being communicated, and they help to clarify the meaning of vague or unfamiliar terms (Newhill et al., 2020).

Stephen Covey (2004) in the book *7 Habits of Highly Effective People*, lists as the fifth habit, "seek first to understand and then to be understood." Covey refers to this as "empathic listening." Empathic listening "gets inside another person's frame of reference. You look out through it, you see the world the way they see the world, you understand their paradigm, you understand how they feel" (p. 278).

Respect Schedules

Respecting schedules is quite simple. If you have a meeting or an appointment, be there on time and come prepared, even if you are the only person that is on time. By doing so you are showing that you respect people's time and see it as valuable.

Respecting schedules is not just about showing up on time, it is also about how the time is utilized. Only call meetings when there is an expressed purpose and let the other party or parties know what the purpose or agenda is. If you are calling a meeting, then the people who come to that meeting must feel that they have had input and that they have gotten something out of the meeting. If they can walk away with the sense that it was worth their time, you have increased the chances of their coming back the next time a meeting or interview is scheduled.

Offer Something Useful

Leadership in community meetings can be seen as transactional. When attendees receive a perceived benefit, they reciprocate with heightened responsiveness emphasizing a more active role. "one implication of this is to allow more latitude for inputs from various sources," bringing more people into the process (Hollander, 2009, p. 72). Incremental progress can increase people's engagement in the work. Researchers Amabile and Kramer (2011) found that "when we think about progress, we often imagine how good it feels to achieve a long-term goal or experience a major breakthrough. These big wins are great – but they are relatively rare." They also report that "Many of the progress events our research participants reported represented only minor steps forward. Yet they often evoked outsize positive reactions."

This research tells us that in order to keep people engaged in the change effort, they need to feel that they are making progress. Amabile and Kramer have termed this the *Progress Principle*. While their research focused on business, it opens a window into human nature. If people feel that progress is being made, and that they have had some small part in it, they will be energized to continue. Not only will they want to stay involved but they will feel better about their involvement.

Foster-Fishman et al. (2006) report that

> most, if not all community-building efforts strive to encourage resident involvement in neighborhood and community affairs with the belief that through such involvement, individuals can gain personal skills and greater self-confidence, improve their relationships with their neighbors and community institutions, increase mastery over their own lives, gain a sense of power in influencing the broader community, and ultimately gain greater access to and control over resources.
>
> (p. 143)

With this in mind, the best way to keep people engaged in the process is through this sense of accomplishment. If someone feels that their involvement helped lead to change or improvement, they are more likely to remain involved based upon the positive feelings that accrue to them, this is the *Progress Principle* in action.

The takeaway from this is that planners should look for small changes and improvements along the way that can help lead to this sense of progress. The earlier in the process that these small steps are achieved the greater the chances of increased involvement in the ongoing change effort. This progress need not be major or monumental, just noticeable and provide a sense of accomplishment. There should also be an understanding of how these smaller accomplishments lead to the change that is being sought

Participatory Planning

Following Stonewall's framework and striving for cultural humility provides a foundation for participatory planning. Participatory planning is a process whereby broad representation of everyone that has a stake in the intervention has the opportunity for a voice with real input into the planning, either personally or through representation. Often, marginalized people and communities feel that they do not have a voice in matters that impact their lives or that they are not heard when asked for their input. If human service program planners are seeking real participation from impacted individuals and communities, then it must be clear from the outset that all voices will be acknowledged. "Involvement in the decision-making process is a public right and should be exercised to influence and promote sustainable decisions that acknowledge the needs and interests of everyone in the community" (Toor et al., 2014).

The Value of Disagreement and Debate

While people may be in agreement that change is needed, there may be differences of opinion and disagreement on how to get there and what that change should look like. This means acknowledging the inherent value of disagreement and debate.

Participatory Planning

- Provides a sense of ownership and builds a strong base for the intervention in the community.
- Provides credibility for the intervention in all segments of the community, organization or target population.
- Brings a broader range of people to the planning process providing access to a wider range of perspectives and ideas.
- Involves important participants right in the beginning of the process.
- Provides an opportunity for disenfranchised groups or individuals to be heard.
- Helps develop valuable skills that can be utilized well beyond the planning process.
- Builds community by bringing together and establishing ties among disparate community members who may not normally have meaningful interactions.
- Builds trust between planners and participants and among participants.
- Demonstrates respect for community members.

(University of Kansas, n.d.)

> Acknowledgment also implies having enough respect for another's opinion to argue with it. All too often, low-income or minority members of a planning team or governing board are treated with reverse condescension, as if anything they say must be true and profound. A truly participatory process would include not only everyone being heard, but also everyone thrashing out ideas and goals, and wrestling with new concepts.
>
> (Community Tool Box, n.d.)

In order for planners to make this happen, participants with less expertise or status may need additional support to learn the process and to feel that their input is valued.

Embrace Both the Means and the End

Participatory planning requires that we do not come to the table with an end goal in sight and then move everyone in the direction that we have pre-chosen. Yes, the shortest distance between two points is always a straight line. But it may not be the most interesting or productive. If we invite people into a process where we have predetermined the end result then we may be losing out on ideas and input that can lead us to another, perhaps more effective result. Think of a road trip for example. The fastest way to get where you are going is to stay on the interstate highways and travel at 60–70 miles per hour. That route will get you to your destination faster, but you will also be missing out on many sights and adventures that await you on the side roads. The same is true for participatory planning. If we are involving people, we must be open to their input and not move them in our predetermined direction. There may be other end goals that should be sought. It is a messier process, but one that can reap rewards that perhaps were not seen at the beginning.

Figure 2.4 illustrates how being open to ideas and inputs of others and allowing the process to unfold, may bring you to a different place than the

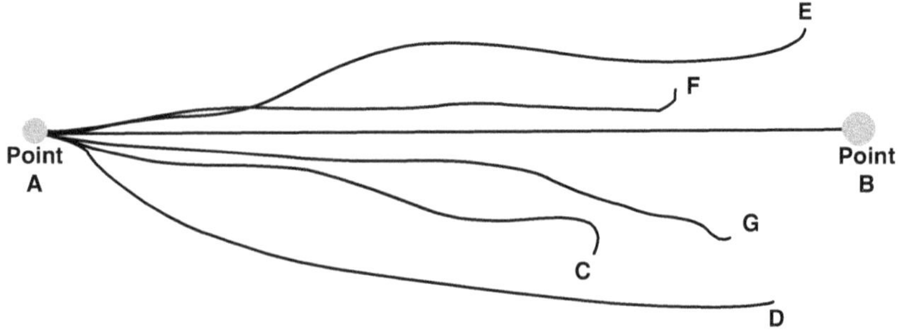

Figure 2.4 Getting from Point A to Point B

one that was planned at the outset or develop other ideas that will get to the same end point. This illustrates how instead of seeking that straight line to a predetermined end result, if we allow the process to unfold there may be several possible paths or end results that address the inequity.

To be successful, participatory planning requires that the planners be willing to see their constituents as equals, with expertise in what they need and are given voice with true input. This means that the planners see themselves as facilitators and not the experts with all the information. While it may seem easier to just move forward and plan the program or intervention because you are the planner with the requisite skills, if you are truly a social justice planner you will not look for the easy road but instead seek the most effective path forward.

Getting Started

The first step in a participatory planning process is to get the word out. Determine who the target population is and then investigate the best ways to reach out to inform them at the beginning of the effort. Next, schedule an initial meeting and determine who the best person or organization would be to serve as convener. In choosing a convenor it should be someone who is known in the community and has established both trust and respect and does not come with an agenda of their own or represent one constituency over another in the community. It may be best not to have one large meeting at first, but rather several smaller meetings so that more voices can be heard and more people feel included. This initial meeting, or meetings, should be scheduled at a time and place that is convenient to as many people as possible. It is always helpful to provide refreshments and to determine if translation is needed. Organize the meeting agenda so there is ample space for attendees to express their opinions and insights. Finally, this meeting and all subsequent meetings should end with action steps. Participants will become more engaged when they leave a meeting feeling there is a role for them and that it was worth their time and effort. Ensure that there is a free and equal flow of information from planners and organizers to the participants and from participants to the planners and organizers.

Figure 2.5 shows the three types of information flow between program planners and participants. The first type is when participants provide information to the planners but receive no feedback. The second is a one-way flow of information from the planners to participants, informing them but receiving no feedback. Finally, we see communication as a constant flow of information from planners to participants and participants to planners.

Once you have involved members or representatives of the target population you can begin planning the change effort. The planning process will be the subject of the remainder of this book. But once the process has

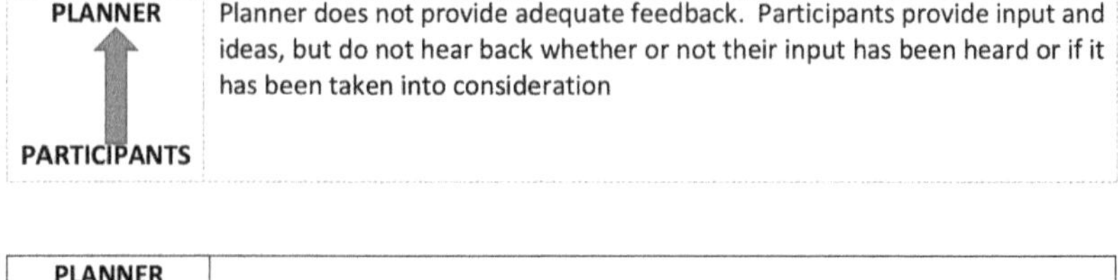

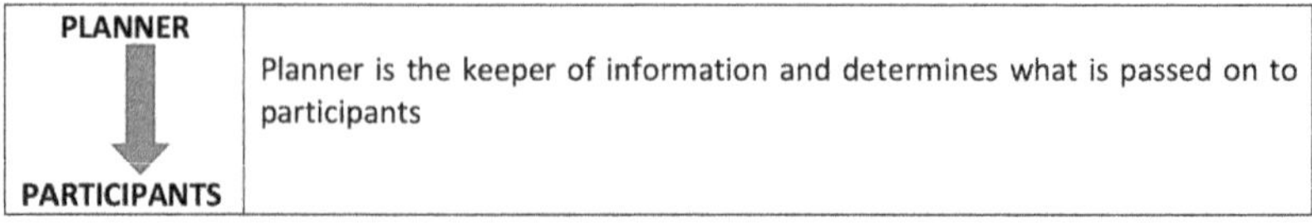

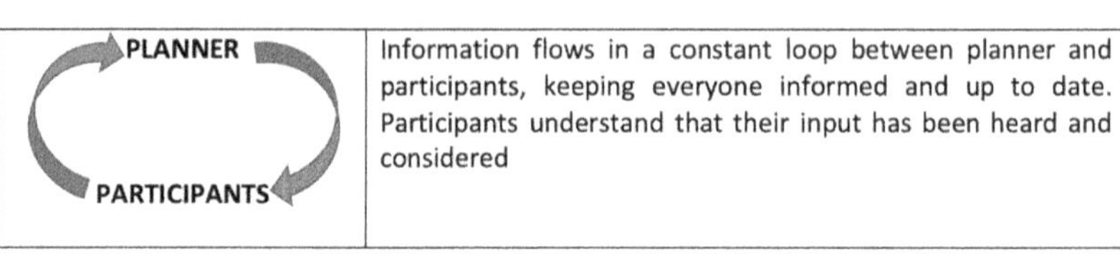

Figure 2.5 Flow of information

begun it requires working with the convenor to ensure that a high level of interest and input is maintained. People need to be kept informed of the process and how they can have input. As the planner you will need to work closely with the convenor and committee chairpeople to ensure that a feedback loop is maintained. Information, input and feedback forms a circular loop; it should never go in only one direction.

Maslow's Hierarchy and Program Planning

You may remember Maslow's Hierarchy of Needs (1943) from your undergraduate Introduction to Psychology class and are probably wondering *what does this have to do with human service program planning?* Maslow provides insight on how to approach program planning based upon the needs of the people who comprise the target population. Maslow presents three categories of needs contained in five stages. The lower category, basic needs, is divided into two stages – physiological needs and safety and security needs. The next category going up the pyramid is psychological needs, also divided into two stages – belongingness and self-esteem. Finally, the top of the hierarchy is self-actualization or achieving one's full potential and being part of something greater than oneself, or self-fulfillment.

Figure 2.6 illustrates Maslow's Hierarchy of Needs. The lower level or basic needs are physiological and safety, the next level or psychological needs are belongingness, love and self-esteem and the top level or self-fulfillment needs is self-actualization.

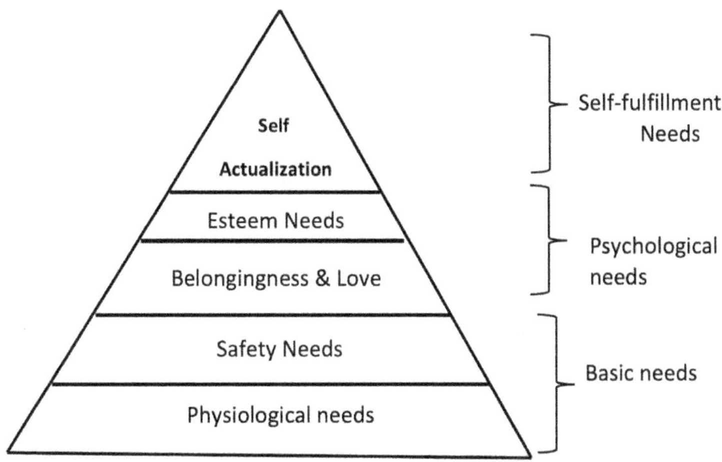

Figure 2.6 Maslow's hierarchy

In the case study that we will be using in later chapters, the identified challenge is the reading gap between low-income children and their middle-class peers that increases during the summer when school is not in session. When investigating how to start our approach it may be helpful to fall back on an old social work dictum, *start where the client is at.*

Basic Needs

For example, if the issue is defined as an increase in the reading gap during the summer, the solution is a summer reading program. However, using Maslow's hierarchy it may be helpful to determine where the intervention should begin. If many of the families in the community are experiencing food insecurity and students are not getting sufficient nutrition, their schoolwork may become more challenging. Edefonti et al. (2014) documented the impact of hunger on academic performance and school behavior. Children who are hungry have lower test scores in math, attend school less frequently and are more likely to repeat a grade.

Therefore, the success of an educational support program during out of school time would be highly unlikely if the participants' physiological needs were not being met. Concurrently, if the neighborhood is not safe, parents may not want their younger children walking alone to school when older youth are out on the streets with much unstructured time. Some of these children may be tasked with watching younger siblings during their parents working hours and older students may need to work to provide additional income.

It is important to understand the primary needs of the target population before trying to address higher-level needs. While parents want their children to succeed in school and in life, when their primary focus is on providing the basic necessities, they may not have the time, energy or language skills to support their child's academic growth. Older children may be forced to drop out of high school to help provide for their families, further complicating efforts to increase high school graduation rates. Any one of these could be contributing factors to the growing disparity in the reading scores and its impact on the lives of these children.

Psychological Needs

Moving further up Maslow's hierarchy, when the basic needs of people are met, they have the ability to address the higher-level needs of belongingness and esteem. In order to join into a change effort individuals must be hopeful that it will produce a positive change and also feel that their participation in the change effort will be meaningful. Depending on the target population, the planner may be up against a community-wide sense of hopelessness that feeds helplessness. This comes about when individuals or a community continually, over a long period of time, face negative situations that they have not been able to impact. This could come from schools that fail their children, daily experiences of racism and discrimination, feeling ignored by city hall or actively trying to improve things and finding time and again that the conditions they are trying to impact do not change.

The challenge here is to construct a planning effort that is inclusive. People who are marginalized have the desire to improve their lives, but may be discouraged by failures of past attempts at improvement or they may feel so marginalized that they do not know where to begin. This so-called *learned helplessness* is a legacy of powerlessness (Barber, 1986). In addition to this desire to improve their lives, people want to feel a sense of belonging and purpose. This is the next stage of Maslow's hierarchy.

With this understanding, engaging in an inclusive planning process will provide opportunities for belonging and being with their neighbors in positive change activities. This sense of belonging and being in concert with others boosts self-esteem and the sense that by working together with others, not only does the individual have value but there is a sense that positive change can be achieved.

Self-Fulfillment Needs

At the top of Maslow's hierarchy is self-actualization. This is when a person feels that they are part of something greater than themselves. People who are engaged in activities to better their lives and that of their neighbors will also feel an increased sense of self-esteem deriving from the feeling that they can control their lives and participate in positive change. Planning is not just about moving forward and getting things done; it is not a contest of product versus process. We must pay attention to the process that engages people and brings them along, helping to create a sense of hopefulness that they can have a positive impact. Without the full engagement of the community or potential participants, we run the risk of not defining the issue correctly and trying to engage the community in an effort that does not meet their desired future.

Motivating Others: The Importance of Why

As Simon Sinek (2009) succinctly states it "people don't buy what you do, they buy why you do it." But we are not selling anything. Planning is not a product. So why think in these terms.

Well, to put it bluntly, you are selling a product. If you cannot get people to buy into what you hope to achieve, your efforts will go nowhere. Let's explore this distinction between "what" and "why." Once you can tap into the "why" of your efforts it becomes easier to develop momentum toward the goal by inspiring people, motivating them to become engaged and to stay with the effort through the hard work that lies ahead.

The Problem with What

When we engage in planning efforts most of us focus on the "what." Which is what we will be doing or creating. In the case study that we will be following in subsequent chapters, the goal of a summer reading program is to eliminate the increase in the reading gap between low-income students and higher income students that occurs during the summer months. If we ask the planners what they hope to achieve, their answer is to maintain reading levels over the summer, thereby reducing the increase in the reading gap.

Not very inspiring.

This explains what they are doing or what they hope to accomplish but what is missing here is why this is important. If that is all we are seeking to accomplish, it may raise the question for many people "why should I care?" What is the impact of this reading gap? If the goal is only to hold the line over the summer months, then we are merely supporting the gap that already exists. What is the real issue here? What happens to poor children and children of color as a result of this reading gap between them and their peers? Isn't that the real issue? Why is this effort important? If all we do is maintain the pre-summer gap, in essence, aren't we justifying it?

Refocusing on the Why

Focusing on the what does not answer the question that potential funders or the supporters that you hope to engage need answered – the all-important "*why should I care enough to invest in or become involved in the effort?*" Your project will need monetary support as well as community support to be successful. If you are unable to answer this simple question, the needed support may not materialize. So, the question that needs to be answered is "why should I care that there is a gap in the reading levels between low-income students and their higher income peers?" To answer this, you need to look down the road at the consequences of this reading gap as the children move ahead in their education and in life, and how it can impact their movement up Maslow's hierarchy. As these students fall further behind it can have a negative impact of their self-esteem, thereby making it more difficult to achieve their self-actualized self.

Research has shown the importance of early childhood education in predicting school outcomes and lifelong outcomes, including career and work options, economic stability, health, and social opportunities (Sanders-Phillips et al., 2009). Therein lies the why of addressing the reading gap. If this gap is allowed to continue without being addressed, there is a much higher likelihood of dropping out of school and being impacted for the rest of their lives through limited choices that can steer them into low-income work with poor health and social outcomes. The "why" of this intervention then becomes *if we do not impact this inequity these children will be cast into low wage jobs and lowered chances for healthy productive lives.* If anybody still has the question in their mind of why they should care, the why can be extended to the costs to society from academic failure and limited economic opportunity, and higher rates of involvement in the criminal legal system for people with limited education. People who are incarcerated average less than twelve years of education, limiting their economic opportunities and increasing chances of living in poverty (Pettit & Western, 2004).

Improving reading scores, while important, is not very inspiring. However, steering children away from a future of limited economic opportunity and the social and economic impacts that go along with this should inspire people to act. Once we get at the why, we are tapping into what will inspire and motivate people to act, or at least believe that there is a need for the intervention.

According to Simon Sinek "Why" may be the most important message that can be communicated to inspire others to action. When we start with "Why" we are able to explain our purpose and the reason to address an existing inequity. Sinek's (2009) theory states that by communicating the "Why" we are communicating with the listener's limbic brain. This is the part of our brain that processes feelings such as trust and loyalty, and decision-making. When we successfully communicate the "Why" that informs "what" we hope to accomplish, we are speaking directly to the part of our brain that influences behavior. This forms the basis of a strong value proposition that can engage others to act.

Chapter Summary

- When engaging people in the planning process, an important step in identifying the need is understanding the impact of marginalization on individuals and communities. A framework is presented to engage people in the planning process that includes establishing trust, identifying gatekeepers, inclusiveness, communication, respect and offering a vision for the future.
- When the issue is defined as lack of a resource or a program, the solution has been simplified to providing that which is lacking. For example, if the issue is lack of food or food insecurity then the solution is to provide food. This approach, however, only serves to address symptoms and does not address the underlying inequity.
- Participatory planning invites participation of a broad representation of the community. It is a process whereby a cross section of the community has opportunity for a voice with real input into the planning, either personally or through representation. When human service program planners are seeking real participation from impacted individuals and communities, it should be clear from the outset that all voices will be acknowledged.
- Maslow's Hierarchy of Needs presents a taxonomy to understand how and why people become engaged. Understanding this hierarchy can help planners to determine where their interventions are most needed and where to begin to successfully engage people.
- Focusing on *why* the intervention is needed, rather than *what* it will do can help to inspire and motivate people to become involved in the effort.

Key Terms

Lack of
Cultural competence
Cultural humility
Marginalized populations
Communicate for understanding
Participatory planning
Maslow's Hierarchy of Needs
Why

Discussion Questions

1. How does defining a challenge as "lack of" lead to simplistic solutions that do not address underlying causes?
2. Why is it important to understand the inequities underlying an issue or inequality before defining the issue to be addressed?

3. How does blaming the victim, or placing the locus of "social problems" on the people experiencing them absolve society of responsibility to address the underlying inequities?
4. How can an understanding of Maslow's Hierarchy of Needs help the planner to understand the needs of the community, its people and the level of intervention that is most appropriate?
5. Discuss the importance of articulating the "why" of what you are hoping to achieve and how this can help to motivate people to care and to become involved in change efforts.
6. Which do you see as more helpful to guide cross-cultural work, cultural competence or cultural humility and why?

References

Alakhunova, N., Diallo, O., del Campo, I.M. & Tallarico, W. (2015), Defining marginalization: An assessment tool, The Elliott School of International Affairs at the George Washington University, htttps://elliott.gwu.edu/sites/g/files/zaxdzs2141/f/World%20Fair%20Trade%20Organizati on.pdf, retrieved 9/10/20

Amabile, T.M. & Kramer, S.J. (2011). The power of small wins, *Harvard Business Review*, https://hbr.org/2011/05/the-power-of-small-wins, retrieved 7/12/21

Barber, J.G. (1986) The promise and the pitfalls of learned helplessness theory for social work practice. *The British Journal of Social Work*, 16(5), 557–570

Betancourt, J.R., Green, A.R., Carrillo, E. & Ananeh-Firempong II, O. (2003) Defining cultural competence: A practical framework for addressing racial/ethnic disparities in health and health care, *Public Health Reports*, 118, July–August, 293–302

Chavez, V. (2018) Cultural humility: Reflections and relevance for CBPR. In N. Wallerstein, B. Duran, J. Oetzel & M. Minkler (eds.) *Community-based participatory research for health: Advancing social and health equity* (3rd ed.) (pp. 357–362). San Francisco, CA: Jossey-Bass

Community Tool Box (n.d.) Participatory approaches to planning community interventions, University of Kentucky, https://ctb.ku.edu/en/table-of-contents/analyze/where-to- start/participatory-approaches/main, retrieved 7/11/21

Covey, S.R. (2004) *The 7 habits of highly effective people*. New York, NY: Simon & Schuster

Dominelli, L. (2002) *Anti-oppressive social work theory and practice*. Basingstoke: Palgrave, MacMillan

Dutko, P., VePloeg, M. & Farrigan, T. (2012) Characteristics and influential factors of food deserts. *USDA Economic Research Service*, https://www.ers.usda.gov/webdocs/publications/45014/30939_err140_reportsummary.pdf?v=9867.8, retrieved 7/1/21

Edefonti, V., Rosato, V., Parpinel, M., Nebbia, G., Fiorica, L., Fossali, E., Ferraroni, M., Decarli, A. & Agostoni, C. (2014) The effect of breakfast composition and energy contribution on cognitive and academic performance: A systematic review. *The American Journal of Clinical Nutrition*, 100(2), August, 626–656

Fisher-Borne, M., Caine, J.M. & Martin, S.L. (2015) Mastery to accountability: Cultural humility as an alternative to cultural competence. *Social Work Education*, 34(2), 165–181

Foster-Fishman, P.G., Fitzgerald, K., Brandell, C., Nowell, B., Chavis, D. & Van Egeren, L.A. (2006) Mobilizing residents for action: The role of small wins and strategic supports. *American Journal of Community Psychology*, 8(3–4), December, 143–152

Hollander, E.P. (2009) *Inclusive leadership*. New York, NY: Routledge

Horton, W. (1993) The almost universal language: Graphics for international documents. *Technical Communications*, 40(9), 682–693

Maslow, A.H. (1943). A theory of human motivation. *Psychological Review*, 50(4), 430–437

NASW (2015) *Standards and indicators for cultural competence in social work practice*. Washington, DC: National Association of Social Workers, htps://www.socialworkers.org/LinkClick.aspx?fileticket=7dVckZAYUmk%3D&portalid=0, retrieved 2/17/21

Newhill, C.E., Muvaney, E.A. & Simmons, B.F. (2020). *Skill development for generalist practice*. Thousand Oaks, CA: SAGE Publications

Otten, J.J., Cheng, K. & Drewnowski, A. (2015). Infographics and public policy: Using data visualization to convey complex information. *Health Affairs*, 34(11), 1901–1907

Penn State College of Agricultural Sciences (n.d.) The keys to building trust, https://aese.psu.edu/research/centers/cecd/engagement-toolbox/role-importance-of-building-trust, retrieved 4/3/21

Pettit, B. & Western, B. (2004) Mass imprisonment and the life course: Race and class inequality in U.S. incarceration. *American Sociological Review*, 69(2), April, 151–169

Prusia, K. (2019) Planning for trust: A relationship-centered approach to community engagement in city planning practice, University of Washington, ProQuest Dissertations Publishing, https://digital.lib.washington.edu/researchworks/handle/1773/44931, retrieved 9/10/20

Reily, L. (2020) U.S. faces shortage of up to 8 billion meals in next twelve months, leading food bank says, *Washington Post*, 10/2/20

Rogers, E.M. & Bhowmik, D.K. (1971) Homophily-heterophily: Rational concepts for communication research. *Public Opinion Quarterly*, 34, 523–538

Sanders-Phillips, K., Settles-Reaves, B., Walker, D. & Brownlow, J. (2009) Social inequality and racial discrimination: Risk factors for health disparities in children of color. *Pediatrics*, 124 (Supplement 3), S176–S186

Sinek, S. (2009) *Start with why: How great leaders inspire everyone to take action*. Penguin Group

Stonewall J., Fjelstad, K., Dorneich, M., Shenk L., Krejci C. & Passe U. (2017) Best practices for engaging underserved populations, *Proceedings of the Human Factors and Ergonomics Society Annual Meeting*, 61(1), 130–134

Sue, D.W. (2006) *Multicultural social work practice*. New Jersey: Wiley and Sons

Trevalon, M. & Murray-Garcia, J. (1998). Cultural humility versus cultural competence: A critical distinction in defining physician training outcomes in multicultural education. *Journal of Health Care for the Poor and Underserved*, 9, 117–125

Toor, P., Cox, J. & Wycoff, M. (2014) A guidebook to community engagement: Involving urban and low-income populations in an environmental planning process, Michigan State University Planning and Zoning Center, https://www.canr.msu.edu/uploads/375/65790/GuidebooktoCommunityEngagement_FINAL_Sept2014.pdf, retrieved 7/14/21

University of Kansas (n.d.) Participatory approaches to planning community interventions, https://ctb.ku.edu/en/table-of-contents/analyze/where-to-start/participatory-approaches/main, retrieved 10/15/20

USDA (n.d.) Food security and nutrition assistance, https://www.ers.usda.gov/data-products/ag-and-food-statistics-charting-the-essentials/food-security-and-nutrition-assistance/, retrieved 9/15/20

USDA (2005) People, partnerships and communities, Natural Resources Conservation Services, Social Sciences Team, https://www.nrcs.usda.gov/Internet/FSE_DOCUMENTS/stelprdb1045582.pdf, retrieved 7/12/21

Weisskirch, R.S. & Alva, S.A. (2002). Language brokering and the acculturation of Latino children. *Hispanic Journal of Behavioral Sciences*, 24(3), 369–378

W. K. Kellogg Foundation (n.d.) Grassroots leadership development: A guide for grassroots leaders, organizations, and funders, www.wkkf.org, retrieved 7/11/21

3 Determining Need

Learning Objectives

1. Understand the value of the needs assessment as an early step in program planning.
2. Articulate how the definition of an issue to be addressed sets up the intervention and the goal to be achieved.
3. Articulate the importance of naming and investigating assumptions that are brought into the planning process.
4. Understand the impact of exploring assets and avoiding a singular focus on deficits.
5. Articulate the four different types of need, how they are investigated in the needs assessment and how each can impact the planning process.
6. Gain an introductory understanding of Appreciative Inquiry.
7. Understand the role of relational organizing and force field analysis in the needs assessment process.

Chapter Overview

The needs assessment helps program planners understand the issues to be addressed, the needs of the people and the community, and how best to proceed. Through this process, program planners can develop a definition and understanding of the issues and gain valuable information about the community and the people to be served. The definition helps to set the stage for the planned intervention, making this an all-important beginning step. However, prior to researching the need, assumptions about the community and factors contributing to the identified inequity should be named and interrogated.

When researching the community, uncovering assets as well as deficits is a critical step. Once identified, these assets, or community strengths, can be called upon to address the identified inequity. Four types of need are discussed, these include:

1. **Normative need**, when an individual or group does not meet certain agreed upon standards of living,

DOI: 10.4324/9781003148777-3

2. **Perceived need**, a need or want that is felt by people,
3. **Expressed need**, when people put a felt need into action by seeking or demanding a service or the availability of a commodity, and
4. **Comparative need**, when a group of people or a community do not receive the same services as a comparable group or community.

Methods of gathering information are discussed, including interviews, surveys, community meetings, focus groups, asset mapping and force field analysis. Brief overviews of Appreciative Inquiry and Relational Organizing are discussed as information gathering tools.

Defining Need

As stated earlier, how the issue is defined determines the intervention and solution. For example, if the problem is identified as hunger and food insecurity, the need is defined as food and the intervention is to provide food banks. When defining the need, we must look deeper than the obvious to uncover the underlying inequity.

Assessing the Need

The needs assessment is the first step in the planning process, determining the actual need to be addressed. This is the process through which planners determine the nature of the issue, how it presents itself and the causes and impacts of the inequity. The needs assessment is also where assumptions are interrogated to determine their impact on the issue to be addressed. Once planners have developed a more complete understanding of the issue they are addressing, they can go about determining the outcomes and the impact to work toward, and how best to get there. Jonas Salk, the developer of the first Polio vaccine, placed this into context, "What people think of as the moment of discovery is really the discovery of the question" (O'Brien et al., 2019).

Before designing the intervention, the needs assessment will help to develop a more complete understanding of the issue to be addressed. When planners skip this step and assume that they understand the inequity they wish to address, it lessens the possibility that the intervention will succeed. There are no real shortcuts to planning and developing a successful intervention based upon social justice. As the late John Lewis, Congressmember and civil rights activist wrote, "Take a long, hard look down the road you will have to travel once you have made a commitment to work for change. Know that this transformation will not happen right away. Change often takes time. It rarely happens all at once" (2017).

While all change efforts take time and commitment and success is never guaranteed, skipping the needs assessment will make success much less likely. We do a shortened version of this type of assessment in our daily lives without thinking that this is what we are doing. As an example, let's assume that you are traveling to class by bus and it gets stuck in standstill traffic. The teacher has scheduled a quiz for the beginning of class, and you do not want to miss it and fall behind. Now that you have identified the issue, the next step is to assess the situation by gathering as much information as possible. You may check your phone hoping to hear something about the traffic. Next you will try to determine exactly where you are and how far it is to school. If it is too far to walk you will realize there is nothing you can do to avoid being late to class and missing the exam. Next, you plan how best to deal with this situation. This may include texting a classmate asking them to explain your situation to the professor. You may write to the professor to ask if there is any way that you can make up the missed exam. After you have explored all of these options, you can then begin to calculate the impact of this exam on your grade and steps you may be able to take to overcome it.

Following each of these steps will provide sufficient information to help determine the extent of the challenge that is being faced, the possible contributing factors, alternative courses of action and the possible outcome of each of these compared to not taking action. First, the possible outcomes and impacts of different courses of action are assessed. Next, based upon this information, the intervention that is apparently most effective is decided upon and designed. Then you launch the intervention. Finally, you evaluate whether or not the chosen intervention is working and whether you need to rethink or adjust your plan of action. If this were a human service program and not a personal issue, you would then reassess the need based upon your evaluation of the intervention. Figure 3.1 illustrates how this is a circular process where you understand and define the issue, design an intervention, launch your intervention, and then address the issue through implementation based upon the plans that you have developed. The implemented intervention is then evaluated and reassessed to determine if further intervention or a modified intervention is needed.

A Case Study in Program Planning

Throughout the remainder of this textbook, a case study will be used to help illustrate concepts presented. OurKids AfterSchool is an organization providing after-school educational, recreational and cultural activities to elementary and middle school children in four communities bordering a major northeastern city. These communities consist of largely working- and middle-class families with significant immigrant populations. The issue the organization identified to be addressed was a growing achievement gap between low-income and middle-income students. To learn more about this issue and to begin the process of developing a

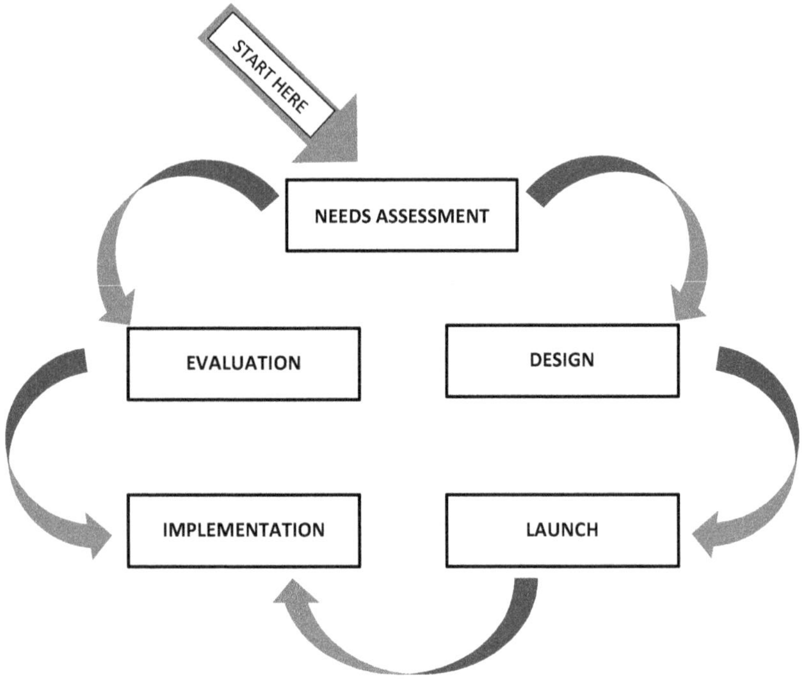

Figure 3.1 Program planning flow chart

program to address this inequity, they engaged in a needs assessment. Through this needs assessment they found the following:

- A higher percentage of low-income students at risk of failing than their middle-class peers;
- Lower student growth percentile for low-income students than their middle-income peers;
- Lengthy waits for financial assistance to attend summer learning programs;
- An increase in the number of referrals to their programs from teachers, guidance counselors and principals; and
- Low-income students' reading skills progressing at the same rate as their middle-class peers during the school year, but losing ground during the summer break.

Figure 3.2 shows the achievement gap between middle- and low-income students remains the same during the school year but increases during the summer months. It also illustrates that the gap already exists when children first begin their schooling. Illustrating reading growth from kindergarten through the fifth grade, the chart demonstrates that the gap widens each year, with low-income students falling further and further behind each summer.

Based upon the needs assessment, OurKids AfterSchool determined that a summer reading program was the best course to follow. While this program would help reduce the loss low-income students were experiencing over the summer, it would not serve to reduce the gap. As Figure 3.2 illustrates, while reading levels progress at similar rates during the school year, low-income students begin their school careers behind in reading levels when they enter kindergarten. Therefore, merely eliminating the summer loss would serve to stop the gap from growing but it would not eliminate it. This is an example of how the definition of the issue determines the intervention. The definition established by OurKids AferSchool focused on the reading loss over the summer. A summer reading program is not designed to reduce the school-year gap or to address the inequity, its causes or its impacts.

Defining the Underlying Inequity

This limited definition by OurKids AfterSchool is based upon the organization's failure to engage in a full needs assessment, only investigating the outcomes of an existing inequity. The needs assessment did not investigate causes of the gap, nor did it research the impacts of the gap if allowed to continue to grow. This incomplete needs assessment begged the question – why is it important to address this gap? What is the impact on these students if the gap is allowed to continue? Does the reading gap impact a number of outcomes including the school dropout rate, the

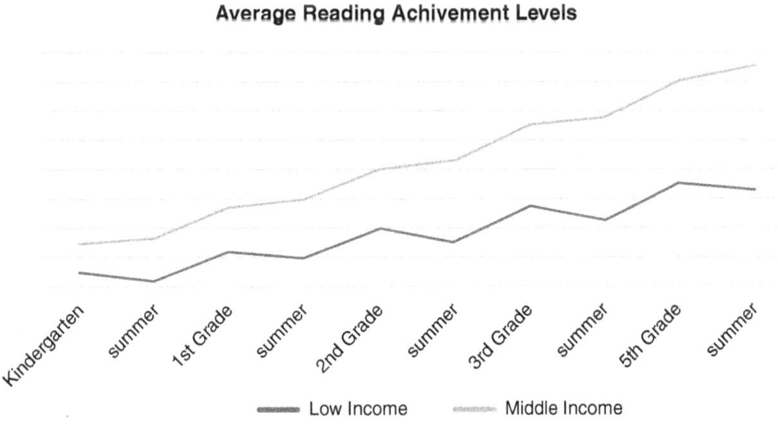

Figure 3.2 Summer learning loss and the achievement gap

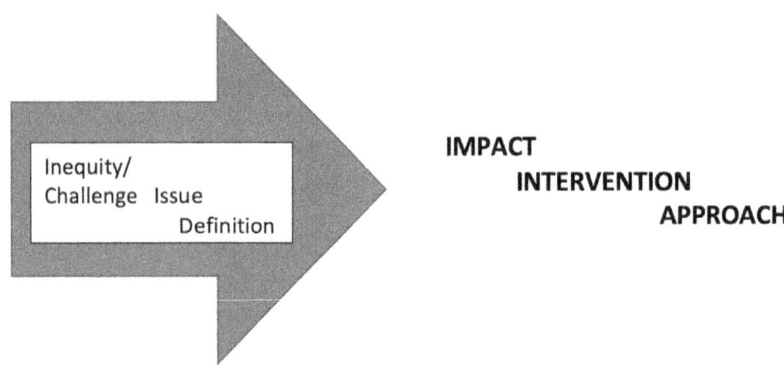

Figure 3.3 Defining the issue

life chances and success rate of these students, future involvement in the criminal legal system, etc.? It would appear that in this case OurKids AfterSchool developed an intervention that was predetermined to fit what was already believed to be helpful. This illustrates how the definition of the issue determines the intervention that you will take and the outcomes you will seek. The issue was defined as the loss of reading levels over the summer break contributing to the achievement gap. If OurKids AfterSchool's summer reading program was successful and low-income students did not lose progress over the summer, they still would remain behind the reading levels of their middle-income peers, leaving all of the negative impacts of low reading scores intact.

Figure 3.3 illustrates how the definition of the inequity or challenge determines the intervention and impact sought. Once you have determined the definition, you have set up the impact that you hope to achieve and the approach and intervention that you will implement.

Investigating Assumptions

We all carry with us assumptions about the way things are and what if anything can or should be done about the current state of affairs. An important function of the needs assessment is to interrogate the assumptions that are brought into the process. Naming these assumptions, and then investigating to see their impact and validity, is an important step in determining the interventions that are needed. Following is a sample of possible assumptions that can impact the design and outcome of the inequity that OurKids AfterSchool is addressing. This is not a complete list, but only serves as an example of possible assumptions that should have been investigated in the needs assessment to determine how best to impact the identified achievement gap. While this list is presented here as an example, it will be further analyzed to see possible impacts on the intervention in the following chapter.

- *The achievement gap exists and should be addressed.* The needs assessment should investigate whether or not this gap exists, how pronounced it is, and the short and long-term impacts. The concept of "achievement gap" must also be investigated. Defining this issue as an achievement gap can suggest that the students themselves are not achieving at the rate they should due to some personal failing or inadequacy. This is an important distinction, as the answer can determine different interventions.
- *The achievement gap is not a product of lower abilities but rather the result of some action or inaction on the part of lower and higher income students.* This assumption can be addressed through research focusing on the resources, supports and activities that are available to higher income students to help them to achieve that may not available to their lower income peers.
- *An intervention would be needed to help reduce this gap.* To address this assumption the needs assessment investigates other school districts to determine if there are existing programs that address the gap, how these interventions are designed and if they have met with success.
- *The achievement gap is not the result of any inequities in the classroom that privileges higher income students over their lower income peers.* It appears that this assumption is based upon the fact that the children, regardless of economic status, progress at similar rates during the school year. To investigate this, the planners can meet

Addressing the Achievement Gap: Intervention Assumptions

- The achievement gap exists and should be addressed.
- The achievement gap is not a product of lower abilities.
- The gap is the result of some action, or inaction, on the part of lower and higher income students.
- An intervention is needed to help reduce this gap.
- The achievement gap does not result from inequities within the classroom.
- Students are engaged in activities over the summer that contribute to the gap.
- Reading scores are an indicator of future success.
- Schools are failing lower income students.
- The community can act to change systems that contribute to the inequity.

with teachers, school administrators, parents and students to help determine if there are structures in the school and in the classrooms that contribute to the gap.

- *Higher income students and lower income students were engaged in activities that increase the gap over the summer months.* Investigating student experiences over the summer months can help to determine if there is something that higher and lower income students are engaging in, or not engaging in, differently that contributes to the growth in the gap.
- *Reading scores are an indicator of success in school and in future life.* A meta-analysis of research found in the literature can help to uncover the impacts of the reading gap on future school and life success.
- *The schools are failing low-income students and that is where the reform should focus.* A similar meta-analysis of previous studies can help to determine if it is indeed the schools that are failing students. Does this reading gap exist in predominantly wealthier communities or is it a function of lower expectations for low-income students, differential treatment of students or inadequate skills on the part of teachers and administrators.
- *The community has the ability to create and/or change systems that are currently disadvantaging low-income students.* Surveys of, and meetings with, community residents can help determine if the community has the resources and whether or not people are willing to engage in working toward change.

When you hold onto your assumptions as correct you open the possibility that you will use the needs assessment to support the beliefs you already hold about the inequity. Through identifying assumptions and then thoroughly interrogating them in the needs assessment, you will develop a deeper understanding of the issues that may impact the inequity. Using the needs assessment to investigate and understand the assumptions that are brought into the process will help to provide a deeper understanding of the issue and how best to address it. Uninvestigated assumptions can have a lasting impact on the intervention and may lead the program planning in a direction that is not effective. These assumptions will be discussed further in the next chapter, looking at how they can affect the impact of an intervention.

Assets vs. Deficits

In a popular YouTube talk, author and speaker Marcus Buckingham (n.d.), provides an example of strengths versus deficits. Speaking to parents, he presented the following scenario:

> Your child comes home with the following grades, English A, Social Studies A, Biology C and Algebra F. Which grade deserves most of

> your attention? Seventy-seven per cent of American parents say the F. So, the sad fact is most conversations around most kitchen and dinner tables are around the child's flaws and how to fix them. Most children in this country are characterized, by the people who love them the most, by who the child isn't, rather than who the child is.

Let's extend this thinking to a community needs assessment or intervention. Going by its name alone – needs assessment – planners tend to look to uncover the needs of the community. *What is wrong with this community that we can fix?* Just like the parents who focused most of their attention on the F, planners tend to focus mostly on what is wrong. Staying with the Buckingham example, how might parents react to this report card from a strengths or asset-based perspective? The answer is clear, do not spend most of your time focusing on the F, but what should a parent do instead?

If the parents' wish for their child is to get good grades and succeed in life, focusing on the failure only serves to give their child attention for what they don't want the child to do, reinforcing negative feelings and diminishing the child's self-esteem. A strengths-based or asset-based approach can be very useful here. From the report card, it is obvious that the student knows how to do well in two of their subjects. In order to build upon the child's strengths, the parents can focus on the two As. Focusing on the two As, does not suggest they ignore the other grades. The issue here is where do they spend most of their time. The first step is to reassure their child that they are proud of those two grades and then help the child investigate what they did in those two classes to earn As and what lessons can be learned that might help improve the other grades. At this point you might be asking "what does this have to do with human services program planning?"

Focusing on what is wrong can serve to overwhelm and disengage people who may see the challenges they are facing as too big and too many to overcome. This is also true working with individuals. This is not to say that we ignore challenges. Rather, the challenges faced by the community should not be the sole focus of discovery. Just as in the example above, Buckingham did not ask about what would parents only address, but where would they spend most of their time. As social justice planners we must spend at least an equal amount of time and energy uncovering strengths and assets as we do challenges and inequities.

As a reviewer for proposals for grant funding, it became evident that many applicants build their case for funding based on highlighting what is wrong in the communities they wish to serve. As the prospective grantees described the community or population that they wanted to serve, they focused on the shortcomings, hoping to make a strong case for need. These descriptions would focus on the negative aspects, such as crime rates, teen pregnancy, single-parent families, high-school dropout rates, unemployment, substance abuse rates, homelessness, poverty, abandoned housing, garbage-strewn vacant lots, etc. When only the negative aspects are focused on, it begs the question: "is this community so far gone that a grant, no matter how large, cannot change things?" An equal focus on community assets and strengths demonstrates that there are real challenges in the community or population of people, but there are also assets and strengths that can be built upon to improve conditions. If social justice planners do not make the effort to identify assets, there is nothing to build upon. It would be like building a house without a foundation and sheltering inside during a tornado hoping it will stand and provide protection.

Every community contains within it a unique combination of assets and strengths that are available, and often untapped, that can be mobilized in building a desired future. Kretzmann and McKnight (1993) point out that when planners take the time and make the effort to uncover and identify these, they

> will discover a vast and often surprising array of individual talents and productive skills, few of which are being mobilized for community-building purposes. This basic truth about the 'giftedness' of every individual is particularly important to apply to persons who often find themselves marginalized...

The authors continue,

> Beyond the individuals and local associations that make up the asset base of communities are all of the more formal institutions which are located in the community. Private businesses; public institutions such as schools, libraries, parks, police and fire stations; nonprofit institutions such as hospitals and social service agencies – these organizations make up the most visible and formal part of a community's fabric.
>
> (p. iv)

Asset thinking provides a more positive view of a community than when the focus is on what is missing. Asset thinking is a strengths-based approach that guides social justice program planners to identify and uncover the social capital within the community that can be built upon. Figure 3.6 compares some of the benefits of asset thinking with the disadvantages of deficit thinking. Through this approach we see people as producers rather than consumers, as the community becomes engaged in a mutual learning exercise that relies on both local knowledge and experience, and outside experts. Looking at communities in this way, engages people in a process where they are in control of their own lives rather than being seen as passive and dependent upon outside expertise and experience.

ASSET THINKING	DEFICIT THINKING
Identifies opportunities and strengths	Responds to problems
Strenghts-based	Needs based
What can we build on	What is missing
People have answers	People are the problem
Looks within the community for leadership and resources	Examines gaps deficits and what is not working
People as producers	People as consumers of services
Bottom-up organic solutions	Top down solutions
Mutual learning – local knowledge and outside experts	Focus on outside experts and professional expertise
Helps people control their own lives	People are passive

Figure 3.4 Asset thinking vs. deficit thinking

The focus on community assets in the planning and development process has been termed Asset-Based Community Development (ABCD). Mathie and Cunningham (2003) define ABCD as based upon the

> premise that people in communities can organize to drive the development process themselves by identifying and mobilizing existing (but often unrecognized) assets, thereby responding to and creating local economic opportunity. In particular, ABCD, draws attention to social assets: the particular talent of individuals, as well as the social capital inherent in the relationships that fuel local associations and inform networks.
>
> (p. 474)

Categories of Need

There are four categories of need that can help guide the research for the needs assessment to help understand the inequity, its causes, why it still remains and how to address it.

Focusing on the case study illustrates how each of these concepts of need can help to understand the issue being addressed. All children should be reading at or above grade level as a normative standard. In this case the needs assessment determined that there is a gap in reading levels and this gap widens over the summer months, demonstrating that this normative standard is not being met. Students who are not reading at grade level can begin to feel left behind and less than their peers, who are reading at or above grade level. Parents of children whose reading is not

Table 3.1

Normative	*Perceived*	*Expressed*	*Comparative*
When an individual or group does not meet certain agreed upon standards of living	A need or want that is felt by people. This may represent a service or commodity that is not available to them, but they believe that it is needed.	When people put a felt need into action either by seeking or demanding a service or the availability of a commodity	When a group of people or a community do not receive the same services as a comparable group or community.

advancing at the rate that it should can feel that their children are failing or being failed. In both cases, there is a felt need that something is wrong.

OurKids AfterSchool also found that there was an increase in referrals to their programs for reading assistance from teachers, guidance counselors and principals. This, in addition to the fact that they found a long waiting list for financial aid for summer programs, demonstrates a strong expression of need for some type of reading assistance. Finally, the fact that the needs assessment showed a growing gap between reading levels of low-income and middle-income students serves as a measure of comparative need.

Normative Need

In determining normative need, the planner begins by collecting as much data as possible that will provide a clearer picture of the population or geographic area to be served. Census data that is already available is a good starting point. The Census Bureau conveniently puts a lot of information online that can be helpful. Census data can be accessed by state, county, town or city, with comparative numbers to statewide data. Population data can be accessed by census tract in order to gather statistics by a specific community or a portion of a community. A census tract is a small, statistical subdivision of a county or other geographic entity. This information can be accessed at the Census.gov website. The Census Bureau collects a plethora of usable information that can be found on this website. Charts list specific categories that include social, economic, housing and demographic characteristics by geographic area. Drilling down to the census tract level accesses maps that show the boundaries of the census tract(s) comprising the community being researched. Once the specific census tracts have been located, there are charts with detailed information, or, if preferred, this information can also be accessed in a narrative description of each census tract that includes all of the information in the charts. This census data will help to create a more complete

Characteristic	Percent of Population
Children between the ages of 5-14	13.1%
Latinx	70%
Non-citizen	34%
Enrolled in College	Less than 3%
Ages 18-24	9%
College graduates	12.5%
Households where English is not the primary language	69%
Households below the poverty level	18%
Households receiving food stamps/SNAP	22%
Households without a computer or internet	10%

Figure 3.5 Demographic data for the community (U.S. Census Bureau)

picture of the community and its residents. Figure 3.5 is illustrative of a small sample of the type of information that can be useful in gaining a fuller picture of the community.

Reviewing the information in Figure 3.5, gathered from the U.S. Census Bureau website, it becomes evident that there are a number of areas where the community served by OurKids AfterSchool does not meet normally acceptable quality of life standards, thereby demonstrating normative needs. The chart reveals:

- A high poverty level and also a high dependence on food stamps, with more than one in every five households relying on this government program.
- English is not the primary language in more than two-thirds of households. This could suggest that adults in these households would be at a disadvantage when it comes to helping their children improve their reading skills.
- The low percentage of people with college degrees and young people attending college shows that the majority of community residents do not go on to advanced education, thereby reducing their future earning power.
- Fully one-third of the population of the community are not citizens. While this in and of itself is not suggestive of a challenge, it can point to the fact that people who are new to the country or undocumented might be wary of reaching out to those in authority to seek help for their children. Additionally, their undocumented or

noncitizen status can often relegate them to low-wage and physically demanding jobs, leaving less time and energy to help with their children's schoolwork.

- Finally, the data shows that 10% of households do not have internet or computers. In today's world, computer ownership and internet access are considered agreed upon standards. However, this is an example of where more information is needed before we choose to use specific data. The raw data only tells us that 10% of the households are without this access, but it does not tell us who lives in these households. Therefore, we cannot assume that this reflects the number of school-age children without such access, but it may be an area for further investigation.

Once helpful information has been gathered through the census data, the next step is to determine the areas that are considered to be agreed upon levels of living. Note of caution, and a reminder, when creating a profile of the community or population to be served, do not only look for descriptors or statistics that highlight negative aspects. As discussed earlier, it is also important to understand the strengths and assets of the community and its residents. Research on community conditions on children and families "has been largely individual and deficit focused" (Mowbray et al., 2007, p. 667). Rapp et al. (2005) write of the "developing realization that our focus on aberrations and problems has not yielded much in the way of social betterment" (p. 80). As social justice planners and human services workers, it is our responsibility to uncover community strengths and assets as well as needs.

In addition to the available census data, there are other sources of information that help determine normative need. Interviewing community leaders and experts within or outside of the community can provide much needed insight. However, the limitations of this approach, must also be taken into consideration. People who are considered experts may come to the interview with their own preconceptions, stereotypes and biases. As such, these experts may, at times, view the inequities being researched through a limited or more myopic lens. The planner must also be aware if they are coming to the interview with their own solutions to the issues and, as a result, only consider information that supports their predetermined ideas.

Community Asset Mapping

Completing a survey of the community can help to paint a more complete picture of whether or not the community has the services and supports needed to provide what would be considered to be a normal standard of living. Some of the areas to investigate can include:

- *Community economics* – Are there jobs that provide employment for families and for young people entering the job market. Do these

jobs pay a living wage? Are community members forced to cobble together more than one job so that they can support themselves and their families? Are residents working in jobs that provide benefits and health care? Can residents shop for food and other necessities in the community or must they travel outside of the community to shop.
- *Education* – What is the quality of the schools? Is there a high drop-out rate, large teacher turnover, limited resources, appropriate materials, parent involvement, etc. Are young people graduating high school and continuing in their education?
- *Other resources* – These may include religious, civic and nonprofit organizations. Do they exist and are they providing services to the community? Can they be a resource in addressing identified community needs?

This section of the needs assessment swill serve to provide a more complete picture of the community. To understand the community further, it can be helpful to create a community asset map. Asset mapping is a tool for documenting both the tangible and intangible resources of a community, seeing it as a place with assets to enhance and preserve and not deficits to be remedied. Community asset mapping is based on the belief that all individuals, physical structures, natural resources, institutions, businesses or informal organizations can play a role in addressing community issues (Kerka, 2003). There are three types of assets when engaging in community asset mapping. These include 1) the skills, and capacities of individuals in the community, 2) citizen associations where people come together to work for common goals, such as tenant and block associations, and 3) community institutions such as businesses, local government, hospitals and clinics, schools and technical training, and nonprofit and human service agencies (Griffin & Farris, 2010).

Asset mapping is part of a strengths-based approach to community development. Approaching community change efforts through an asset approach emphasizes the capabilities and capacities of communities to identify and develop workable solutions that build upon the strengths of community members, institutions and structures. The asset approach is in contrast to a deficit orientation to community change that has traditionally focused on problems or risks faced by the community and its residents that require professional resources and interventions (Morgan & Ziglio, 2007). An asset-based approach

> involves community members in defining the boundary of a community, exploring and identifying community assets, conducting an inventory of the community assets, and composing a physical and/or conceptual map of the community's assets that also highlights the interconnections and relationships among the assets. This in turn leads to community interventions that build directly on the assets in the community.
>
> (Lightfoot et al., 2014, p. 59)

Figure 3.6 illustrates examples of community assets by category, including community associations, physical spaces, institutions, the local economy and individuals.

Perceived Need

Perceived need is determined by what the people themselves see as needed. To determine this need, it is helpful to get out and interact with the residents of the community or the target population. After all, who better to inform you of their needs than the people themselves? This can

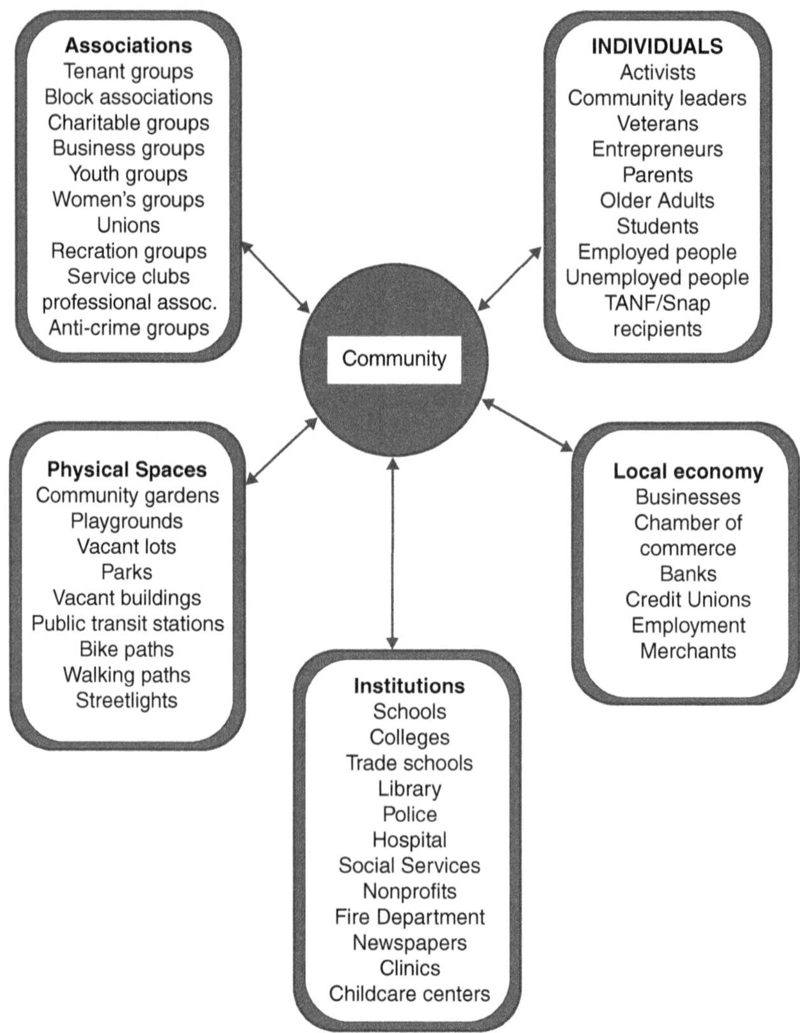

Figure 3.6 Community asset map

help to understand if the community has the resources to address a need that is perceived by the people. It is also important to determine if this perception of need is based upon a lack of information of services available in the community. There are several methodologies to help you to gather this information, including in-person interviews, community surveys, focus groups and public forums.

Gathering Information Through Interviews

In-person interviews engage people where they are the most comfortable. Performing such interviews in formal settings such as an office or government building can be stifling and intimidating for some people. In these settings you may find that the interviewee attempts to give you the answers they think you want as a way of pleasing an authority figure. Much of what is discussed below pertaining to in-person interviews can also be applied to surveys done by questionnaire.

Choosing the people to interview is an important step. It is crucial to get the input of a cross section of the community, not just community leaders and not just people who step forward volunteering to be interviewed. Some people who come forward and are eager to be interviewed may have an agenda that they wish to put forward. While it is important to include such people, they should not be representative of the entire sample. So, it is important to create a representative sample that includes a variety of opinions and insights. A representative sample includes people of various ages, income levels, community involvement, genders and professions. Shop keepers, community leaders, religious leaders and everyday residents are an integral subset of a representative sample. In order to locate these people, the planner will have to get out into the community, spend time talking to people and develop trust to achieve a truly representative sample.

Investigating Perceived Need

- What needs are identified by the residents?
- Have people sought services and were unable to find them within the community?
- Are services available in the community?
- Do community residents know that the services exist and are available?
- Are services fully utilized?
- Do existing services have waiting lists?
- Have people been turned away without being placed on a waiting list?

Are service seekers being referred outside of the community?

There are preliminary steps to ensuring the questions asked will elicit the interviewee's perception of need and their knowledge of existing services. Before administering a questionnaire or interview questions, it is helpful to pretest the survey instruments to ensure that the questions are understandable and are culturally acceptable. A careful review will help to ensure questions are constructed in such a way to gain needed information. Another consideration is the sample size, which is flexible and will be determined by time and available resources. Too small a sample will not provide actionable information and too large a sample can create logistical problems to gather and interpret the data.

Open-ended questions for interviews or focus group discussions will help to spark conversation and thoughtful answers. Following are some examples aimed at learning more about the achievement gap described in the case study example.

Sample Interview Questions

- What do you feel is unique about your community?
- What do you like about the education your child(ren) is getting in school?
- What are the most significant educational concerns in your community?
- What are the most significant educational needs of the children in your community?
- Are there community programs that focus on helping children to succeed?
- What concerns about the schools do you believe are significant in your community?
- What do you think is needed to address those concerns?
- How would you like to see the educational experience that children are getting in your community improved?
- What educational support services or programs don't exist that you believe should?
- What are some barriers that people face to increase opportunities for young people?
- What would it take for you to become involved in a community change effort?
- Please tell me about the last time you tried to make a change to impact your community or to improve your life or that of your family.
- What would you like us to know about your community or the schools that we have not asked?

Reviewing the questions above you will note that positive feelings are also being sought. This is consistent with a strengths-based approach where the investigator determines both the strengths of the community as well as what is needed through the eyes of community members. As discussed earlier, uncovering community assets and strengths is an important part of the discovery and planning process.

Focus Groups and Community Meetings

Focus groups and community meetings are additional ways to gather information and perceptions from community members. Community meetings were discussed in Chapter 2 under participatory planning. Focus groups are small groups of people, usually no more than six to eight in a session, representing the target population or a particular segment of it.

> A focus group isn't just a bunch of people getting together to talk. A focus group is a special type of group in terms of purpose, size, composition, and procedures. The purpose of conducting a focus group is to better understand how people feel or think about an issue, idea, product or service. Focus groups are used to gather opinions.
>
> (Krueger & Casey, 2015, p. 2)

By keeping the group small it is less intimidating and easier for all group members to participate. Through the use of a set of open-ended questions, similar to the questions used in the individual interviews, participants are guided through a facilitated discussion. These groups are interactive, and it is up to the facilitator how focused on the prepared questions the group remains. Sometimes it can be just as valuable to follow the discussion where the participants take it.

There are several benefits to focus groups that are not available in one-on-one interviews and surveys. Group members may help jog memories or insights of others in the group or expand on ideas put forth by others. When the discussion strays from the prepared questions, the facilitator may gain valuable information and insights that were not identified when constructing the interview guide. Giving space for the discussion to go beyond the prepared questions can be quite helpful to understanding the perceptions of community members. Focus groups also help to reach more people and gain detailed information using fewer resources.

Each of these methods of gathering data – in-person interviews, surveys and focus groups – have equal value, no one method is preferable or better than the others. You do not have to choose only one method as they are not mutually exclusive. Engaging in all three methods can provide a rich amount of data that will be helpful in determining the issue at hand and the best course of action, while reaching the greatest number of people with limited resources.

Expressed Need

A felt or perceived need becomes an expressed need when people put their desired need into action. Two measures of expressed need are noted in the OurKids AfterSchool needs assessment, where they found long waiting lists for financial assistance for students to attend summer programs and an increase in referrals to their programs from teachers, principals and guidance counselors. The fact that the waiting list exists demonstrates an expressed need as does the increase in referrals. These highlight how to measure expressed need. Program planners can survey community services to determine how many people they are serving, whether or not they have excess capacity and whether or not there are waiting lists. The survey can be used to collect data on the number of requests for services that are not offered or if people have been turned away without being placed on a waiting list. The one shortcoming to be aware of when measuring expressed need is that it is based on the assumption that people with a need will seek the appropriate services. There are many reasons why a person may not seek a service or express a need. In assessing expressed need, program planners should also determine how well the available services and programs are known in the community. If people are not aware that a service exists, they cannot seek it out.

As Marosszeky et al. (2006) point out,

> A community or person who uses a lot of services is assumed to have high need. A community or person who does not is assumed to have low needs. However, expressed need is influenced by the availability of services – if one community has many, well distributed resources, its population is likely to use more services than a community with few services.

Additionally, in communities with large immigrant or marginalized populations, residents may be reticent to seek out help because they assume that the help is not there, or they are not eligible, or they do not want to repeat negative experiences when they sought help previously. Perhaps the biggest deterrent for undocumented immigrants seeking assistance is the fear of deportation. When working in communities with large immigrant or undocumented populations the planner must be aware of this and protect individual information. Researchers for the U.S. Department of Health and Human Services found a number of barriers to accessing health and human services by immigrants. These include:

- Complexity of Application, Eligibility Rules, and Verification
- Administrative Burdens and Errors
- Language, Literacy, and Culture
- Transportation and Other Logistical Barriers

- Climates of Fear and Mistrust
- Special Challenges for Mixed-Status Families and Refugees

(Pereira et al., 2012)

Comparative Need

Comparative need is determined by the gap in levels of service existing in one community, geographic area or services available to a specific population compared to those existing in a similar community, geographic area or group of people. However, just because another community has a service that is not available to the target community is not sufficient to determine need.

To determine comparative need for OurKids AfterSchool there are a number of areas that can be researched.

One note of caution here. If OurKids AfterSchool only looked at similar communities or school districts, they would not be looking at wealthier communities or better funded school districts to determine a comparison. They would only be comparing to other low- to middle-income and immigrant communities. If the comparison were only made to similar districts and communities, the researchers could determine that there is no comparative need, thereby institutionalizing a system that denies lower income and immigrant communities the same resources as their wealthier neighbors. The case for comparative need should be made by comparing low-income or immigrant communities to higher income communities to determine the services that are being denied to these children and their communities that are available to their wealthier neighbors.

Program planners engaged in comparative needs research tend to follow the definition of comparative need focused on comparing similar communities or populations. This is where a social justice planner should be cautious. If we are comparing low-income community to low-income community, we may be comparing two communities that are equally disadvantaged. For example, let's apply this to school funding. The United

Investigating Comparative Need

- Comparative reading scores in other school districts;
- Reading programs available in other districts;
- Supportive services available after-school and summer;
- Per pupil funding levels in contiguous school districts;
- Available youth services in other communities;
- Financial assistance available in other localities for summer reading programs.

States has an unequal formula for funding schools, based upon property taxes. According to the Tax Policy Center, 30% of school funding comes from local property taxes (Zaretsky, 2018). Therefore, higher income communities have the ability to spend significantly more per pupil on public education due to higher property values. If only similar low-income communities are compared, a reasonable finding might be that the level of school funding is consistent. However, if we compare a low-income community with a higher income community, we may establish that a funding difference exists, which could be a contributing factor to the issue being studied.

The key to determining comparable need is defining the term "comparable." For example, this can mean similar size, population density, size of student population, or contiguous or nearby geographic locations. In the case example of OurKids AfterSchool, we would want to look at higher income communities located in the same metropolitan region to determine if there are differences in funding, teacher training, class size or available resources, for example. Do these differences have an impact on the reading levels of low-income students compared to their higher income peers in these wealthier districts? For example, the average per pupil expenditure in the communities served by OurKids AfterSchool is approximately $13,000, compared to the average expenditure per pupil in a contiguous town of $16,100 (MA Department of Education, n.d.). While clearly different, these two school districts are located in the same geographic area and are therefore comparable.

In this case example, to determine comparative need the researcher may also want to determine if there are similar school districts where the reading gap is not as prominent or has been reduced significantly. Locating such a school district with a similarly high percentage of immigrant and low-income families can help to determine a path forward. Gathering sufficient information during the needs assessment will serve to provide a clearer picture of the issues to be addressed and to determine a path forward.

Appreciative Inquiry

Appreciative Inquiry (AI) is another tool for involving people in the change process. It is a positive approach to change efforts that engages a wide range of stakeholders and can help move participants to a shared vision of the future.

Cooperrider and Whitney (n.d.) describe AI this way:

> AI is about the co-evolutionary search for the best in people, their organizations and the relevant world around them. In its broadest focus, it involves systemic discovery of what gives "life" to a living system when it is most alive, most effective, and most constructively

capable in economic, ecological, and human terms. AI involves, in a central way, the art and practice of asking questions that strengthen a system's capacity to apprehend, anticipate and heighten positive potential.

Focusing on Strengths

AI focuses on strengths and the future rather than problems and the past. In this way, AI modifies the types of questions asked, thereby changing the answers given while helping to build a positive and trusting relationship. Building on what has been discussed in previous sections, AI enhances a strengths-based approach. Through a problem focus we try to identify what is wrong, what caused the problem, how do we fix the problem and what are the action steps to take. To the contrary, an AI approach attempts to identify assets, capacities, capabilities, resources and strengths, thereby creating new possibilities for change (Luderma et al., n.d.).

When used correctly, AI is an inclusive process of inquiry, understanding and planning that leads to action. It can serve as an invitation for people to come together to co-create the future that they would like to live. Future here does not mean a sci-fi fantasy, but to co-create a real vision of an attainable future.

The Appreciative Inquiry Process

Cooperrider and Whitney (n.d.) delineate a "Four-D Approach" to Appreciative Inquiry:

- **Discovery**, appreciating what is;
- **Dream**, envisioning results of what might be;
- **Design**, co-constructing what should be, or the ideal future; and,
- **Destiny**, sustaining the change.

Program planners may not follow all of the steps in AI, but it is important to be aware of the process and to at least incorporate some of the concepts into the work. With that in mind, let's drill down to some of the specifics that can be helpful in learning more about the community and engaging people.

AI is based on exploring six basic questions that lead us through the Four-Ds.

- *Think back to a time when you first moved to the community or were old enough to go out on your own. What attracted you to the community or what were your initial impressions of the community?* This question can serve as a warm-up and also help elicit positive qualities about the community.

Six Basic Questions of Appreciative Inquiry Focused for OurKids AfterSchool

- Think back to a time when you first moved to the community or were old enough to go out on your own. What attracted you to the community or what were your initial impressions of the community?
- As a community member, you have probably experienced some ups and downs. Please take a moment to think about an experience that you consider to be a high point. What happened in this experience? What about it do you remember that made it a high point?
- What do you value most about yourself? If you were to ask other people about you, what are the greatest strengths they would recognize in you?
- What do you see changing in the community that would help children succeed in school and as adults?
- What is the best possible future that you can imagine for the community where all children can look forward to a positive future for themselves and their families?
- Thinking about the vision you just described, what would be the three most important strategies in the next two to three years that would launch us toward your vision?

- *As a community member you have probably experienced some ups and downs. Please take a moment to think about an experience that you consider to be a high point. What happened in this experience? What about it do you remember that made it a high point?* This question recognizes that there have been low points, but by asking to remember a high point it maintains focus on the positive and on moving forward. While interviewing, it is important to draw out more detail and ask clarifying questions. Think of this as helping the interviewee to construct a story, rather than merely guiding them through a series of questions.
- *What do you value most about yourself? If you were to ask other people about you, what are the greatest strengths they would recognize in you? What do you value most about the work that you do, this can be paid work, volunteer work, community work or work in the home?* The interviewer may have to coax the answers to these questions as many people are shy about discussing their positive attributes.
- *What do you value most about your community? If we were to move forward with change, what would you like most to preserve in the*

community? Through these questions the focus is on success rather than failure, and on community assets rather than deficits, while helping people to identify that they have something to contribute to the change effort.

- *What do you see changing in the community that would help children succeed in school and as adults in life?* This question gives the participant the opportunity to think about and identify changes that can impact the community and its children. Identifying these changes, whether they are deemed positive or negative, lays the foundation for moving forward and determining direction. This helps to move the conversation from the past to the future.
- *What is the best possible future that you can imagine for the community where all children can look forward to a positive future for themselves and their families? If you were to leave and return in three to five years what changes would have taken place in your imagined future so that you could truly say that this is the community of your dreams where all children have the opportunity to succeed?* Help the interviewee to elaborate and share as much detail as they can. Ask clarifying questions to help them to go deeper. Framing the question in a nonjudgmental and nonthreatening way allows the interviewee to stimulate their imagination and describe their construction of the best possible future.
- *Thinking about the vision you just described, what would be the three most important strategies in the next two to three years that would launch us toward your vision?* The answers to this question will help to begin fleshing out strategies that will engage the community (Luderma, et al., n.d.).

No one person is going to provide the key to understanding the issues facing a community or how to move forward. The purpose of interviewing is to uncover common themes that are expressed by the interviewees. Analyzing the answers to these questions can help to see where there are commonalities among respondents. Are there similar issues that people identify? Do they have similar dreams for the community? Collecting this data can help community members see they are not the only ones with hopes and dreams for their community, and it can help to identify where these dreams and hopes will converge. Identifying commonalities can help to develop strategies and plans to move toward an imagined future.

Additional Discovery Tools

In addition to the tools and processes discussed in this chapter, there are two additional tools that can be helpful components in the social justice planner's tool belt: relational organizing and force field analysis.

Relational Organizing

Developed as an organizing tool for electoral campaigns, relational organizing can also be useful for engaging people in the discovery and program planning processes. As such, it can be a valuable tool to help identify people for information gathering and to engage them in the process. Relational organizing utilizes individuals to harness their personal relationships to encourage others to agree to be interviewed, answer a survey or participate in a focus group. It is a way that you can reach out to people in the community through others who have stepped forward or shown interest in becoming involved in the change effort (Fuld, 2018). This is also known as *snowball sampling* in qualitative research, where study subjects are used to recruit future subjects among their acquaintances.

In relational organizing, the planner/researcher asks people who have already been engaged in the needs assessment reach out to their contacts in the community informing them of the change effort and encouraging them to become involved. Through relational organizing, volunteers develop a list of all of their community contacts, including relatives, friends, neighbors, businesses where they shop, associates in organizations, their place of worship, etc. Then, from this list, they create a list of priority people whom they think would be interested in participating and they reach out to them in person, by phone, text or email. In these conversations they inform their contacts about the change effort, ask about their concerns and hopes for their future and then invite them to be interviewed, complete a survey, join a focus group or attend a community meeting. People will respond better to people they know and trust. The hope is that the response will be "if you believe in this effort and think it is worthwhile, then I will give it a try."

The next step is to encourage these folks to post on social media or talk to others, giving information about the change effort and encouraging their contacts to come to a meeting, respond to a survey or agree to be interviewed. This effort then becomes exponential, as new people become involved, they are then encouraged to reach out to their networks. Unlike snowball sampling, the hope here is that these people will also become involved in the change effort. This is not a new method of organizing or reaching people, it was used quite effectively in the Civil Rights and United Farm Workers social justice movements and in grassroots political campaigns.

Figure 3.7 Illustrates relational organizing where one person reaches out to their contacts and then one or more of those contacts reach out to their own contacts, expanding the number of people who are informed about the change effort and encouraged to participate. Everyone that is reached through relational organizing may not agree to be interviewed or attend a meeting, nor will all reach out to their networks. But, having

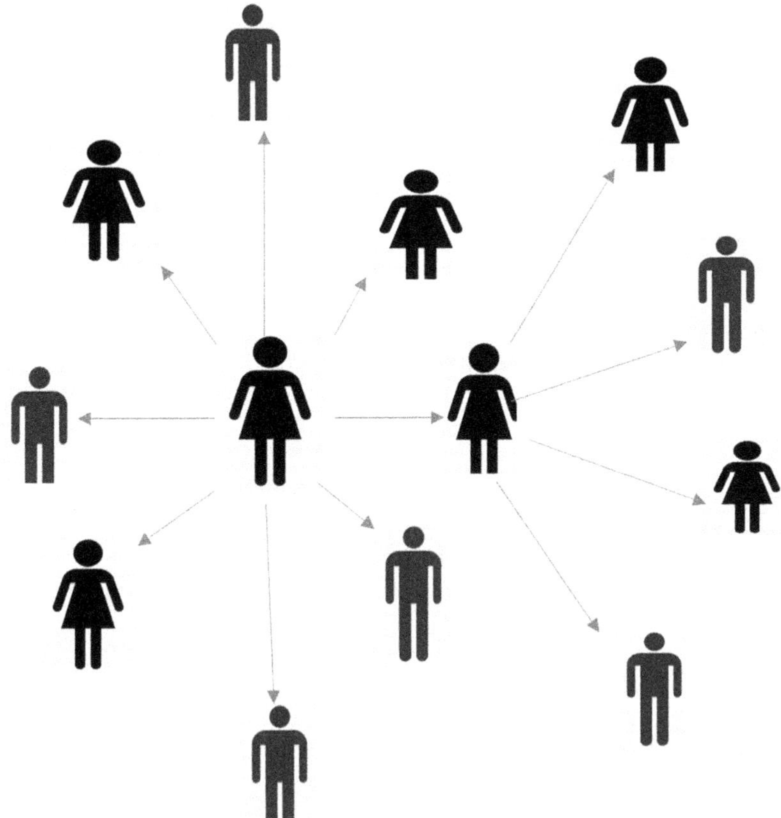

Figure 3.7 Relational organizing

been reached by someone they know and trust, people will at the very least become aware of the change effort.

Force Field Analysis

In the words of so many Star Wars characters, "may the force be with you." A force field analysis, first introduced by Kurt Lewin (1951), is a way of determining if the force is with you or against you when implementing a planned change effort. Identifying possible supporters and detractors is an important component of the needs assessment. A force field analysis can help to develop a balancing of the forces that support the change effort and those forces that may oppose it. By identifying the forces for and against, it gives the program planner a sense of where the work is needed to move the project forward. As part of the needs assessment this can help the planner to determine if the time is right to move forward, if there is sufficient support for the change effort or if education and community outreach work is necessary to build support for the change effort.

In a force field analysis, the planner enumerates two forces, restraining and driving. Restraining forces are those forces that are against the change, and driving forces are those that support the change. Change takes place best when the sum of the driving forces is greater than that of the restraining forces. This is not to suggest if the restraining forces are greater than the driving forces change is not possible. Rather, by analyzing these forces the planner can identify restraining forces to be addressed, and the driving forces that can be strengthened and used to move the change effort forward. Lewin (1947) suggested that the strength of these forces could be identified, mapped and measured to help provide an understanding of the potential to plan change at any level. With this understanding, a force field analysis can accomplish the following to help move the planned change effort forward:

- Present the positives and negatives of a situation so they are easily comparable.
- Consider all aspects of making the desired change.
- Encourage agreement about the relative priority of factors on each side of the balance sheet.
- Encourage honest reflection on the underlying roots of a problem and its solution.

A force field analysis for the change effort implemented by OurKids AfterSchool could include the content of Figure 3.8.

In Figure 3.8 we see a sampling of the possible forces that could be harnessed to drive change, and the countervailing forces that need to be addressed in order to move the change forward. For example, while parents are on both sides of the equation, they appear to be more of a driving force than a restraining force. This suggests that the planner might want

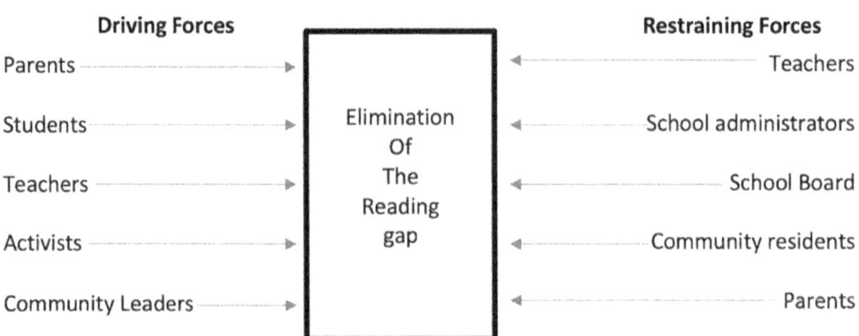

Figure 3.8 Force field analysis

to set up a dialogue between both sets of parents and uncover the reasons some parents support the change while others oppose it; these concerns can help to inform the design of the change effort. The parents favoring the change effort can impress upon the opposing parents the importance of the extra summer help for their children. Perhaps the opposition is based upon a sense that their children will lose out if additional resources are targeted for others. Perhaps there is an unsaid fear that their children will face more competition if others can improve their reading scores. These perspectives can only be addressed if they are identified. Parents who are concerned about their children's progress and success in school can also be among the restraining forces because they may fear that the effort will only serve to raise hopes and not succeed in impacting the gap.

A further discussion of the force field analysis, as illustrated in Figure 3.8, could help identify that the strongest driving force is parents, and the strongest restraining force is teachers. Teachers may oppose the change because it could reflect negatively on them, suggesting that they are failing their students if the gap exists and a summer reading program is needed. Identifying these forces can help the planner to determine who must be involved in the planning. If it is determined that some teachers are opposed to the program and as indicated above, some favor it, then bringing teachers from both sides together in the planning phase can help to overcome the opposition. Including the input of teachers in the planning can help provide them with a sense of ownership and their input would be valuable in planning an effective program that goes beyond a summer intervention and into the classroom during the school year.

Quantitative Measures

The discussion of the needs assessment so far, has focused on uncovering new information through qualitative methods. Existing data can add important information as well. The example given in the section on normative need cited census statistics as one source to help provide information to help understand the issues involved in the reading gap. In addition to the data available through the Census Bureau, there are other government sources of data online that can be helpful in determining normative and comparative need. Two examples are the CDC's National Center for Health Statistics (cdc.gov/index.htm), which maintains databases providing a trove of information on the nation's health, and the Bureau of Labor Statistics (bls.gov), providing a range of statistics and information on employment that can be drilled down to localities.

As demonstrated earlier in Figure 3.4, not all information that can be obtained is useful and some can be subject to misinterpretation. In this example, the fact that 10% of households do not have computers or Wi-Fi access can be misinterpreted if the planner generalizes this to include 10% of households with school-age children as well. Since this statistic does not describe which 10% of households are referred to, it would be an incorrect assumption that this also applies to households with school-age children. An incorrect assumption such as this could lead you down the wrong road to pursue an objective that would not help move you toward your goal. For example, it may lead you to assume the lack of computer and Wi-Fi access is a contributing factor to the reading gap. While this may be true, it is not supported by the available data. Therefore, further research would be needed to determine if this is a contributing factor and one worth addressing.

In addition to utilizing existing data, quantitative research can also gather new data through the use of surveys and interviews. While qualitative data relies on open-ended questions, quantitative surveys utilize close-ended questions, through a mix of multiple choice and rating scales. Data collected through surveys should be anonymized and generalized so that specific answers are not traceable to individuals. Through the promise of anonymity, respondents may be freer to respond honestly without fear of condemnation or retribution.

Surveys used in needs assessments are cross-sectional, studying a representative sample at a particular point in time. The goal is to collect specific information from a sample of people who are representative of the target population. In addition to the use of surveys, planners may engage in one-on-one interviews as well. These interviews include the same close-ended questions as the surveys, but the interviewer also has the opportunity to seek clarification and additional information.

The social justice program planner must be diligent using statistics and information gathered in the needs assessment, and take precautions that personal biases do not interfere when analyzing and interpreting data. It would be a mistake, and a disservice to the people you hope to serve, to only look for and use information that supports a predetermined sense of the need. The needs assessment should be an objective investigation into the topic. Allow it to lead where the facts and information take you to help develop a deeper understanding of the issues, their impact and possible alternatives. Once sufficient information has been obtained to develop an understanding, then, and only then, are you ready to develop the theory of change. This will be discussed in the next chapter.

Chapter Summary

Main Points

1. The needs assessment is the important first step in developing an understanding of the issue to be addressed. It will provide the planner with insight into the inequities that contribute to the condition. Once you have developed a deeper understanding of the inequity, you are

in a better position to determine the appropriate interventions and the impact to work toward.

2. There are four categories of need to be investigated in the needs assessment, these include: normative need, defining an acceptable standard of living to be compared against; perceived need, a need that is felt by the target population; expressed need, a perceived need that is put into action; and comparative need, the need of the target population compared to others.
3. When studying the need of a target population or community, it is important to identify and recognize assets and strengths that can be built upon. All communities and individuals possess strengths, it is critical that these be investigated in the needs assessment as well. An asset-based approach engages people in positive action compared to a deficit-based approach that focuses on what is missing or past failures. Appreciative Inquiry is used as an example of an asset-based approach engaging people in forward thinking and focusing on building upon that which already exists.
4. It is important to enter the needs assessment with an open mind, putting aside any preconceived ideas and remaining open to and learning from the process to uncover new ideas and a broader understanding of the issues to be addressed.

Key Terms

Needs assessment	Expressed need
Assets vs. deficits	Comparative need
Asset mapping	Appreciative Inquiry
Normative need	Relational organizing
Perceived need	Force field analysis

Discussion Questions

1. What are the possible challenges that a human services program planner may face if a thorough needs assessment is not completed before beginning to address existing inequities?
2. Discuss the importance of uncovering and investigating assumptions about the issues, the people and the intervention as part of the needs assessment.
3. When determining comparative need, what are some of the pitfalls that researchers can fall into that would limit the actual measure of comparative need?
4. Why is an asset-based approach an important consideration when investigating need?

5. When utilizing statistics to determine need, why is it important to ensure the statistics are leading you to the correct interpretation and you are not making premature conclusions or looking to support preconceived ideas?

References

Buckingham, M. (n.d.) www.youtube.com/watch?v=wuZBJQAFOfM&t=4s

Cooperrider, D.L., Whitney, D. (n.d.) A positive revolution in change. *Appreciative Inquiry*, http://www.tapin.in/Documents/2/Appreciative%20Inquiry%20-%20Positive%20Revolution%20in%20Change.pdf, retrieved 12/8/20

Fuld, J. (2018) What is relational organizing and how can it help my campaign? 8/16/2018, https://www.thecampaignworkshop.com/blog/pillar/campaign-tactics/relational-organizing, retrieved 12/10/20

Griffin, D. & Farris, A. (2010) School counselors and collaboration: Finding resources through community asset mapping. *Professional School Counseling*, 13(5), 248–256

Kerka, S. (2003) Community asset mapping. *ERIC Clearinghouse on Adult, Career, and Vocational Education*, 47, https://www.virtualcap.org/downloads/VC/US_Needs_Assessment_ERIC_Community_Asset_Mapping.pdf, retrieved 7/16/21

Kretzmann, J.P. & McKnight, J.L. (1993) *Building communities from the inside out*. ACTA Publications

Krueger, R.A. & Casey, M.A. (2015) *Focus groups, A practical guide for applied research, 5th ed.* Thousand Oaks, CA: SAGE Publications

Lewin, K. (1951) *Field theory in social science*. Harper and Row

Lewin, K. (1947) Frontiers in group dynamics. In D. Cartwright (ed.) *Field theory in social science* (pp. 188–237). Social Science Paperbacks.

Lewis, J. (2017) *Across that bridge: A vision for change and the future of America*. Audio Book. Hachette Audio.

Lightfoot, E., McCleary J.S. & Lum, T, (2014) Asset mapping as a research tool for community- based participatory research in social work. *Social Work Research*, 38(1), March, 59–64

Luderma, J.D., Manning, M.R. & Johnson, A.A. (n.d.) Six questions that can lift your leadership, shape your strategy, and transform your organization, https://cvdl.ben.edu/resources-tools/sixquestions/, retrieved 12/8/20

MA Department of Education (n.d.) School and district profiles, https://profiles.doe.mass.edu/, retrieved 7/21/21

Marosszeky, N., Rix, M.D. & Owen, A.G. (2006). Knowing what you need to know about needs assessment, National Health Outcomes Conference Wollongong. Australia: Australian Health Outcomes Collaboration, https://ro.uow.edu.au/cgi/viewcontent.cgi?article=1088&context=gsbpapers, retrieved 4/21/21

Mathie, A. & Cunningham, G. (2003) From clients to citizens: Asset-based community development as a strategy for community driven development. *Development in Practice*, 13(5), November, 474–486

Morgan, A. & Ziglio, E. (2007) Revitalising the evidence base for public health: An assets model. *Promotion & Education*, Supplement 2, 17–22, https://pubmed.ncbi.nlm.nih.gov/17685075/, retrieved 5/1/21

Mowbray, C.T., Woollet, M.E., Grogan-Kaylor, A., Gant, L.M., Gilster, M.E. & Williams Shanks, T.R. (2007) Neighborhood research from a spatially oriented strengths perspective. *Journal of Community Psychology*, 35(5), 667–680

O'Brien, B., Karani, R. & Park, S.Y. (2019) Foreword: The moment of discovery: How do you know when you hit a question that's pure gold? *Academic Medicine*, 94(11s), si–siii

Pereira, K.M., Crosnoe, R., Fortuny, K., Pedroza, J.M., Ulvestad, K., Weiland, C., Hirokazu, Y. & Chaudry, A. (2012) Barriers to immigrants access to health and human services programs, https://aspe.hhs.gov/reports/barriers-immigrants-access-health-human-services-programs-0, retrieved 7/18/21

Rapp, C.A., Saleeby, D. & Sullivan, W.P. (2005) The future of strengths-based social work. *Advances in Social Work*, 6(1), Spring, 79–90

U.S. Census Bureau, www.census.gov/data.html, retrieved 15/11/21

Zaretsky, R. (2018) School days, school funding haze, Tax Policy Center, Urban Institute and Brookings Institution, https://www.taxpolicycenter.org/taxvox/school-days-school-funding-haze, retrieved 7/18/21

4 From Understanding the Issue to Developing the Impact

Learning Objectives:

- Understand the importance of developing a clear and unambiguous statement of the issue to be addressed.
- Articulate how to develop an intervention hypothesis and how it is used to guide the planning process.
- Understand the importance of identifying and interrogating assumptions brought into the planning process and how these assumptions can impact the focus on the identified inequity.
- Define the impact and how this serves as the vision of the preferred future.

Chapter Overview

Completing the needs assessment lays the foundation to plan the intervention. The next step is to develop a clear statement of the issue to be addressed, based upon the findings in the needs assessment. Once there is agreement on the issue to be addressed the next step is to develop the intervention hypothesis. Throughout the process, it is essential to identify and interrogate assumptions participants are bringing into the planning process. This chapter identifies a number of possible assumptions that could impact the planning process and the impact sought by OurKids AfterSchool.

The theory of change is presented as a guide to creating a road map for the planning process. It is based upon the definition of the issue to be addressed and the impact sought, delineating where you plan to go and how to get there, and includes how progress is measured along the route. Finally, the theory of change is used to develop the logic model, which is the actual road map showing how the planned intervention will be implemented and what is hoped to be achieved.

Statement of Issue to Be Addressed

Once you have completed the needs assessment, and identified and investigated assumptions about the issue or the change to be achieved, you are

DOI: 10.4324/9781003148777-4

ready to develop the intervention hypothesis. The first step in developing this hypothesis is to create a clear and unambiguous statement of the issue to be addressed.

In the OurKids AfterSchool case study, it appears the findings of the needs assessment was not reviewed in sufficient detail to determine the real issue and its importance to parents and the community. As a result, the following issue statement not addressing the underlying inequities was developed: *There is a significant achievement gap between low-income students and their middle-class peers in the communities served by OurKids AfterSchool.* While this is a clear statement of the identified issue to be addressed, it does not address possible causes or ramifications of this achievement gap. If we look back to the discussion of "why" in Chapter 2, this simple statement raises the "why" question. Why should we care? Why is this a problem? A strong issue statement addresses the "why." This statement also lacks a clear understanding or definition of the achievement gap. Without defining the achievement gap there is no way forward to measure success in addressing it. It appears the reading gap and the achievement gap have been conflated into one issue, begging the question of whether the reading gap is the only component of this so-called achievement gap.

The Value of a Clear Issue Statement

The issue statement is used to engage people in addressing the challenge as it is identified and to develop a path forward. While it is widely known this gap exists for children of color, immigrant and low-income children, it has not been eliminated, thereby illustrating knowledge that an inequity exists is not enough to impel society to marshal necessary resources to address it. Addressing the achievement gap through a summer reading program does not eliminate or reduce a gap, only reducing the growth during the summer months. Reviewing Figure 3.2 in the previous chapter, we see low-income students enter school at the kindergarten level already behind their middle-class peers in reading.

Merely stating that the gap exists is reiterating what is already known. When the issue is defined so it also names the impact resulting from the inequity, a stronger case for intervention is made. This highlights why it is crucial for the needs assessment to address the impacts and contributing factors of the inequity. Investigating these will have a bearing on the definition of the issue. An example of a stronger issue statement addressing the gap might read this way: *There is an opportunity gap between low-income students and their middle-class peers leading to lower graduation rates, lower college acceptance and fewer career options experienced by the lower income students.* A more comprehensive statement such as this depends upon engaging in a needs assessment that looks at the impacts on low-income students as they continue in their education and their lives.

Deconstructing the revised issue statement illustrates the value of a vigorous needs assessment and examination of all assumptions.

- It is important to note this revised issue statement uses the term "opportunity gap" instead of "achievement gap." Labeling this as an opportunity gap changes the way the issue is looked at and how it is best addressed. It also removes the stigma of victim blaming. (This distinction is discussed in more detail in the next section.)
- This revised statement clearly delineates the long-term impacts of the issue if it remains unaddressed. Defining the issue as an opportunity gap refocuses the inequity in broader terms, taking it away from the students themselves and broadening it to include the systems denying lower income students and students of color the opportunities they need to succeed.
- The issue statement makes it clear long-term impacts hamper the life opportunities of these students when allowed to remain unaddressed.
- Finally, the statement clarifies that the difference lies between low and higher income students, identifying the low-income students as one target of the intervention. This statement also answers the "why" question – if this gap is not addressed then children will be left behind with fewer life choices.

Intervention Hypothesis

Similar to a research hypothesis, the intervention hypothesis shows how the program planner believes a predetermined intervention will impact the inequity. If the planned intervention is based upon empirical evidence of the success of prior program interventions, then the identified inequity can be addressed through replication of an intervention demonstrating success. However, if the hypothesis is based upon research leading to new ideas of how to impact the identified inequity, this could lead to developing a new model of intervention. In this way, the intervention hypothesis provides the program planner with direction for planning the intervention.

Working with the impacted population, and researching the issues in the needs assessment, the hypothesis is discussed and refined to set the basis for developing the intervention. The program hypothesis is key to a successful program plan. The program hypothesis serves as the foundation to the program and provides the basis for all that follows. It is written in *"if then"* terms; if X intervention is in place, then we can expect Y results. There are two variables, the independent variable, or the intervention you believe will work and the dependent variable or the outcome of the intervention. Figure 4.1 illustrates this process based upon the original issue statement developed by OurKids AfterSchool. The revised issue statement is applied later in this chapter.

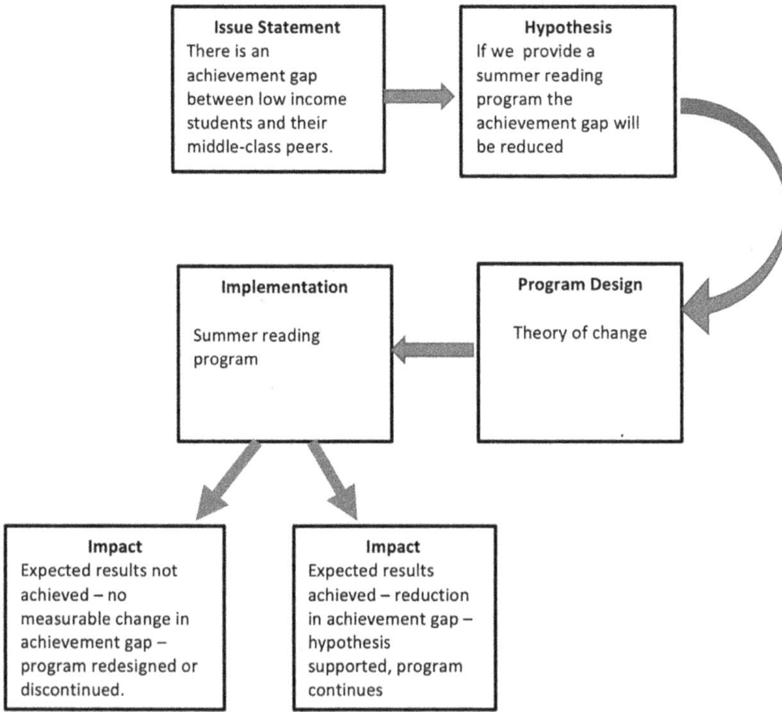

Figure 4.1 Role of the intervention hypothesis

Figure 4.1 Illustrates the role of the intervention hypothesis in the development and expected impact of the intervention in the OurKids AfterSchool.

Assumptions Impact the Theory of Change

As Knowlton and Phillips point out, "the most significant opportunity to improve theory of change models lies in unpacking the knowledge and beliefs employed in assumptions" (2013, p. 24). When developing the hypothesis and the interventions to follow, human services planners have to continue identifying and investigating the assumptions brought to the effort. Engaging in a process with stakeholders to identify assumptions held by various people and constituencies can help uncover different ideas about the goal to be achieved and how to get there. This process can also help to identify the extent to which there is a common vision among stakeholders. Naming and uncovering these assumptions helps create a process whereby stakeholders can get to know each other and identify where their assumptions overlap in order to begin creating shared goals for change. Many of these may be the same assumptions already interrogated in the needs assessment

In the OurKds AfterSchool case study we see several assumptions on the part of the program planners, some of which were investigated in the needs assessment and others that were not identified. Reviewing the assumptions discussed in the needs assessment provides examples of possible assumptions that might be carried into the effort and inform the planned interventions. As pointed out in the previous chapter, one purpose of the needs assessment is to identify and interrogate each of these assumptions to ensure they do not erroneously affect the development of the intervention. Once this has been done, it is time to develop the intervention hypothesis. With this in mind, let's review each of these assumptions and see how they impact the choice of intervention.

Investigating Assumptions

- The achievement gap exists and should be addressed.

This assumption may seem quite obvious. Without agreement the inequity exists, there is no reason to develop an intervention to address it. But this is where the obviousness of the assumption ends. Yes, an inequity exists, but has the actual inequity and its causes been identified? This assumption started the organization on the path to plan an intervention, but like all assumptions this too must be investigated and questioned. Although the work began with this assumption as a statement of what is, it is essential the researcher/planner maintains an open mind to allow their own assumptions to be questioned. This assumption, without further investigation, could lead to a hypothesis such as: If a summer reading program is implemented, then the growth in the reading gap occurring over the summer will be reduced. The independent variable is the summer reading program, and the dependent variable is the reduction in the increase of the gap over the summer.

However, fully interrogating this assumption leads the researcher to question the term "achievement gap." As a social justice program planner this term should be fully investigated and not accepted at face value. Naming the issue as an "achievement gap" places the blame on the children for not achieving, while not looking into the contributing factors of this inequity. This is evident in the intervention pursued in the case study. The plan to address the "achievement gap" is based on addressing the individual students through a summer reading program. In fact, this intervention takes the inequity out of the school system and larger society, placing the focus on students during their summer vacation. Social justice planners are tasked with uncovering all assumptions, whether they are on the part of the planners, or they are generally accepted as part of societal institutions. A reasonable investigation of this term and the perspective it perpetuates raises questions and leads social justice program planners toward a more comprehensive intervention than one focusing on individuals.

Education activists and organizations are working to change the concept from "achievement gap" to "opportunity gap." This is not a mere exercise in semantics. It is an attempt to change the way we look at education and disparities in our educational system.

> The term "achievement gap" is inaccurate because it blames the historically marginalized, under-served victims of poor schooling and holds whiteness and wealth as models of excellence. And, as with all misnomers, the thinking undergirding the achievement gap only speaks of academic outcomes, not the conditions leading to those outcomes, nor does it acknowledge that the outcomes are a consequence of those conditions.
>
> (Royal, 2012)

The importance of this change in perspective is further highlighted by John Jackson, President and CEO of the Schott Foundation for Public Education:

> After decades of education reform, parental income remains the top predictor of student outcomes. This report challenges the notion that school-based reforms alone can provide students a fair and substantive opportunity to learn. If these lives matter, addressing these systemic gaps must matter.
>
> (Schott Foundation for Public Education, 2020)

> "Opportunity gap" refers to the fact that the arbitrary circumstances in which people are born – such as their race, ethnicity, ZIP code, and socioeconomic status – determine their opportunities in life, rather than all people having the chance to achieve to the best of their potential. Low-income students don't have lower tests scores because they lack ability or interest or because of the culture in their community. Rather, it's because, well before they take tests, they face a lack of opportunity from systems, structures, and adults.
>
> (Mooney, 2018)

Changing the focus of the discussion from an achievement gap to an opportunity gap opens up the discourse so people can begin to look at educational policies and broader societal conditions and beliefs directly impacting them and their communities. This change in focus can help to engage people in needed advocacy for policy changes and away from seeing this as an individual problem, or one suggesting certain people are less capable than others. However, a singular focus on the broader policy issues should not deter program planners from investigating ways in which students can be helped in the interim. We cannot focus primarily on the broader macro issues while ignoring the individual impacts these issues currently have on children. Therefore, an example such as this demands social justice program planners look at all levels of intervention micro, mezzo and macro, in order to effect true and lasting change.

Ibram X. Kendi addressed the achievement gap:

> when people commonly think of the achievement gap – and I'm saying when people, I'm talking not necessarily about scholars, but everyday people ... the types of people who are going to support policies, or not – they typically think of this idea that black and Latinx and native children are achieving at a lower level than white and Asian children. And they're achieving at a lower level because there's something wrong with them. Because there's something they're not as individuals doing – there's something that parents were not doing there, [that] teachers are not doing. And so that's why you've had people support accountability measures for students and teachers, but not necessarily be willing to think about and look at these larger structural factors that are actually impacting what's happening in the classroom.
>
> (wbur.org, 2019)

Incorporating this perspective, opens up the opportunity to envision a better future. Professor and abolitionist educator[1] Bettina Love suggests one such vision:

> My vision for schooling would be a school where there's no standardized testing. Yes, there are tests, but they are not high-stakes and have nothing to do with a billion-dollar industry. Second, no

Levels of Intervention

- Micro – An individualized focus providing direct services, interventions, and support to individuals, families, and groups.
- Mezzo –focus centers on problem-solving on behalf of groups of clients, or client systems, such schools, social service agencies, or specific populations such as at-risk elderly in a particular community or location.
- Macro – the focus is on addressing societal inequities to improve the quality of life locally, nationally, and internationally, confronting issues at the systems-level.

> police, no dogs, no metal detectors. Children walk into beautiful, bright buildings that look like someone is ready to love them in that space. There would be as many therapists and healers and counselors as teachers, because what we don't talk about is the generational and everyday trauma, regardless of race and nationality, that children are dealing with.
>
> (Stoltzfus, 2019)

If OurKids AfterSchool had looked into the contrasting concepts of achievement gap and opportunity gap, this could have determined a more far-reaching path forward. Incorporating social justice concepts into the planning process demands a comprehensive understanding that uncovers more than just individual issues but seeks to determine if there are institutional barriers to overcoming the issues to be addressed. While a summer reading program is designed to help those individual students who are able to enroll in and complete the program, it does not change the institutional inequities causing the gap. If these are not addressed, then little is done to prevent more low-income students and students of color from experiencing the negative consequences of this opportunity gap.

- *The achievement gap is not a product of lower abilities but rather the result of some action or inaction on the part of lower and higher income students.*

On its face, this assumption suggests lower income children are not engaging in some activity their higher income peers are doing, thereby causing the increase in the gap. Both sides of this assumption – higher income students are engaging in activities to maintain their reading levels while lower income students are not – need to be investigated. This assumption also assumes there is no difference in abilities between these two groups of students. If the needs assessment debunks any difference in abilities, it can help to put to rest the assumption that this is the cause, and an intervention is not needed. The second part, investigating whether or not higher income students engage in activities supporting their reading while lower income students do not, or do not have access to these resources, is a critical aspect of understanding why the gap exists and why it continues to grow. It could also help to support the notion that this is an opportunity gap rather than an achievement gap. This assumption, as it stands, leads us to a similar intervention hypothesis as above: If we implement a summer reading program, we can level the field and reduce the growth in the reading gap occurring over the summer.

Interrogating this assumption with a view toward the opportunity gap changes how we respond. Rather than trying to make up for some deficit existing between lower and higher income students, the planner would investigate the opportunities not available to low-income students enjoyed by their higher income peers. By focusing on the opportunities that may or may not be available to all students we are not looking for individual flaws which place blame on low-income students. This type of thinking moves away from individual interventions designed to address individual shortcomings.

Even though the concept of achievement gap has been discussed earlier and hopefully discredited, the term is still used here because it is based on the use of the term in the case study. This is in no way meant to support achievement gap as an acceptable concept. As the case study is further critiqued in later chapters, the use of the term "achievement gap" is changed to "opportunity gap."

- *An intervention is needed to help reduce this gap.*

Interrogating the assumption that an intervention is needed provides the impetus to investigate other school districts to see if other interventions have succeeded or failed. Examining this comparative need provides information about interventions that might work as well in this community. There is no need to develop new ideas when there is evidence of successful interventions that can be implemented. This is an essential part of any needs assessment, learning from what already exists, what has succeeded and what has not worked. There is nothing wrong with building on the experiences of others by avoiding failures or duplicating successes.

Investigating other interventions that have succeeded or failed, or those currently implemented, but have not achieved results can be helpful in determining how to proceed. Once the assumption an intervention is needed is identified, then it is incumbent upon the planner to fully investigate what has and has not been done to impact the inequity. There can be lessons to learn from other districts who have tried to impact this inequity and there may also be approaches that have not been tried but look promising. Once committing to the need for an intervention, research helps to determine the levels of intervention, whether the issue is best addressed on the micro, mezzo or macro levels, or some combination of these. As noted in the discussion above, focusing only on the micro level, as in the case study, the onus of the problem is on the individual and the larger policy and institutional issues do not get addressed.

- *The achievement gap is not the result of any inequities in the classrooms that privileges the higher income students over their lower income peers.*

As part of the needs assessment the researcher/planner also investigates what is happening in the classroom. In the case study, it is clear the assumption is that the cause of the reading gap is not due to any differential treatment in the classroom. This suggests there are other contributing factors. Since it is not due to classroom activities or differential treatment, then it may be due in part to individual capabilities or actions. A summer reading program would have little impact when there is differential treatment in the classroom. However, when there is no evidence of differential treatment and the gap is due to individual capabilities or behaviors, a summer reading program could have the desired impact. This assumption is based upon the statistics showing the reading gap grows during the summer months, but reading levels advance at the same rate during the school year. While this is a fair assumption, it should not prevent a deeper dive into classroom content to determine if there is any differential treatment between lower and higher income students. However, without further investigation, this assumption once again leads to the same intervention hypothesis: If we implement a summer reading program, we can reduce the growth in the reading gap occurring over the summer.

- *Higher income students and lower income students are engaged in activities that increase the gap over the summer months.*

This assumption provides the basis for the design of a summer reading program. It appears to be based upon the belief the increase in the reading gap over the summer is due to the higher income students having access to resources or activities not available to their lower income peers over the summer. The needs assessment should investigate this assumption to learn if there are in fact resources and activities disproportionately available to higher income students. Learning if these exist and identifying these resources provides insight into the program design. If they do not exist, this would raise the question "what is causing the increase in the gap" and it may suggest a summer reading program is not the best intervention. Once again, an individual approach only tackles a small part of the inequity. This assumption suggests there is an opportunity gap. However, addressing this by providing increased opportunity and support for students over the summer does not address the causes of an opportunity gap.

A summer reading program should not duplicate the resources higher income students have access to, while at the same time merely accepting that these differences exist. This calls for an approach at all levels of intervention; micro, mezzo and macro. The micro aspect is served by the intervention chosen by OurKids AfterSchool. On the mezzo level teacher training and parent activism can help to increase resources for lower income students. Intervention at the macro level can involve organizing parents, students and community members to demand changes in the way schools are funded and increasing opportunities for low-income families to have the same resources as their higher income neighbors.

- *Reading scores are an indicator of success in school and in future life.*

In order for people to become engaged in the change, a level of agreement that it will have a long-range impact is necessary. The assumption that reading levels are an indicator of future success begins to address the "why" question, discussed later in this chapter. This assumption, once interrogated, can be used to gain support for the intervention giving people a cogent reason to care and become involved. It also helps define the long-term change to be sought. Once this change is defined, the impact is no longer merely maintaining reading levels over the summer but preparing students for greater success in life, eliminating the reading gap, not just preventing an increase over the summer.

This assumption, if found to be correct, leads to a more significant intervention than a summer reading program. The appropriate intervention includes activities to help children succeed beyond the leveling of reading scores. With this in mind, the impact sought would include improved reading scores and also focus on increased high school graduation, increased college or trade school admissions and better career opportunities resulting in reduced poverty.

- *The schools are failing low-income students and that is where the reform should focus.*

The assumption that the schools are inadequate and failing low-income students suggests an intervention to impact systems and policy changes. Investigating this assumption can provide another direction for program planning to follow. System level or policy change is not mutually exclusive from direct programming to address the issue. While this can be identified as the most effective path to follow, current students cannot be sacrificed for the betterment of future students. If this is a widely held assumption and is supported in the needs assessment, then it creates an additional set of objectives to work toward in addition to direct programming. Such an intervention on the macro level addresses an issue greater than only the limited number of students who are served by a summer reading program. Focusing on this assumption leads to the desired impact of improved schools supporting all children to function at or above grade level, leading to increased graduation rates, fewer behavioral issues and increased opportunities for meaningful careers helping lift families out of poverty.

- *The community has the ability to create and/or change systems that are currently disadvantaging low-income students.*

This assumption is important since it forms the foundation for the planning effort. When stakeholders do not believe they can implement the change they may sit out the effort and watch from the sidelines. This is where community asset mapping and an Appreciative Inquiry approach become tools to help stakeholders identify community strengths and a vision for the future that can help build confidence in the community's capacity to engage in the change effort. The impact sought as a result is an active community working together to improve the education of their children, resulting in increased graduation rates, increased acceptance to higher education and improved opportunities for meaningful employment.

Assumptions Impact the Focus on the Inequity

Each of these examples demonstrate how assumptions on the part of stakeholders and the researcher/planner when not interrogated in the needs assessment can lead to an ineffective intervention or one not addressing the causes of the inequity. Awareness of the assumptions brought into the planning efforts helps to inform the direction of the needs assessment. Once identified, each of these assumptions is vigorously researched to determine if they are true or are they are contributing factors to be addressed. Knowlton and Phillips (2013) caution us that exploring assumptions is foundational to the planning process, and failure to do so without due diligence "can lead to diffuse or dilute programs that lack the focus or intensity needed to produce intended results. Because of these implications, omitting this 'foundation' for your idea, program, or social change effort undermines its potential for success" (p. 35).

Figure 4.2 illustrates the bearing assumptions have on the focus of the intervention and the impact sought. The locus of the inequity, or the location of the cause of the inequity, is identified for each assumption. The chart demonstrates that five of the seven assumptions discussed place this with the individual students. This preponderance of placing the cause within individuals leads to an intervention based upon changing individual students. In the impact column, only two of the seven assumptions lead to interventions focused on the long-term impacts of the so-called achievement gap.

From Social Inequity to Determining Impact

Once the issue to be addressed has been identified, the next step is to define the impact, or the broader change being sought. This helps define the preferred future resulting from the change effort. When you have developed a strong issue statement, the impact becomes the inverse of the statement. In the case of OurKids AfterSchool, the inverse of the issue statement is a reduction in the achievement gap. Note here it states a reduction, not elimination of the achievement gap. The problem as stated is the existence of a "significant gap." This could be interpreted to mean if the gap were not significant it would not be a problem. While this may seem like parsing words, the inverse of a significant gap is the reduction

Assumption	Locus of inequity	Intervention	Impact sought
Achievement gap exists and should be addresses	Individual students	Summer reading program	Reduction/elimination of achievement gap
Achievement gap is not a product of lower abilities but the result of action or inaction on the part of low and middle-income students	Individual students	Summer reading program	Reduction/elimination of achievement gap
Not result of inequalities in the classroom	Individual students	Summer reading program	Reduction/elimination of achievement gap
Students engage in activities that increase the gap over the summer.	Individual students	Summer reading program	Reduction/elimination of achievement gap
Reading scores are an indicator of success in school and future life	Individual students	Summer reading program, year-round tutoring and homework help	Reduction/elimination of achievement gap, increased high school graduation and secondary education rates, improved career opportunities and reduction in poverty rate
School is failing low income students	Educational policies and resources	Summer reading program, new in-school and after school supports, and improved school policies and resources	Reduction/elimination of achievement gap, changes in school policies, increased school resources, increased high school graduation and secondary education rates, improved career opportunities and reduction in poverty rate
The community has the ability to create and/or change systems that currently disadvantage low income students	Educational policies and resources	Organizing the community to impact the school system and policies to equalize educational opportunities and resources for all children.	Changes in the schools that result in the reduction/elimination of achievement gap, improved school policies, increased school resources, increased high school graduation and secondary education rates, improved career opportunities and reduction in poverty rate

Figure 4.2 The impact of assumptions

of the gap; the inverse of an achievement gap is elimination of the gap. But neither of these provides us with any idea of the benefit of reducing or eliminating the gap.

In the previous section interrogating the assumptions, it was determined the existence of an achievement gap is not the real inequity to be addressed. The social inequity the program is addressing is the "opportunity gap." In recognition that achievement is an individual issue while opportunity is a social issue beyond the realm of any one individual to change, all future references to this gap are identified as an opportunity gap.

Defining the Issue Determines the Impact

The impact is the broader or long-term change being sought as a result of the program activities, usually occurring after the conclusion of the project or several years after participants have completed the intervention.

The impact can be defined as organizational, community or systems-level changes expected to result from the intervention. These can include improvements in conditions, capacity or overarching policies. The impact is not the expected changes participants in the intervention experience. Rather, it is the collective and wider ranging changes resulting from these individual changes.

Engaging participants in a visioning process helps to determine the appropriate impact to strive for. This was touched upon briefly in the discussion of Appreciative Inquiry in the previous chapter. This process leads to a vison of the preferred future, or what would it look like when the opportunity gap no longer exists. Engaging people in visioning or exploring their preferred future increases chances of discovering the possibility of a number of people sharing a similar vision of the preferred future and the various paths to get there. The social justice program planner risks nonengagement of key stakeholders and the loss of possible alternative paths to addressing the issue when this step is skipped.

Engaging stakeholders in this aspect of the process, using tools discussed earlier, can also be seen as a creative process. Together, the planner and participants create a pathway to a preferred future for the community and its people. Involving people in this creative process helps build momentum, buy-in and excitement, ensuring the wishes and dreams of the people form the foundation of the planning efforts.

With the amended definition in mind, we can determine the impact based upon the rewritten issue statement in the previous section. Inverting this statement, the impact becomes: *Elimination of the opportunity gap between low and middle-income students, resulting in students better prepared to succeed as adults with increased high school graduation and college acceptance and greater career options.* The original and amended issue statements and the impacts they can lead to are illustrated in Figure 4.3. These examples illustrate how the inverse of the issue statement leads to a statement of the impact to be sought.

The key to determining impact is that it is the longer-term changes we hope to see as a result of the intervention. The understanding of how to develop the impact is based upon the needs assessment. Through the needs assessment we can understand more clearly the issue we are planning to address, how it came to be, why it is continuing and what a desired future might look like if we are successful.

Answering the "Why" Question Helps to Articulate the Impact

Let's take a moment to revisit the "why" question before moving on. The simple problem statement, *there is a significant achievement gap between low-income students and their middle-income peers*, states the issue but begs the question "why should something be done about it?" While most people might agree this is a problem, it does not translate to agreeing

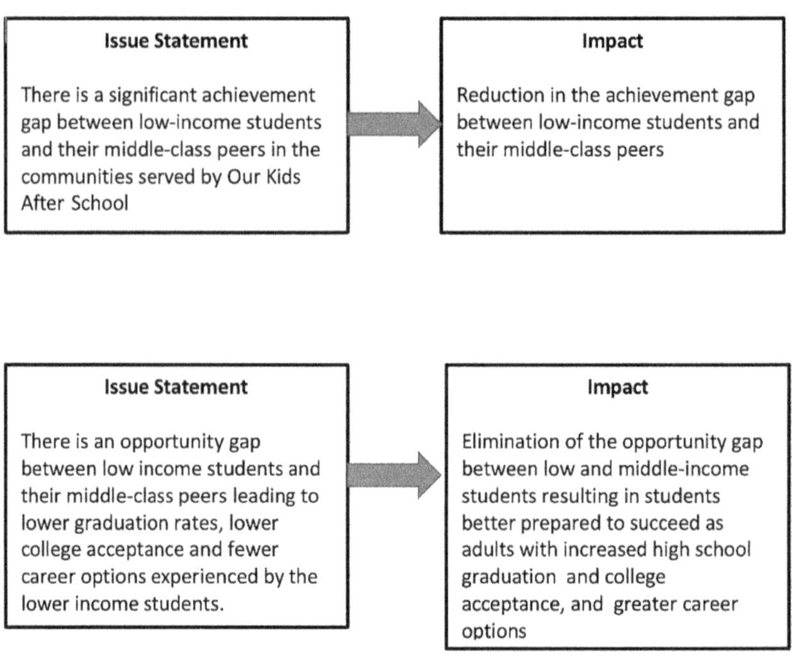

Figure 4.3 How the issue statement leads to impact

something should be done about it. As discussed earlier, it can also be interpreted by some as an individual problem resulting from individual failures or lack of initiative. What this comes down to is answering the question "why should I care?" It is incumbent upon human services program planners to make a clear case an intervention is needed and to develop broad support for addressing the issue. The existence of an achievement gap by itself may not translate to urgency for some people, or the implications of such a gap may not be clearly understood. The first step in answering the why question and underscoring the urgency of addressing this issue is changing the nomenclature from achievement gap to opportunity gap. By taking the focus and blame away from individuals experiencing the inequity, and making it more of a universal concern, the issue is defined in such a way that community members feel they have a stake in addressing it. Additionally, the amended issue statement makes clear this gap exists while also enumerating some of its longer-term effects. These effects are clearly delineated, so they are easily understood and unambiguous.

This rewritten issue statement addresses the "why" by enumerating some of the impacts of the inequity and moving it away from victim blaming such as, *"oh, if only they worked harder, they would succeed."*

When children continue to fall further behind in their reading skills, there can be life-long consequences. The specter of these negative consequences, that are greater than the individuals experiencing the inequity, can help to engage and motivate people to care enough to want to do something about it.

This illustrates the importance of answering the why question. This could be asked in different ways, such as why should I care or why is this important enough to invest resources of time or money. These questions are best asked throughout the planning process. Why is this important? Why should people care about the long-term impacts? Keeping these in mind helps to focus on why you are involved in this planning project, while helping to keep the planning focused on the future and the change being sought. Focusing on the impact of what you are doing, in this case helping to create a path for young people to have more opportunity for success as adults, helps to keep you aware that those who are involved are in it for long-term results. Since the impact of the planning work can be further into the future, understanding this helps to keep the momentum going while focusing on the changes and interventions moving in the direction of the preferred future.

Theory of Change

Once the first three steps have been completed – 1) identify and define the issue or inequity to be addressed, 2) a full needs assessment and, 3) the impact or change sought has been determined – the next step is to specify the theory of change. This is an illustration of how you will address the identified inequity. It might be easier to think of it as road map to point the path forward to achieve the change being sought. "Every community needs a road map for change. Instead of bridges, avenues and freeways, this map would illustrate destinations of progress and the routes to travel on the way to achieving progress" (Annie E. Casey Foundation, 2004, p. 1).

Developing the Road Map Forward

The theory of change delineates where you plan to go and how to get there, and also builds in ways to measure progress along the route. One way to illustrate this is if you are planning a road trip. While map reading is no longer a skill some of us have, the GPS on smart phones or in cars can serve as an example. You begin by entering your destination, or the goal of your trip. When you don't know where you are going it does not matter how you get there. This point was illustrated by Lewis Carroll in the iconic story *Alice in Wonderland.* At one point in their journey Alice comes upon a fork in the road. Alice sees a Cheshire cat in the tree and asks which way they ought to go. The cat responds, "that depends on where you want to get to." Not knowing where they are going,

Alice responds, "it really doesn't matter," and to this the cat says, "then it really doesn't matter which way you go." This advice is echoed by the baseball legend Yogi Berra: "when you come to a fork in the road take it."

Once you have entered your destination, the GPS calculates the starting point and then provides several options of how to get to the end point. In addition, it specifies how many miles to the destination and how long before you arrive. As progress is made it is marked by the GPS calculating how many miles are left in the trip and an approximate time of arrival. Based upon an ongoing evaluation of traffic and road conditions the estimated time of arrival is updated as you travel. The GPS provides evaluation points all along the route, warning of traffic or construction ahead and offering alternative routes if they exist. A well-developed theory of change provides all of these to guide program planners along the journey of planned change.

Theory of Change Logic Model

The theory of change clearly defines the issue being addressed and the impact or long-term change you hope to achieve as a result of the intervention. This is based upon the intervention hypothesis and it is called a theory because it is built upon the assumption of a specific outcome of a planned intervention. When a funding source requires a theory of change, they are usually asking for an illustration of the proposed process or a logic model. This chart delineates the process being proposed to achieve the desired results. If a picture is worth a thousand words, then the logic model is that picture, illustrating the theory of change. The logic model has five main components. These include:

- the inputs or resources required to successfully implement the intervention;
- activities offered based upon the inputs;
- outputs or quantifiable products or participation numbers realized through the activities engaged in;
- outcomes or short and medium-term changes occurring as a result of the intervention;
- overall impact or the long-term, larger changes resulting from the intervention.

Figure 4.4 illustrates the components of the theory of change comprising the logic model. It is noted the final component, the impact, is also illustrated as an arrow pointing forward. This demonstrates that the impact is what occurs going forward. It is not a definable end result that can be measured at the termination of the intervention, but rather it is what is hoped to be achieved in the future resulting from the changes put in place by the intervention.

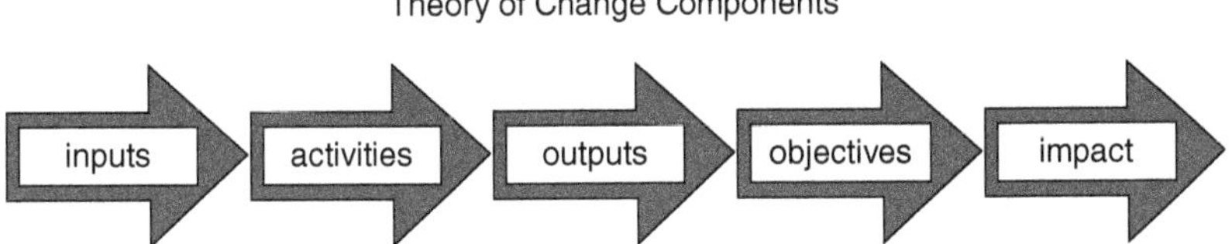

Figure 4.4 Theory of change components

The following chapters build a logic model based upon the OurKids AfterSchool case study, focusing on each of the components illustrated above. Through this step-by-step process each element of the logic model is discussed and shown how they are all interconnected and form the theory of change, delineating the changes expected to be achieve through the planned intervention.

Chapter Summary

Main Points

1. Developing a clear, unambiguous statement of the issue to be addressed in a way that specifies the inequity is an essential step in developing a planned change effort.
2. The intervention hypothesis clearly defines the program intervention stated as: if X intervention is implemented, we can expect Y results. This is a hypothesis because it delineates the direction the planned change effort will take, based upon the needs assessment and the understanding of the inequity.
3. To successfully develop a working hypothesis leading to the theory of change, the social justice program planner names and unpacks assumptions brought into the planning process. These assumptions, if not interrogated, can lead to an intervention not targeted to the actual inequity the program planner is addressing.
4. The theory of change is introduced as a five-step process delineating: 1) inputs or resources needed to implement the planned change, 2) activities planned using these resources, 3) outputs or products of the activities, 4) outcomes or expected changes as a result of the intervention, and 5) impact or long-term, systems-level changes that will result.
5. Identifying and naming the social inequity properly leads the planner to determining the final impact being sought.
6. The issue and impact statements also illustrate the importance of answering the "why" question to help motivate and engage people in the planned change effort.

Key Terms

Issue statement
Assumptions
Intervention hypothesis
Theory of change
Needs assessment
Logic model
Inputs
Activities
Outputs
Outcomes
Impact
Why

Discussion Questions

1. Discuss the implications of the term achievement gap versus opportunity gap.
2. Why is it important to develop a clear and focused issue statement?
3. Why add the step of developing an intervention hypothesis when you already think you know the intervention required?
4. What is the possible impact of not uncovering and naming assumptions before developing a program intervention?
5. How does answering the "why" question help engage people in the planned change effort?

References

Annie E. Casey Foundation (2004) Theory for change: A practical tool for action, results and learning, https://www.aecf.org/resources/theory-of-change/, retrieved 12/29/20

Friere, P. (1970) Pedagogy of the oppressed. Herder and Herder

Knowlton, L.W. & Phillips, C.C. (2013) *The logic model guidebook: Better strategies for great results, 2nd ed.* SAGE Publications

Mooney, T. (2018) We say opportunity gap instead of achievement gap, 5/11/18, https://www.teachforamerica.org/stories/why-we-say-opportunity-gap-instead-of-achievement-gap, retrieved 12/29/20

Royal, C. (2012) Please stop using the phrase "achievement gap," 11/10/12, https://www.good.is/articles/please-stop-using-the-phrase-achievement-gap, retrieved 12/29/20

Schott Foundation for Public Education (2020) National report highlights root cause of pervasive racism and inequality in America's most populated cities, 7/8/2020, http://schottfoundation.org/search/content2/opportunity%20to%20 learn%20index, retrieved 12/29/20

Stoltzfus, K. (2019) Abolitionist teaching in action: Q&A with Bettina L. Love. *Education Update*, December, 65(1), http://www.ascd.org/publications/newsletters/ educationupdate/dec19/vol61/num12/toc.aspx, retrieved 12/29/20

wbur.org (2019) Achievement gap, or opportunity gap? What's stopping student success, *WBUR On Point*, aired 11/9/19, https://www.wbur.org/onpoint/2019/09/09/achievement-gap-opportunity-education-schools-students-teachers, retrieved 3/01/21

Note

1 Abolitionist educators fight injustice within their schools and communities. Utilizing the intellectual work and direct action of community organizers, abolitionist teachers organize and take action for educational freedom. This approach builds upon the work and lessons of early abolitionists and the writings of Paolo Friere (1970), a Brazilian educator, philosopher and leading advocate of critical pedagogy. He authored the influential work *Pedagogy of the Oppressed*, a foundational text of the critical pedagogy movement.

5 The Process of Program Planning

Theory of Change and Logic Models

Learning Objectives

- Articulate the steps to follow in rational decision making.
- Demonstrate an understanding of structured decision making.
- Understand the concepts of "unintended consequences" and "benefit-cost analysis" and how they impact program planning.
- Articulate the difference between "evidence-based" and "evidence-informed" planning.
- Demonstrate an understanding of the role of logic models in human services program planning.

Chapter Overview

Building upon the theory of change and logic models, this chapter defines logic models, demonstrating the usefulness in program development while serving as a working illustration of the "how" and "why" of a planned change effort. Beginning with an exploration of the rationality of planning, the chapter explores how logic models serve as the bridge between the activities of the intervention and the desired impact. The concepts of unintended consequences and benefit-cost analysis are explored as part of the planning process.

Planning as a Rational Process

Rational planning can be seen as the ability to control the future consequences of actions taken in the present (Wildavsky, 1971), based upon "the deliberate social or organizational activity of developing an optimal strategy for achieving a desired set of goals" (Alexander, 1979, p. 111). To be rational, planning "emphasizes goal setting, identification of alternatives, and evaluation of means and ends with a focus on implementation of decisions" (Hudson, 1979). Julian and Lyons (1992) describe rationality in planning as

> a choice of future actions governed by the rules of logic… Goals are defined and strategies are generated that hold a high probability of leading to the desired outcome. The strategy thought to be the most

DOI: 10.4324/9781003148777-5

> likely to produce some desirable outcome at an acceptable cost is designated, implemented and evaluated supporting future iterations of the planning process.
>
> (pp. 248–249)

As the definitions above suggest, rational planners engage in a process of due diligence exploring alternatives and strategies leading to an approach with a high probability of success. The logic model lays out the change effort in a linear and logical format, following a rational path to the impact sought. Social policy planning highlights three approaches that can be followed in a rational planning process. While these approaches were developed for social policy planning, exploration of these approaches applies to program planning as well.

Rational-Comprehensive Approach to Program Planning

Leoveanu (2013) describes a rational approach to public policy decision making. It is worth exploring this approach as it can be applied to human services program planning as well. According to Leoveanu, to be truly rational all of the following must be available and considered:

- The inequity can be identified and there is agreement on the need to resolve it.
- All values of the community and the larger political systems can be identified and weighed.
- All alternative approaches can be identified and considered.
- The consequences of each alternative can be fully understood in terms of benefits and costs for the target group and the larger community.
- The benefit-cost analysis for each possible approach can be calculated.
- Planners can choose the approach maximizing the net gain – the alternative that achieves the most benefit at the lowest cost.

Forester (1989) terms this approach "rational-comprehensive." He lists six assumptions this approach is based upon:

1. a well-defined problem;
2. a full array of alternatives to consider;
3. full baseline information;
4. complete information about the consequences of each alternative;
5. full information about the values and preferences of citizens; and
6. fully adequate time, skill and resources.

(pp. 49–50)

While a fully rational or rational-comprehensive approach sounds like the best way to approach planning or problem-solving processes, let's take a look at the basis of this approach. All planning is based upon the assumption that the inequity can be identified and there is a need to resolve it. However, while it seems the ideal approach would be truly rational, there are certain drawbacks to this approach.

To follow a rational-comprehensive approach to planning, there are a number of factors to be considered:

- Is it possible to identify all of the values held by the community? In an attempt to do so, when do you know you have successfully identified all of the values held by community members and leaders, and if you are able to do this, do these values support a need for intervention?
- Is it ever possible to know you have identified all of these values?
- Trying to identify and consider all alternative approaches can lead to a never-ending search to ensure you have considered every possible alternative. In fact, this one aspect can make a truly rational approach a nonstarter because it is not possible to know you have identified all possible alternatives.
- Assuming you have been able to identify a range of alternative approaches, it is not possible to name all of the possible consequences of each approach and then figure out the costs and benefits for each. Each possible alternative is investigated to determine the benefits

Rational-Comprehensive Approach

- Identify all values held by the community.
  - When do you know that you have successfully identified all values held by community members and leaders?
  - Is it possible to know that you have identified all of these values?
- Identify every possible alternative approach.
  - Is it possible to know that you have identified all possible alternatives?
  - Even if this is possible, how do you know that you have identified all possible alternatives?
- Determine the costs and consequences of each alternative approach.
  - Is it possible to determine all of the costs and possible consequences of every alternative approach?
- Sufficient time, skills, and resources exist to accomplish all of the above.
  - Will the planners have access to all needed resources and unlimited time?

and costs before choosing the best approach based upon the most benefit for the least cost.
- Is the best approach always the one costing the least?

While each of these steps, on their face value, sound rational, they are indeed onerous and can lead to endless investigation, and still fall short of identifying and interrogating every possible alternative. To be truly rational in our approach to planning would in fact be detrimental to the process, by preventing the planner from moving forward. Therefore, having established that a fully "rational" approach to the planning effort is not possible, we can look at other approaches based on rationality.

Bounded Rationality

Another such approach is "bounded rationality," whereby planners consider a limited number of alternative interventions and choose the one(s) appearing to achieve the most essential goals, with a balance between costs and benefits that satisfies the appropriate interested parties. Bounded rationality recognizes the ability to plan is constrained by the available information. Simon (1990), who coined the term, writes "bounded rationality is used to designate rational choice that takes into account the cognitive limitations of the decision maker" (p. 915).

Based upon the work of March and Simon (1958) and Perrow (1986), Forester (1989) provides six examples of constraints on the rational approach suggesting a "bounded" approach, these are:

1. problems are ambiguous or poorly defined,
2. available information about alternatives is incomplete,
3. information about the background of the inequity is incomplete,
4. consequences of possible alternatives are unknown,
5. insufficient information about the range and content of values, preferences, and interests, and
6. limited time, skills and resources.

(p. 50)

Political Approach to Program Planning

Finally, there is the "political approach," focusing on the reality of the challenges faced by planners in getting a diverse group of people on board to address the issue. This approach has been developed as a response to the assumptions of the rational planning model. Without the advantage of absolute rationality, the political approach is governed by a constrained rationality limited by the abilities and cognitive biases of those involved (Favoreau et al., 2015).

Bounded Rational Approach

Is useful when:

- The inequality may not be easy to define
  - *Different community members or supporters can have differing perspectives on the issue to be addressed.*
- All possible alternatives cannot be identified.
  - *Is it possible to know you have identified all possible alternatives?*
- Even if this is possible, how do you know you have identified all possible alternatives.
- Consequences and benefits of all possible alternatives cannot be identified.
  - *If you cannot identify all possible alternatives, it is not possible to determine all of the costs and possible consequences of every alternative approach.*
- All values of the community and community leaders cannot be identified.
- Time and resources are limited.
  - *Planners often have limited resources and are under time constraints to address the identified inequity.*

Political Approach

- There may be conflicting values among community members and leaders.
- Community members and/or leaders do not agree upon the inequity to be addressed.
- Costs cannot always be identified or compared.
- Other community needs or priorities can cause conflicts about costs and resources allocation.
- Those with power and influence in the community may make it difficult to discern the values and needs of other community members who have less power and influence.
- Progress can be impeded by holding on to the old way of doing things.

The political approach points out a number of realities to be taken into consideration when beginning the planning process. These include:

- We cannot always identify the agreed upon values of specific groups and individuals who may have conflicting values and goals.

- People do not always agree on the issue, an inequity to one group can be a benefit to another.
- There can be many conflicting costs and values that cannot be compared or weighed.
- Planners cannot always predict the consequences of alternative interventions or calculate the true costs.
- The political environment of power and influence within the community or organization makes it difficult to discern the inherent social values, especially those not supported by people with power and access within the community.
- The way things were done in the past can often create barriers to change and moving forward.

Rational Decision Making

As illustrated by Figure 5.1 and suggested by the three approaches, planning cannot always be a truly rational process. Through the needs assessment the planner/researcher collects as much relevant information as possible, addressing many of the concerns or challenges raised above. Once the planner believes sufficient information has been collected, then it is time to move forward based upon what is known. If the planner/researcher is focused on gathering all available information, investigating all alternative interventions and exploring the benefits and costs of each, the effort can get mired down in collecting information and exploring alternatives, without any way of knowing when the end point has been reached. There may be possible interventions that have not been identified and unknown costs and possible benefits that cannot be identified at the outset. However, there is a point where the planner/researcher has gathered and analyzed sufficient information to move forward.

	Rational Comprehensive	Bounded Rationality	Political Approach
Inequity to be addressed	Inequity is well defined	Ambiguous, poorly defined	Issue not always greed upon
Community values	All community values can be agreed upon and weighed	Cannot know all values	Different groups may have conflicting values
Alternative interventions	All alternatives can be identified and considered	Limited alternatives considered	Cannot identify all alternatives
Consequences of alternatives	Consequences can be identified for each alternative	Consequences are unknown	Can only investigate limited number of alternatives and their consequences
Net gain	Choose one approach that maximizes net gain	Choose among limited alternatives	Choose among limited alternatives that best meet identified community values
Benefit cost	Compute benefit cost of all alternative interventions	Explore benefit cost of limited number of interventions	Choose among limited alternatives one that provides greatest benefit cost ratio
Time, resources & skills	Adequate time, resources and skills available	Limited time, resources and skills	Must move forward within limited time frame with available resources and skills

Figure 5.1 Three approaches to rational planning

Julian and Lyons (1992) have developed helpful criteria to guide rational decision making based upon a combination of the political and bounded rational approaches as defined above. These are:

- Involvement of a broad cross-section of stakeholders in the decision-making process. The importance of this for social justice planners has been discussed in previous chapters.
- Emphasis on implementation. Throughout the process, the emphasis should be focused on those alternatives with a reasonable expectation of success as viable options to be pursued.
- Degree of strategic thinking. Focus is placed on exploring and analyzing strengths, weaknesses, opportunities and threats.
- Emphasis on consensus building. Consensus is reached when there is a point of agreement among stakeholders. Building consensus means taking into consideration minority opinions and views, and not just the will of the majority.
- Likelihood innovative programming will result from problem-solving activities. To address existing inequities often requires innovation based upon research, prior knowledge and experience.
- Exercise of collective power. This builds upon consensus decision making and involvement of a broad cross-section of stakeholders becoming empowered through the planning process.

Structured Decision Making

Whether following a bounded rational or political approach in the decision-making process, there still needs to be a structure to follow to determine the information needed to help make the best decisions. One such possibility, structured decision making (or SDM), is growing in usage. Gregory et al. (2012) define structured decision making as

> an organized, inclusive and transparent approach to understanding complex problems and generating and evaluating creative alternatives. SDM is founded on the idea that good decisions are based on an in-depth understanding of both values (what's important) and consequences (what's likely to happen if an alternative is implemented). (p. 6)

SDM has been used most recently in environmental decisions impacting communities, with a range of community values affecting the decision-making process. In SDM, planners evaluate and respond to community values transparently, articulating clear and unambiguous objectives while dealing with uncertainty. Every decision is based upon objectives to be achieved, decision options and predictions of decision options. By analyzing each of these separately "within a comprehensive framework, it is possible to improve the quality of decision making" (USGS, n.d.). Whatever decision-making process or tool is utilized, program planners should keep in mind that

> most strategies, plans, management actions and decisions ignore that the ability to implement them does not lay on the decision maker, but on common citizens, workers and other stakeholders who end up predominantly ignored and even disregarded in the decision-making process.
>
> (Fernandes, 2019, p. 564)

Keeping this in mind helps to ensure stakeholders are involved in every step of the decision-making process. Gregory et al. (2012) suggest seven questions to help guide structured decision making.

Considering each of these questions helps to move the planning process forward by focusing on necessary considerations. When following a bounded rational or political approach, this series of questions helps to organize the data gathering needed. The final question emphasizes learning over time and the ability to modify plans throughout the implementation phase.

Figure 5.2 illustrates the sequence of structured decision making. Once the inequity has been identified the next step is to determine what you want to achieve, or the desired impact.

Step three is to investigate possible interventions and to determine if there are other impacts that should be sought. Once you have identified one or more interventions in step three, the expected and unintended

Questions to Guide Structured Decision Making

- What is the context for (scope and bounds of) the decision?
- What objectives and performance measures will be used to identify and evaluate the alternatives?
- What are the most promising alternative actions or strategies under consideration?
- What are the expected and possible unintended consequences of these actions or strategies?
- What are the critical uncertainties and how do they affect choices?
- What are the key trade-offs among consequences?
- How can the decision be implemented in a way that promotes learning over time and provides opportunities to revise actions and decisions based on what is learned?

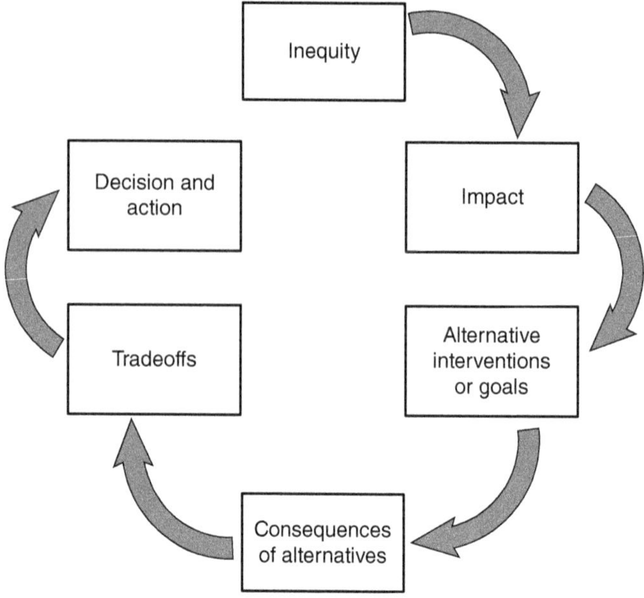

Figure 5.2 Structured decision making

consequences of each of these are explored. After identifying some of the consequences of the preferred alternative interventions, the tradeoffs (or benefits and costs) for each alternative are analyzed. After exploring the alternatives and the benefits and costs then it is time to make a decision about which intervention appears to be the most effective and then this is acted upon or put into motion.

Two terms were introduced in the discussion above – unintended consequences and benefit-cost analysis.

Unintended Consequences

The so-called "Law of Unintended Consequences," makes it clear there may be consequences of your actions you have not planned for or could not have been aware of. In a paper first published in 1936, "The Unanticipated Consequences of Purposive Social Action," sociologist Robert Merton (1936) described unintended consequences as follows: "the consequences of purposive action are limited to those elements in the resulting situation which are exclusively the outcome of the action, i.e., those elements which would not have occurred had the action not taken place." He further explains these consequences are the result of "the interplay of forces and circumstances which are so complex and numerous that prediction of them is quite beyond our reach."

Unintended consequences are not necessarily positive or negative. They merely result from the work the planner engages and were not anticipated in the planning process. In the OurKids AfterSchool case study there are a number of unintended consequences that could be experienced as a result of the intervention. Some of these possibilities are enumerated below as examples, not to suggest these are actual outcomes. However, they can serve to illustrate outcomes that are not part of the intended program, some are positive and some not so positive. These possible examples include:

- As students improve their reading scores, they become more engaged in the classroom and there is a noted reduction in behavioral issues.
- The administration begins rating teachers on their students' improvement in reading scores. As a result, teachers begin teaching to the reading test and sacrifice learning in other academic areas.
- As the reading gap is reduced, teachers begin to focus less time on reading skills resulting in another increase in the gap.
- Parents see their children improving and as a result they become more involved in their children's schoolwork and spend more time reading on their own as well.
- Parents for whom English is not their primary language see their children improving in school and develop their English skills so they can help support their children's education.
- Schools with lower reading scores are allocated additional funds by the school board resulting in parents in other schools in the district fighting back because they feel their children are now being disadvantaged.

As you see from these examples, unintended consequences can be both positive and negative, but in one form or another all result from the intervention. Each of these would likely not have occurred if the intervention, or as Merton (1936) termed it "purposive social action," was not put in place.

Benefit-Cost Analysis

A benefit-cost analysis is a process whereby planners determine the direct and indirect costs of the planned change effort and compare these to the proposed benefits. This process has been traditionally termed a "cost-benefit" analysis. However, through a social justice lens it is preferable to engage in a benefit-cost analysis, elevating benefit to a higher priority than cost.

The benefit-cost analysis is used to determine whether the advantages of a particular action outweigh its costs or drawbacks. Through this, planners compare alternative intervention options by quantifying their

Table 5.1.

	Intended/Expected	Unintended/Unexpected
Desireable	• Reading scores improve • Students more engaged • High school graduation increases • College acceptance increases	• Reduced behavioral issues • Parents more involved in children's schoolwork • Improved English skills among parents • Teachers become more energized • Improvement in other courses
Undesireable	• Teacher resistance • Parents unprepared to assist students	• Reduced learning time focused on other subjects • Long-term increase in reading gap • Parental resistance • Reduced funding in other areas of education

impacts, identifying positive changes as benefits and negative changes as costs. The projected costs are then subtracted from the increased value or proposed benefits. When the increased value or savings are greater than the proposed costs, then the intervention is deemed to be cost effective. However, it is important to note not all benefits can be quantified in dollar amounts, especially in the human services where this exercise can raise the question, how much is a human life worth?

> The use of money (or willingness to pay) as a measure of value indicates that cost-benefit analysis is firmly rooted in neoclassical economic theory, which conceive of human well-being in terms of utility (or preference satisfaction), and focus on the price (or exchange) value of goods and services.
>
> (Wegner and Pascual, 2011, pp. 492–493)

When computing the benefit-cost shows the costs are high, but the benefits are low, because they do not benefit a significant number of people, does that mean the intervention is not viable? When a program is successful in improving the conditions of some people's lives, but at a high per-person cost, does that mean the intervention does not go forward because it is not cost effective? We must ask ourselves about the people the program is able to help. Are they not worth the expense? These questions are not posed to suggest the costs and benefits of a program are not to be taken into consideration. Yes, there should be a clear idea of the costs of the program, but when we are working with people, we cannot project all of the benefits. In any human services intervention, some participants may accrue more of the benefits than others.

Benefit-cost questions to be considered by social justice planners.

- Does high cost and low or moderate benefit automatically cancel a planned intervention?
- Does a low success rate mean an intervention is not viable?
- What is the determining factor between cost and benefit?
- What is the value of improving one person's life?
- What is the value of a human life?

Let's look outside of human service programs to explore the advantages and disadvantages of such an analysis. There is an expectation that public transit in most urban centers pays for itself through the fare box. However, all public transit depends on government subsidies to make up the shortfall between the income from fares and the actual costs of running the system. Across the country however, there are demands that riders pay more of the costs of operating these systems to avoid increasing taxes. The assumption here is that the costs of public transit should be borne by the riders, because they are the direct beneficiaries of these systems. However, engaging in an extensive analysis of the benefits would show public transit users are not the only ones, nor are they the largest group of beneficiaries from mass transit. A true benefit-cost analysis would take into account benefits accruing to non-mass transit users such as reduced automobile traffic, resulting in less pollution thereby contributing to a possible reduction in the number of related illnesses and lost days at work. These numbers are difficult to enumerate because it is unknown how many people would commute by car if there was no mass transit, nor how many people might succumb to lung disease or other ailments caused or exacerbated by pollution. Finally, the benefit of reduced traffic on climate change would have to be enumerated, as well as the cost of increased traffic and burning of fossil fuels as contributors to climate change.

On the other side of this discussion, if fares are kept low to increase ridership and reduce auto usage, the increased ridership and crowding could cause delays making more people late for work and have a negative impact on productivity. As these examples demonstrate, it is difficult to predict all unintended consequences and costs or benefits in order to develop a complete benefit-cost analysis.

A benefit-cost analysis focused on OurKids AfterSchool would look at the costs of running a summer reading program, including all hard and soft costs, and the projected benefits. While some of the projected benefits have cost savings attached to them, many do not. What is the cost that can be attributed to a student's increased self-esteem? We know a high school graduate can expect greater lifetime earnings than someone who does not graduate, and it is known there is a lower incarceration rate for high school graduates than nongraduates. The Bureau of Justice Statistics reports that 41% of all incarcerated people in the U.S. did not complete high school, while 22.6% are high school graduates (Harlow, 2003). These cost savings can be projected based upon a prediction of how many additional students would graduate high school and how many fewer would enter the criminal legal system. However, while projecting the reduction in the opportunity gap will result in increased graduation rates, we cannot predict what this increase will be. Students who participate in the program might indeed improve their reading scores and school grades, but there are a number of intervening circumstances that can prevent individual students from graduating, and these cannot be predicted at the outset. For example, it is impossible to predict how many, or whether or not, some students might be forced to drop out to help support their families.

Vining and Weimer (2019) make the point that it is difficult to quantify the social value of high school graduation, which is not straightforward for several reasons. This is due to the fact that investments in educational increments, whether quantity or quality, are multidimensional, long-term, and non-linear, making them difficult to measure. Without clear numbers, a dollar amount of cost savings cannot be attributed to participation in the program. Instead, we can predict there will be greater earnings, less poverty and reduced incarcerations as a result, but a hard number cannot be computed for these benefits. Therefore, to make the case, planners need to focus on the benefits that are expected to accrue, even if a dollar amount cannot be associated to them. Then, based upon the importance of these benefits determine whether or not the costs associated with the program seem reasonable.

In the human services, where we are working with people who are individuals with individual capacities and life situations, it is difficult to enumerate the benefits as compared to the costs. That is the key, we are working with individuals who cannot be easily categorized into a box so that we can predict how they will use the benefits afforded them through the intervention. Therefore, costs can be computed, but benefits are best described in descriptive prose to demonstrate they are worth the investment in the intervention.

Using Evidence/Research in Planning

Evidence-Based Planning

The currently accepted standard for human services interventions is Evidence-Based Practice (EBP), with originates in the medical field. EBP has been described as "a problem-solving approach to the delivery of health care that integrates the best evidence from well-designed studies and patient care data and combines it with patient preferences and values and..." practitioner expertise (Melnyk & Fineout-Overholt,

2010, p. 51). The National Association of Social Workers describes EBP as "a process in which the practitioner combines well-researched interventions with clinical experience, ethics, client preferences, and culture to guide and inform the delivery of treatments and services... These are interventions that, when consistently applied, consistently produce improved client outcomes" (The National Association of Social Workers, n.d.). This definition however, begs the question of whether when working with people who are unique individuals in unique circumstances, can we ever predict an intervention will always result in improved client outcomes? The evidence can show that a particular intervention or theory has proven effective in the past, but this is not a guarantee of successful replication in other circumstances and with different populations. Webb (2001) offers a definition of EBP applicable to the human services field: "the conscientious, explicit and judicious use of current best evidence in making decisions regarding the welfare of service users and carers" (p. 61). This definition focuses on the decision-making process and does not suggest EBP is predictive of the outcome. Instead, the focus here is on a decision-making process based upon evidence.

Rubin (2007) delineates five phases of evidence-based practice. These are:

1. Formulate a question,
2. Search for studies providing evidence about the question,
3. Critically appraise the evidence,
4. Select and implement an intervention that is supported by the best evidence, and
5. Monitor progress.

(p. 541)

The Ministry of Local Government and Rural Development of the Republic of Botswana (2013) has developed an evidence-based planning toolkit building upon these phases with a focus on planning that describes six steps to guide planners.

While evidence-based planning seems a rather simple concept underscoring human services program planning based upon available data and knowledge, it is not without its critics. Rubin (2007), while defending the EBP model, summarizes four disadvantages they have found in the literature. These are:

1. It ignores idiosyncratic client and practitioner factors, and thus makes EBP look too mechanistic,
2. It lacks transparency and uncertainty, makes inflated claims about the evidence base for the EBPs, and hides flaws in the research,
3. It is hard for social work practitioners to implement the EBPs in light of resource limitations regarding time, training and supervision, and

4. The fluid, ever-changing and self-correcting landscape of scientific advances can make any list of EBPs outdated by the time it appears in print.

(p. 542)

Davoudi (2015) addresses this when they write "in the messy world of planning and policy making, evidence can be best considered as playing an enlightening rather than determining role" (p. 317) suggesting that program planning is more appropriately informed by rather than being based on evidence.

Nemo and Šlonim-Nevo (2011) question EBP, writing it

> is neither determinative nor exclusive. In fact, practice is as much an art as it is a science, and as much a dialogue as it is an application of empirical findings to clients' unique characteristics and context. The wisdom appropriate to it is practical wisdom rather than that of scientific rationality.

Based upon this perspective, they propose "a comprehensive conception of practice as informed by but not adequately based on evidence" (p. 1178). Haight (2010) proposes a wider range of research methodologies including "a richly contextualized analysis of social phenomena through practices such as sustained engagement and use of multiple methods – including direct observations and in-depth interviewing…" (p. 102). Social justice planners include the judgments, knowledge, experience and creativity of stakeholders and practitioners. EBP is a research-informed process, while social justice planners follow a process that is stakeholder informed.

Evidence-Informed Planning

Taking these criticisms into consideration, a social justice approach to planning is best described as Evidence-Informed Planning (EIP). This is based on the idea that the best use of evidence in the planning process is to serve as a guide to help planners determine the best course of action based upon available information, practice experience and the needs and desires of the community. EIP does not require that planners only limit themselves to empirical evidence and research that demonstrates what has been found to be effective, but that this information is used as a guide to inform the planning process. Nevo and Slonim-Nevo (2011) suggest that through an EIP approach, practitioners "become knowledgeable of a wide range of sources – empirical studies, case studies and clinical insights – and us them in creative ways throughout the intervention process" (p. 1176).

Figure 5.3 illustrates the sequence of steps followed in evidence-informed planning. The steps that are followed in evidence-informed

Evidence-Informed Planning

- Step 1. **Planning**: is not done before the "real" work is started, planning *is* part of the real work.
- Step 2. **Evidence gathering**: investigating and gathering available data, information, knowledge, practice experience, and insights and experiences of stakeholders.
- Step 3. **Results oriented planning**: using evidence gathered to inform what should be done.
- Step 4. **Preparing the plan**: based upon the priority issues, determined goals and objectives, chosen strategy and activities, in this step these are brought together into the logic model format.
- Step 5. **Implementation, monitoring and reporting**: the activities that have been decided upon are implemented in an organized manner. This step also includes monitoring the activities and outcomes to make adjustments as needed.
- Step 6. **Evaluation**: determining the effectiveness of the intervention, outcomes achieved and lessons learned.

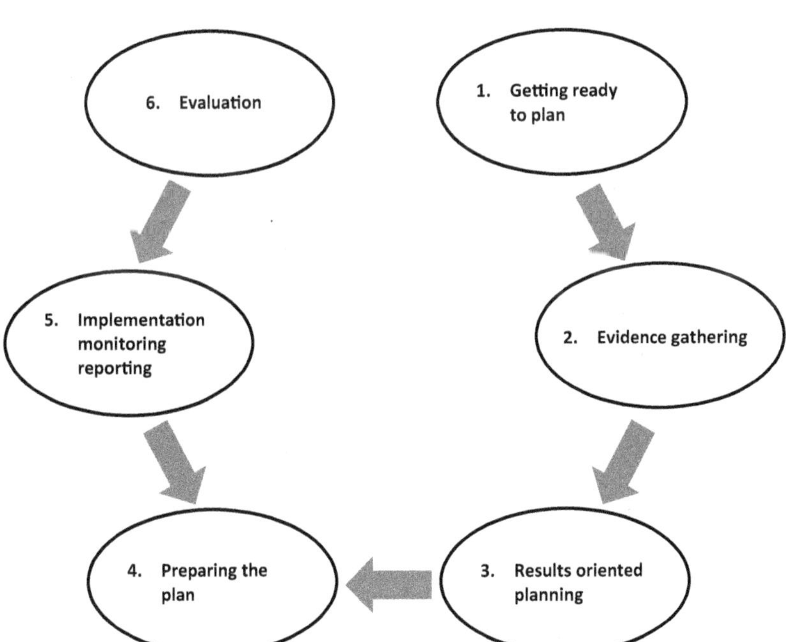

Figure 5.3 Evidence-informed planning

planning are equivalent to the steps followed in developing the theory of change and program logic model.

Building on the Theory of Change

The theory of change can serve multiple purposes. It is a powerful tool for the stakeholders to articulate ideas and to build consensus around a planned change effort. When complete, a theory of change serves as a guide for implementation, ensuring plans are true to their original intent. A well-developed theory of change helps facilitate the evaluation of program results by comparing a clearly articulated plan to what has actually occurred in the implementation of the planned change effort.

Theory of Change and Logic Models

The logic model, based on the theory of change, serves as a guide whereby planners can compare the planned approach with what actually occurred, enabling the ability to reflect on the strategies implemented and their results. Logic models based upon the theory of change also serve as a point of reference. During implementation of the change effort the original theory of change can be adapted and changed over time as new understanding and ideas based upon the experience of implementation surface. Therefore, it is crucial to see the theory of change and the logic model as a guide, not a set course of action that cannot be changed.

> Logic models can be seen as maps with guideposts that help keep the intervention or program on course. In most social work interventions, however, regardless of the type and the experience of the practitioner or staff, the actual implementation activities deviate from the plan. As every direct service worker knows, an agreement with a client does not necessarily mean that the reciprocal responsibilities are always remembered and enacted. As every experienced program developer also knows, the best laid plans usually slip during the first month or two of implementation. A well-written logic model can stabilize an intervention or program during times of flux and can allow for revisions if situations should warrant.
>
> (Alter & Murty, 1997, p. 103)

Theory of Change Phases

Hernandez and Hodges (2006) delineate three phases to the development of a theory of change. These are:

- Phase 1. *Pre-planning.* During this phase, those involved in the planning effort come together to define the process, allowing the

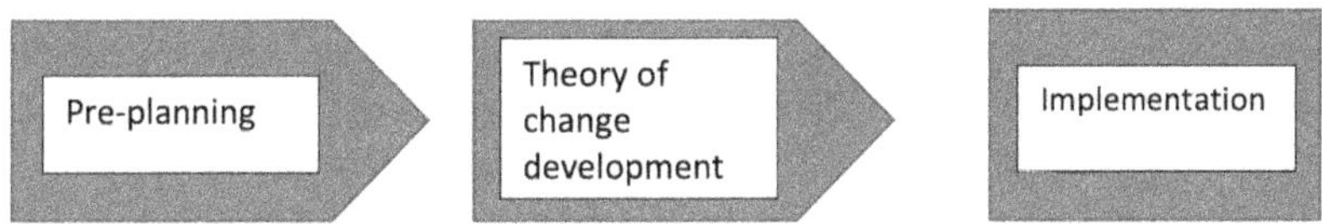

Figure 5.4 Theory of change phases

participants to build trust, rapport and group identity. The authors delineate four steps to be accomplished during this phase: work-group formation, articulation of the mission, identification of goals and the guiding principles for the group to follow.

- Phase 2. *Theory of change development.* During this phase, participants determine the characteristics, needs and strengths of the population to be served, the outcomes desired by the population to be served, and the strategies employed to achieve these outcomes. This informs the logic model.
- Phase 3. *Implementation.* There are two stages to this phase, the first is implementing the planned change effort and the second is process evaluation or tracking the progress and revising the intervention where necessary.

The clear articulation of a theory of change requires making explicit the linkages between the identified populations, intended outcomes and planned strategies. Once the elements of a theory of change are clearly articulated, stakeholders have an informed understanding of what should be implemented in their community and what is expected to be accomplished.

(Hernandez & Hodges, 2006, p. 166)

The "Why" of Logic Models

In its simplest terms, the logic model is a visual presentation of the theory of change, demonstrating the relationship among the resources needed to create and implement the planned intervention, the activities these resources will support, the outcomes as a result of the planned activities and finally the long-term impact resulting from the planned intervention. As a visual representation, the logic model serves as a road map logically leading to the desired outcomes and impact. It is a useful framework that supports critical thinking to help design programs that are results based while also providing a structure for evaluation. "Logic models support design, planning, communication, evaluation and learning... They can untangle and clarify complex relationships among elements or parts" (Knowlton & Phillips, 2013, p. 3).

Building the Logic Model

As a tool for successful program planning, logic models present in diagrammatic form a clear understanding of the planned change effort that is being proposed. By filling in the if/then of the program hypothesis and illustrating the connections between the components of the planned change effort, the logic model provides the capacity to evaluate the probability of success. It also serves the purpose of clearly demonstrating the steps to be taken and the progress made in order to achieve the desired results. In its diagrammatic format, the logic model presents a clarifying sequence of events to be followed, thereby providing a full understanding of the planned change effort. Logic models provide a usable format for evaluations to help guide program progress and support remedial actions when the outputs and intermediate outcomes are not met during the implementation phase (Millar et al., 2001). As Martin and Carey (2014) point out, "Logic modeling surfaces and summarizes the explicit and implicit logic of how a program operates to produce its desired benefits and results" (p. 456). In this way, logic models establish the interdependence between the elements that cause the change and clearly demonstrate how the inputs and activities lead to the anticipated changes (Zyronski & Mariani, 2019).

Figure 5.5 illustrates the logic model template. As illustrated, the model is divided into two sections, the planned work and the proposed changes resulting from the intervention. Each of these categories is divided into specific sections. The first category, planned work, specifies the work needed to implement the planned change effort. This includes gathering the resources needed to support the program, the activities participants will become engaged in, and the quantifiable outputs of these activities. The second category, proposed results, specifies in measurable terms, the results that are expected to be achieved from the planned change intervention and the long-term impact sought.

The logic model components illustrated in Figure 5.5 are:

- Inputs/Resources: The assets or capital needed to engage in the planned change effort, such as finances, materials, supplies, human resources, and space.
- Activities: What the program will do with the resources specified in the first column of the logic model. These are the actions that form the intentional part of the planned change effort leading to the expected outcomes to be realized as a result of these activities.
- Outputs: The direct products of the program activities. Outputs are quantifiable results such as program participation and the number of planned activities to be delivered by the program activities.
- Outcomes: The changes expected to be realized through participation in the program activities. This can include changes in behavior, knowledge, skills or level of functioning, for example.

LOGIC MODE TEMPLATE
Issue or inequity to be addressed:______________________________

Inputs Resources that will be devoted to or invested in the intervention. What you will need to make the planned change effort work.	**Activities** What you will be doing in the program. What actions, steps or tasks are essential to the intervention	**Outputs** What the program will produce as a result of the activities. What services will be offered, how frequently, to whom and the products that will be produced as a result	**Short-term outcomes** The results that you expect to occur immediately due to intervention	**Medium-term outcomes** The results that will occur next due to the intervention	**Impact** The long-term changes to larger systems resulting from the planned change effort

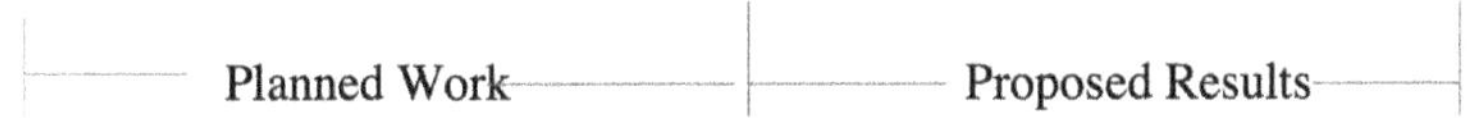

Figure 5.5 Logic model template

- Impact: The long-term change(s) in systems, policies, organizations or communities that can be expected as a result of the planned change effort, often occurring after the program has terminated.

The components of the logic model correlate to the intervention hypothesis. Following the "if–then" hypothesis, the planned work, or the resources/inputs and the planned activities represent the independent variable. If these inputs and activities are engaged in, then we can expect the proposed results, or the dependent variable that includes outcomes and the longer-term impact. As in any research hypothesis, the dependent variable is named as such because it is dependent upon the implementation of the independent variable. In Figure 5.6 a third variable is introduced, the intervening variable. Usually, the intervening variable is caused by the independent variable and has an impact on the dependent variable. For example, in a logic model there can be a correlation between the number of participants or how often they participate in an intervention, defined as outputs, and whether or not the proposed activity leads to the projected outcome. However, while this can influence the outcome it may not be directly causal in nature.

In a research hypothesis, the intervening variable can influence the relationship between the independent and dependent variables. This relationship is illustrated in Figure 5.6. For example, if tutoring is offered as an activity to address the reading gap, then the outputs are the products of that activity. This includes the number of tutors recruited, the number of students participating, how often they participate, and how many sessions are offered over a predetermined period of time. These outputs have an impact on the proposed outcome – improved reading grades. This improvement may be dependent upon the number of times a student participates in tutoring and how often. It can also be impacted by the number of tutors recruited. If the program is not successful recruiting a sufficient number of tutors, then the number of students in tutoring may not be sufficient to achieve the projected outcomes.

The Logic of Logic Models

While named a logic model because it logically illustrates the planned intervention, reading the logic model and developing it do not follow the same logical sequence. Logic models are best read starting with the impact to be achieved, telling the reader what you hope to accomplish in the long-term. Then it is read from left to right, starting with the resources needed and illustrating the planned intervention to achieve the desired impact. Reading it in this way fills in the blanks of the intervention hypothesis. If "X" resources are used to create "Y" activities, then we can expect "Z" results, leading to the desired long-term change. However, logic models are best created working from right to left, beginning with the proposed impact and working back through how you will get there, the activities needed, and resources required. As Hall of Famer and baseball legend Yogi Berra is quoted to have said, "If you don't know where you're going, how you gonna know when you get there?" So, the first step is determining where you want to go, or the impact to be achieved. Once you have determined where "you're going" then you can develop the path to help answer the question "how you gonna know when you get there?"

Millar et al. (2001) point out,

> Starting with the inputs tends to foster a defense of the status quo. One is less likely to challenge the status quo when one starts with the status quo. To engage in reinvention and out-of-the-box thinking, we must reverse the rules for developing the logic model, thereby focusing on the end result to be achieved.
>
> (p. 76)

By developing the logic model in this way, working from the hoped-for impact, following each step back to the inputs needed, we remain focused on what we hope to achieve, rather than what is. When planning is built upon the resources that are already available, thinking can become

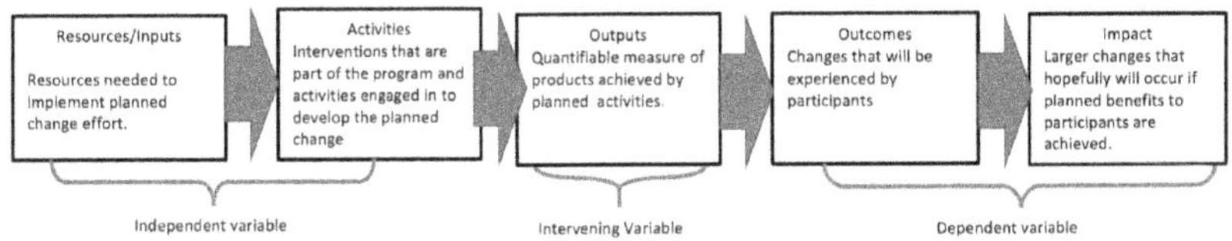

Figure 5.6 Independent, intervening and dependent variables illustrated in the logic model

constrained forcing planners to limit the possibilities to be considered. However, beginning with the end result in mind and working through the changes we wish to achieve and how we plan to get there, we can develop the resources based upon what is needed, not what is already known.

The logic model presents the elements of the theory of change and a clear articulation of the relationships between these elements, providing the stakeholders with an informed understanding of what is proposed to be implemented in the community and what they can expect to see accomplished as a result. With that in mind, the next chapter focuses on developing a logic model for the OurKids AfterSchool intervention, starting with the intended impact.

Chapter Summary

1. To be truly rational, or to follow an approach that is fully rational or rational-comprehensive, requires exploring all possible alternatives and community values.
2. It is not possible to know that all possible alternative interventions and all possible community values have been identified and investigated.
3. Program planners can move forward within recognized limitations, based upon limited intervention options and community values that can be identified and explored.
4. In the planning process, unintended consequences and the benefits and costs of limited alternatives are explored and taken into account.
5. Evidence-informed planning utilizes data, information and previous knowledge to support decision making, while not stifling innovation and creativity by dictating what can be done based upon what has been done previously.
6. Building upon the theory of change, the logic model serves as a visual representation, demonstrating the relationships between the resources needed, proposed activities and the expected outcomes.
7. Each component of the logic model correlates to the intervention hypothesis and the theory of change. As such, the logic model presents a clear understanding of the planned change effort in diagrammatic form.

Key terms

Rational-comprehensive planning
Bounded rationality
Political approach to planning
Rational decision making
Structured decision making
Unintended consequences
Benefit-cost analysis
Evidence-based planning
Evidence-informed planning
Theory of change
Logic model

Discussion Questions

1. Discuss the pros and cons of a bounded rational approach compared to a rational-comprehensive approach in designing an intervention for OurKids AfterSchool.
2. Discuss the implications of a benefit-cost analysis when determining cost while taking into consideration the concept of the value of improving one person's life compared to the idea of the most benefit at the least cost.
3. What is meant by the statement "starting with the inputs when designing a program intervention limits thinking to maintaining the status quo?"
4. How can evidence-informed planning be used to support innovative ideas and interventions?

References

Alexander, E. (1979) Planning theory. In A.J. Cantanese & J.C. Snyder (eds.) *Introduction to urban planning* (pp. 106–119). New York: McGraw Hill

Alter, C. & Murty, S. (1997). Logic modeling: A tool for teaching practice evaluation. *Journal of Social Work Education*, Winter, 33(1), 103–117

Davoudi, S. (2015) Planning as practice of knowing. *Planning Theory*, 14(3), 316–331

Favoreau, C., Carassus, D. & Maurel, C. (2015) Strategic management in the public sector: A rational, political or collaborative approach? *International Review of Administrative Sciences*, 82(3)

Fernandes, J.P. (2019) Developing viable, adjustable strategies for planning and management: A methodological approach. *Land Use Policy*, 82, 563–572

Forester, J. (1989) *Planning in the face of power*. University of California Press

Gregory, R., Failing, L., Harstone, M., Long, G., McDaniels, T. & Ohlson, D. (2012) *Structured decision making: A practical guide to making environmental choices*. Wiley- Blackwell

Haight, W.L. (2010) The multiple roles of applied social science research in evidence-informed practice. *Social Work*, 55(2), 101–103

Harlow, C.W. (2003) Bureau of Justice Statistics special report: Education and correctional populations, January, https://bjs.ojp.gov/content/pub/pdf/ecp.pdf, retrieved 8/2/21

Hernandez, H. & Hodges, S. (2006) Applying a theory of change approach to interagency planning in child mental health. *American Journal of Community Psychology*, December, 38(3), 165–173

Hudson, B.M. (1979) Comparison of current planning theories: Counterparts and contradictions. *American Planning Association Journal*, 45, 387–389

Julian, D.A. & Lyons, T.S. (1992) A strategic planning model for human services: Problem solving at the local level. *Evaluation and Program Planning*, 15, 247–254

Knowlton, L.W. & Phillips, C.C. (2013) *The Logic Model Guidebook*. SAGE Publications

Leoveanu, A.C. (2013) Rationalist model in public decision making. *Journal of Public Administration, Finance and Law*, 4, 43–54

March, J. & Simon, H.A. (1958) *Organizations*. Wiley and Sons

Martin, I. & Carey, J. (2014) Development of a logic model to guide evaluations of the ASCA National Model for school counseling programs. *Professional Counselor*, 4, 455–456

Melnyk, B.M. & Fineout-Overholt (2019) *Evidence-based practice in nursing and health care*. Philadelphia, PA: Wolters Kluwer

Merton, R.K. (1936) The unanticipated consequences of purposive social action. *American Sociological Review*, December, 1(6), 894–904

Millar, A., Simeone, R.S. & Carnevale, J.T. (2001) Logic models: A systems tool for performance management. *Evaluation and Program Planning*, February, 24(1), 73–81

Ministry of Rural Development and Local Government, Botswana (2013) *DMSC evidence based planning toolkit*. National Alliance of State and Territorial AIDS Directors

National Association of Social Workers (n.d.) Evidence-based practice, https://www.socialworkers.org/News/Research-Data/Social-Work-Policy-Research/Evidence-Based-Practice, retrieved 2/22/21

Nevo, I. & Slonim-Nevo, V. (2011) The myth of evidence-based practice: Towards evidence- informed practice. *British Journal of Social Work*, 41, 1176–1197

Perrow, C. (1986) *Complex organizations: A critical essay*. New York, NY: McGraw Hill

Rubin, A. (2007) Improving the teaching of evidence-based practice: Introduction to the special issue. *Research on Social Work Practice*, September, 17(5), 541–547

Simon H.A. (1990) Bounded rationality. In J. Eatwell, M. Milgate, & P. Newman (eds.) *Utility and probability*. The New Palgrave. Palgrave Macmillan

USGS (n.d.) Structured decision making, usgs.gov/center/science/structured-decision- making/qt-science_center_objects, retrieved 2/15/21

Vining, A.R. & Weimer, D.L. (2019) The value of high school graduation in the United States: Per-person shadow price estimates for use in cost-benefit analysis. *Administrative Sciences*, December, 9(4).

Wegner, G. & Pascual, U. (2011) Cost-benefit analysis in the context of ecosystem services for human well-being: A multidisciplinary critique. *Global Environmental Change*, 2(2), May, 492–504

Webb, S. (2001). Some considerations on the validity of evidence-based practice in social work. *British Journal of Social Work*, 31, 57–79

Wildavsky, A. (1971) Does planning work? *The Public Interest*, 24, 95–104

Zyronski, B. & Mariani, M. (2019) Connect the dots: Using a logic model to connect goals with interventions, evaluation strategies, and outcomes. *Professional School Counseling*, 22(1b) 1–11

6 Lasting Change Requires a Detailed Strategy

Learning Objectives

- Articulate how plans and tactics are used to develop a strategy.
- Understand the difference between a theory of change logic model and a program logic model.
- Demonstrate an understanding of the value of utilizing a program logic model to develop a planned change effort.
- Define the components of a program logic model.
- Articulate how to develop SMART objectives.
- Understand the distinction between outcomes and outputs.

Chapter Overview

The chapter begins with a description and discussion of strategy, its role in program planning, and its component parts – plans and tactics. This is followed by an explanation of the distinction between theory of change logic models and program logic models. Focusing on the program logic model, program outcomes are discussed within the context of SMART objectives. Using the OurKids AfterSchool case example, the program logic model begins to take shape with examples of the impact and short- and medium-term outcomes.

Strategy, Plans and Tactics

The previous chapter discussed how the theory of change leads to the creation of a logic model. Some writers have developed two distinct types of logic models: a theory of change logic model and a program logic model. Each of these serves a different purpose, both built upon the theory of change that has been developed. Theory of change logic models provide a conceptual overview of the planned change effort as compared to program logic models that provide the specifics and details, operationalizing the theory of change, filling in the strategy with a plan and specified tactics. To develop a working logic model that will lead you through the steps to achieve the impact you are seeking, it is helpful to understand the difference between strategy, plan and tactics.

DOI: 10.4324/9781003148777-6

Strategy

Strategy defines long-term goals, focusing on the end result to provide a path forward. It is an articulation of the direction you hope to move forward in. Phils (2005) points out that the strategy answers four critical questions:

- What do you want you do and why?
- What are the deepest aspirations of the community?
- Where are we headed?
- How do we prosper?

(p. 13)

Bryson (2010) delineates a ten-step strategic planning process for organizations, with minor tweaking, these can be applied to developing a strategy for program planning. The amended ten-step process refocused to program planning is:

1. Initiate and agree on a planning process.
2. Identify organizational and community mandates.
3. Clarify community values.
4. Assess the environment.
5. Identify the issue(s) facing the community.
6. Formulate strategies to address the issue(s).
7. Review and adopt the strategy to address these.
8. Establish a vision for the change effort.
9. Develop an effective implementation process.
10. Reassess strategies and the planning process.

(p. 232)

The vision for a preferred future or the impact you are seeking, is synonymous with a concept called the public value proposition. "If you want something from others (time, money, information, permission for example) you need a compelling proposal: one that will convince people that their efforts will be rewarded, and their resources spent wisely" (Cels et al., 2012, p. 16). It is difficult to implement change without a vision of why change is both necessary and possible. By articulating a public value proposition, you are establishing the reason for the change and a vision for the future. This is accomplished through a strong statement of the impact you hope to achieve, often been referred to as the "elevator speech." This value proposition is designed to interest others in your proposal with a short, compelling, and engaging statement. A clear impact statement, or public value proposition, becomes the basis of your strategy articulating what you hope to achieve, but without details of how this will be accomplished.

Hickman (2010) writes about the vision for an organization. However if we change the word "organization" in the following quote, and replace it with "community," it is just as relevant to the program planning process as well.

> A vision, much like a compass, points an organization [*community*] toward its end goal, or "true north." It is a realistic, credible and appealing future for the organization [*community*] that sets a clear direction; defines a more successful and desirable future; fits the organization's [*community's*] history, culture and values; and reflects the aspirations and expectations of major stakeholders.
>
> (p. 413)

In program planning, the vision is synonymous with the impact, or the greater change we hope to accomplish.

Weisenbach Keller (2013) divides strategy into two components: planning and implementing. "Planning involves dreaming big, creating a crystal-clear vision of a future place and time, analyzing and understanding the current situation, and estimating and recording the steps needed to traverse from the present to the future envisioned place" (p. 161). This highlights many of the steps discussed in previous chapters. Dreaming big and creating a clear vision follow the steps in Appreciative Inquiry as discussed in Chapter 3. Understanding the current situation is addressed by the needs assessment and estimating the steps to traverse from the present to the preferred future is the logic modeling process.

The University of Kansas Community Tool Box (n.d.) has developed a helpful set of criteria for developing a strategy. A good strategy does the following:

- Gives overall direction: strategy points to a path forward without detailing the specific approaches to be used. The strategy showing overall direction for the OurKids AfterSchool intervention is illustrated in Figure 6.1.
- Fits resources and opportunities: a good strategy takes advantage of current resources, assets and opportunities, while seeking new ones.
- Minimizes resistance and barriers: any effort aimed at changing the status quo will meet with some resistance, therefore a strong strategy attracts allies and deters opponents.
- Reaches those affected: strategy connects the intervention with those who should benefit. In the example of OurKids AfterSchool, the strategy should reach those students who are impacted by the opportunity gap.
- Advances the mission: the strategy should have an impact on the issue/inequity being addressed. In the case example, the strategy reduces the opportunity gap, increasing opportunity for those who have been disadvantaged by it.

The amended strategy or long-range change articulated in the OurKids AfterSchool case study is the "*elimination of the opportunity gap between low and middle-income students, resulting in students better prepared to succeed as adults with increased high school graduation and college acceptance resulting in greater career options.*" This tells us where they hope to go, but not the plan to get there. It serves as the future impact to be sought and as the "public value proposition," making the case this is a worthwhile strategy to pursue. "In order to execute strategy, choices must be made to delineate activities, resource allocation decisions and policies" (Phils, 2005, p. 18). Strategy is the overarching idea defining where you want to go, what you hope to accomplish, and how you will get there. However, in order to implement a strategy more specifics are required; these are the plan and tactics engaged in to fulfill the chosen strategy.

Figure 6.1 illustrates the theory of change logic model, delineating the strategy based upon the articulated theory. The "theory of change logic model" provides few details, with a generic focus that does not provide time frames nor is it measurable. In this example, the goal is the impact being sought. The diagram delineates four parts of the strategy to achieve the goal, these are as follows:

1. Increase reading abilities;
2. Increase parental engagement;
3. Improve teacher skills; and
4. Improve student self-confidence.

While this clearly illustrates the strategy to be followed, it does not include details about how this is to be accomplished. The details are

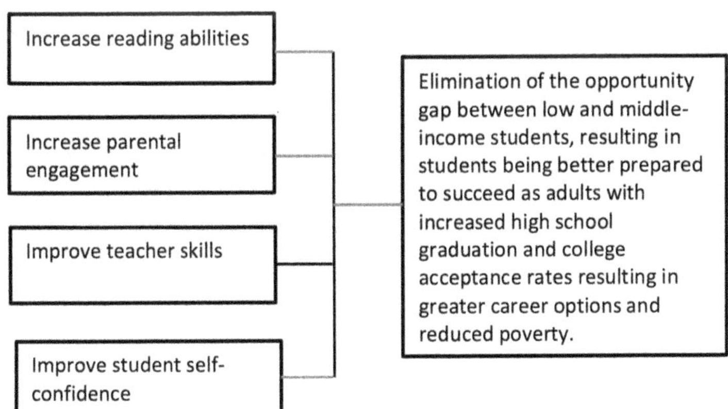

Figure 6.1 Theory of change logic model

delineated in the plan and tactics developed to implement the strategy. These are detailed in the program logic model.

Developing the Plan

Plans and tactics operationalize the strategy. These are the specific steps that will be engaged in to achieve the stated strategy or goal. The plan clearly lays out what is proposed, through a series of steps, to achieve the strategy. Through a carefully thought-out sequence of steps, the plan specifies how resources will be used in service of achieving the proposed outcomes and impact. The plan lays out how you will get to where you hope to go. Let's say you are about to fulfill a life's dream and join an expedition to climb Mount Everest. The strategy is that you are going to train and be in the best physical shape possible to conquer the tallest mountain in the world. The plan is how will you make that happen. This may include some of the following steps:

1. Get into better physical shape.
2. Obtain good quality climbing gear and clothing.
3. Learn about mountain climbing.
4. Take off time from work.
5. Travel to Nepal.
6. Join a guided expedition.
7. Just in case, make sure your last will and testament is up to date.

Developing Tactics

Now you are beginning to flesh out the strategy by determining what you have to do in order to successfully meet your goal of climbing Mount Everest. Just like the strategy, your plan needs more details to answer the operational questions that remain unanswered. Plans do not describe in detail the specific actions you will be taking to make each of these steps happen and how you will know you are getting closer to fulfilling your dream. These questions include: How will you choose the guide company? How will you get into the physical condition needed to make it to the top and back? Where will you purchase your gear and what gear will you need? How will you learn about mountain climbing? When will you take off from work and how much time will you need? How will you travel to Nepal, and, finally, how to update your will? The answer to each of these questions are the tactics to be engaged in to fulfill the plan and realize the strategy.

Tactics are the specific, short-term actions taken to implement the plan. Without tactics, the plan is no more than a wish list of the things you would like to accomplish. In order to accomplish each aspect of the plan, first determine the actions that are relevant to your success. Staying with the example of conquering Mount Everest, the tactics to implement and achieve the specifics of the plan to get to the very top of the world can include some of the following:

1. Get into better physical shape.
   a. Research the physical challenges of the expedition.
   b. Hire a personal trainer.
   c. Develop an exercise regimen with goals.
   d. Purchase exercise equipment or join a gym.
2. Obtain good quality climbing gear.
   a. Research the gear requirements for the trip.
   b. Create a budget for equipment.
   c. Read reviews of climbing gear.
   d. Purchase the gear.
3. Learn about mountain climbing.
   a. Locate and contact people who have successfully climbed Everest.
   b. Locate a climbing school.
   c. Enroll in a climbing course.
   d. Practice climbing increasingly more difficult mountains.
4. Take time off from work.
   a. Determine how much time you will need to be away from your job.
   b. Request the time off.
5. Travel to Nepal.
   a. Research and compare airfares.
   b. Research how to travel from airport to expedition base.
   c. Purchase tickets and make hotel reservations.
   d. Plan out how to get to and from the airport.
6. Join a guided expedition.
   a. Research the various guide companies.
   b. Locate people who have successfully climbed the mountain and solicit their experiences with and opinions of different expedition companies.
   c. Investigate costs and schedules of the different companies.
   d. Read online reviews.
   e. Choose an expedition company and register.
7. Update will.
   a. Research lawyers.
   b. List all assets and determine how you would like them distributed.
   c. Make an appointment with a lawyer.

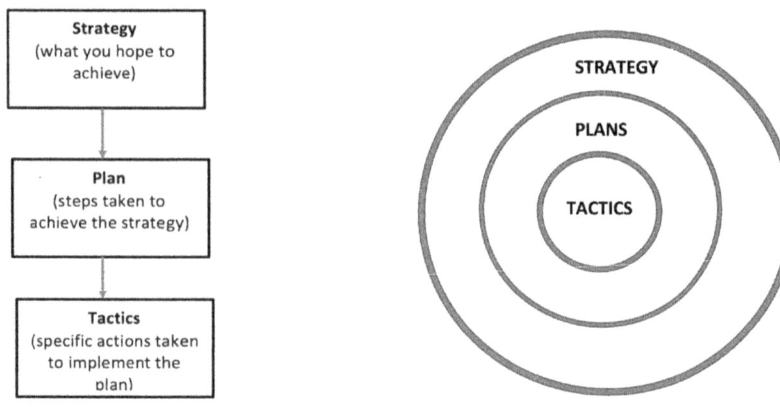

Figure 6.2 Strategy, plans and tactics

Figure 6.2 illustrates two ways of envisioning the relationship between strategy, plan and tactics. The illustration on the left shows the first step is delineating the strategy. Once this has been determined, the plan is developed detailing the steps to be taken to achieve the strategy. Finally, once the plan is in place, the tactics, or the specific actions that will be taken to implement the plan are developed. On the right, we see that the strategy is the overarching goal, including the plans, which in turn include the tactics.

Filling in the Strategy

Bryson (2013) proposes a five-part strategy development that can be used to add detail to the diagrams above:

1. Identify practical alternatives or visions for addressing the inequity.
2. Identify barriers to achieving the identified alternative visions or dreams. According to Bryson, "doing so is one way of ensuring that any strategies developed deal with implementation difficulties directly rather than haphazardly" (2013, p. 202).
3. Develop major proposals for dealing with each of the identified alternatives.
4. Develop actions to implement the major proposals. (These are the plans.)
5. Develop a detailed work program to implement the actions. (These are the tactics.)

Logic Models

To use a much-overused cliché, "a picture is worth a thousand words." Think of the logic model as that picture illustrating the strategy, plans

Strategy

- Defines intent.
- Determines what needs to be done.
- Focuses on developing the preferred future.
- Does not include evaluation metrics.
- Does not include execution details.

Plan

- Consciously chooses a series of actions.
- Maps out what must be done in order to achieve goals.
- Provides clarity.
- Determines resource allocation.
- Helps to keep people on track.
- Improves cooperation.
- Increases buy-in.
- Contains evaluation metrics.

Tactics

- Puts intent into action.
- Defines specific actions.
- Provides concrete actions/steps.
- Contains evaluation and implementation metrics.

and tactics to be followed. A well-developed logic model contains sufficient information and specificity so anyone reviewing it will have a complete idea of the theory of change; what is hoped to achieve and the plan for implementation. Once a working logic model has been developed, the next step is to develop a program narrative providing more detail on the how and why of the proposed intervention. The logic model is completed before the narrative because its structure will help the planner think through all aspects of the program before sitting down to write the narrative. Think of the logic model as the outline used before starting to write a term paper or thesis.

As discussed previously, there are two types of logic models, theory of change and program. For the purposes of creating a program intervention, the remainder of this and the next chapter will be devoted to developing the program logic model. The logic model chart, in Figure 6.3, delineates some of the differences between a theory of change logic model and program logic model, highlighting why the program logic model is the preferred format to follow when developing a targeted intervention. The theory of change model is more conceptual, specifying

Table 6.1 Logic Models

Theory of Change	Program
• Emphasizes theory of change	• Operationalizes theory of change • Strategy • Plans • tactics
• Identifies desired results	• Identifies desired results
• Illustrates strategy to address inequity	• Outlines approach and expectations
• Conceptual view of proposed change	• Illustrates process of program implementation
• Illustrates the big picture ideas	• Shows what will actually be done
• Illustrates how and why the program will work	• Informs management planning activities
	• Informs evaluation

desired results and broadly outlining the proposed intervention. The program logic model provides the details, showing not only what will be done but how and why. The program logic model provides the specificity needed to evaluate program implementation progress toward achieving the desired outcomes.

Program Logic Model Components

There are six components to the program logic model – *inputs, activities, outputs, short and medium-term outcomes, and impact* – that can be divided into three categories: *strategy, plan and tactics* as illustrated in Figure 6.4. As noted previously, the logic model is read from left to right but created from right to left. The first steps include defining the impact and the changes resulting from the intervention leading to the impact, or the outcomes. The impact and outcomes define the strategy. Once you have determined the strategy you will follow, the next step is to determine how you plan to get there, or in this case the activities to be engaged in. However, developing the logic model is not absolutely sequential. When creating the program logic model, we skip the outputs column until we have determined the activities. Outputs, discussed in greater detail in Chapter 7, are the measurable products of the activities. Logically, we cannot determine the outputs until we have developed the activities that will produce them.

The impact as noted in Figure 6.3 is a clear statement of the future hoped to be achieved. This end point is determined first to establish the goal being worked toward. The impact is defined as changes affecting people, the larger community or policies. The impact is aspirational and while it may not be achievable in the near future, progress made toward

Issue or inequity to be addressed: **Achievement Gap Between Low and Middle-Income Students**

Inputs Resources that will be devoted to or invested in the intervention. What you will need to make the planned change effort work.	**Activities** What you will be doing in the program. What actions, steps or tasks are essential to the intervention	**Outputs** What the program will produce as a result of the activities. What services will be offered, how frequently, to whom and the products that will be produced as a result	**Short-term outcomes** The results that you expect to occur immediately due to intervention	**Medium-term outcomes** The results that will occur next due to the intervention	**Impact** The long-term changes to larger systems resulting from the planned change effort
					elimination of the achievement gap between low and middle-income students, resulting in students better prepared to succeed as adults with increased high school graduation and college acceptance resulting in greater career options.

Figure 6.3 Theory of change and program logic models

this through the program implementation should have a significant impact on people's lives. In Figure 6.3, strategy also includes the program outcomes, which are the measurable changes that are part of the impact you are working toward. The plan is represented by the activities, the steps that will be taken to achieve the outcomes. Finally, the tactics are the outputs, or the specific actions to operationalize the plan.

Program Outcomes

There are two types of outcomes in a program plan – *program outcomes* and *process outcomes*. Program outcomes describe changes that will be achieved through participation in the program. Process outcomes describe actions taken during implementation of the program.

> If the objective describes something a staff person or volunteer is going to do, it is almost certainly an activity or process objective. If the objective describes a change in behavior, skills awareness, health status, and so on, by a client or consumer of your services it is almost certainly an outcome objective... One is an ends statement and the other is a means statement.
>
> (Allison & Kaye, 2005, p. 238)

Program outcomes are the specific results or changes that help to realize the stated impact. These are the measurable changes resulting from participation in the program activities. Another distinction to be aware of is the difference between outcomes and outputs.

The distinction between outcomes and outputs is an important one that some may find confusing. As noted above, program outcomes are achievements or changes in areas such as personal growth, understanding, new skills, etc. These are the baby steps to get you to where you want to be. Outcomes are short stepping-stones when achieved bring you closer to realizing the impact. On the other hand, outputs are numerical measures of the products of the activities. For example, if you are having parent discussion groups, the outputs could be the number of sessions over a specified period of time, how many participants, and how often they participate. The outcomes of such a group might be improved parental skills, increased parental involvement with their children, reduced corporal punishment, etc. To be effective outcomes and outputs are stated in measurable terms so progress can be gauged.

Creating effective outcomes helps to keep the program focused on what really matters. Outcomes are written using strong, forward-looking verbs such as "will achieve" and "will produce."

Karsh and Fox (2009) stress the importance of outcomes that meet a set of criteria to be effective, these are:

- Measurable with specific benchmarks;
- Results oriented;
- Realistic, aim high but not too high;
- Change oriented to make a difference.

Outcomes: measurable changes resulting from participation in program activities (i.e., changes in personal growth, understanding or new skills)

Outputs: measurable products resulting from program activities (i.e., number of sessions, volunteers recruited, participants registered, participants attending)

Throughout the literature, and in this discussion, you will see the terms "outcomes" and "objectives" used interchangeably. The Centers for Disease Control (CDC) defines objectives in this way:

> Objectives break the goal down into smaller parts that provide specific, measurable actions by which the goal can be accomplished. Objectives define for our stakeholders and partners the results we expect to achieve in our program or intervention. For our program expectations to be clear, we must write clear, concise objectives.
>
> (CDC, n.d.)

As this quote stresses, objectives are written clearly and define the progress to be achieved while moving toward the eventual goal or impact of the intervention. However, instead of being "measurable actions" as stated by the CDC, they are measurable results or changes resulting from specific actions or interventions. Further supporting the interchangeability of outcomes and objectives, the Merriam-Webster dictionary (n.d.) defines an objective as "something toward which an effort is directed: an aim, goal or end of action," and an outcome as "something that follows as a result or consequence." The distinction being made here is an objective is something you seek to happen as a result of some effort, and an outcome is the result of that effort.

As is clear from this definition, there is little if any distinction between these two terms. Kettner et al. (2017) solve this dilemma for the purposes of program planning and logic modeling by combining the two terms:

> Outcome objectives flow directly from the problem analysis phase in a number of ways. First and foremost, an outcome objective is a statement intended to reflect a reduction in the incidence or prevalence of the problem or need. Outcome objectives state clearly what the effect of the intervention is expected to have on the target population.
>
> (p. 119)

Therefore, for the purposes of our discussion, outcomes and objectives will be used interchangeably, defining both as "specific changes in *attitudes, behaviors, knowledge, skills, status, or level of functioning* expected to result from program activities" (W. K. Kellogg Foundation, 2004, p. 8).

SMART Objectives

Objectives are most effective when written in brief, declarative statements that do not specify how something will be done but rather what changes will be realized. The acronym SMART is used to describe the characteristics of effective objectives.

While Table 6.2 defines each of the SMART components, it is necessary to take a moment to discuss standardized measures referred to in

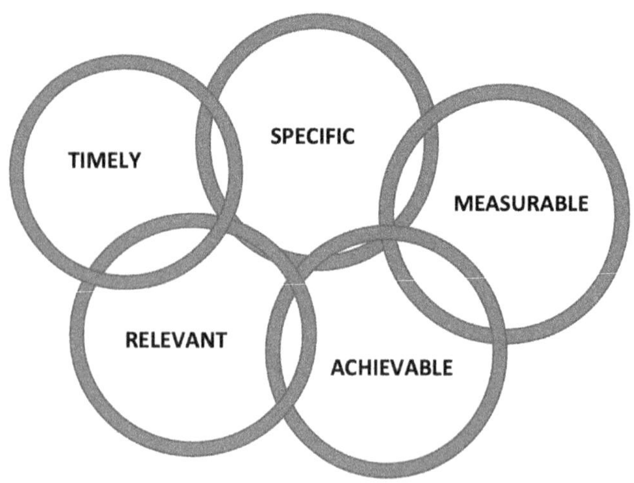

Figure 6.4 SMART objectives

Table 6.2 Smart Objectives

SPECFIC	Objectives are stated in a way that they are clear, understandable and unambiguous specifying what will change and for whom.
MEASURABLE	Creating measurable objectives allows you to track your progress. Measurable objectives answer the questions, how much, how many, and how will we know when it is accomplished? Outcomes can be measured numerically, through levels of functioning, standardized outcome measures, or participant/client satisfaction.
ACHIEVABLE	While it is good to stretch expectations, they must be achievable within the constraints of time and available resources, answering the questions whether the resources and capabilities are available and can be used successfully to achieve this objective.
RELEVANT	Is this an important and worthwhile objective that will help to realize the impact? Is it a benefit for participants or the community? Will it have an effect on the desired impact? Evidence for relevancy can come from the needs assessment or the theory of change.
TIMELY	Is the objective time constrained, with reasonable start and finish dates?

the definition of measurable. These are pre-existing measurement tools that have been tested for reliability and validity. Standardized measures can be in the form of interviews, questionnaires or self-assessments. They are called standardized because of their general acceptance to measure specific phenomena such as client satisfaction, self-esteem or specific knowledge or behaviors. Standardized tests are "designed by experts for wide use and has prescribed content, well-defined procedures for administration and scoring, and established norms" (Waltz et al., 2016, p. 4). These have been tested for reliability and validity and are considered standardized because the people being evaluated respond to the same questions and their answers are assessed according to the same scoring standard. Individual scores are then compared to a predetermined standard to provide an accurate measure of some characteristic.

Outcomes can be short-term, or intermediate. Short-term outcomes can be expected to be achieved soon after the program or intervention is implemented, usually in a one- to three-year time frame. Intermediate outcomes result from and follow short-term outcomes, achieved in longer time frames, usually between three to five years. The impact, which can also be considered a long-term objective, is achievable in five or more years, usually after the intervention has been completed.

Writing SMART objectives helps develop the evaluation plan (discussed in Chapter 8) by identifying indicators and performance measures, determining how progress will be identified and measured. Indicators are used to measure and

> obtain observable evidence of accomplishments, changes made, or progress achieved. Indicators describe the type of data you will need to answer your evaluation questions… A performance measure is the amount of change or progress achieved toward a specific goal or objective. SMART objectives can serve as your performance measures because they provide the specific information needed to identify expected results.
>
> (CDC, n.d.)

Figure 6.5 illustrates the logic model with short and medium-term objectives filled in. The table following each figure reviews a sampling of these objectives, demonstrating how they meet the SMART designation. Following the chart, is a checklist detailing the specifics of SMART objectives.

Tables 6.3 to 6.6 use four of the outcomes in the logic model in Figure 6.5 as examples of SMART determination.

Outcome: Teachers will self-report a 50% increase in confidence in Out of School Time (OST) programming.

Outcome: 85% of participants will improve reading skills by at least one grade level.

Outcome: Students report minimum increase of one hour per week reading independently.

Outcome: Teachers improve teaching of reading skills by 50%.

There are a number of determinants to ensure you are developing SMART objectives. The following checklist provides a guide to writing SMART outcome objectives.

Issue or inequity to be addressed: **Opportunity Gap Between Low and Middle-Income Students**

Inputs Resources that will be devoted to or invested in the intervention. What you will need to make the planned change effort work.	**Activities** What you will be doing in the program. What actions, steps or tasks are essential to the intervention	**Outputs** What the program will produce as a result of the activities. The services offered, how frequently, to whom and the products that will be produced as a result	**Short-term outcomes** The results that you expect to occur immediately due to intervention	**Medium-term outcomes** The results that will occur next due to the intervention	**Impact** The long-term changes to larger systems resulting from the planned change effort
			Teachers will self-report a 50% increase in confidence in OST programming at completion of training 85% of participants will improve reading skills by at least one grade level by end of school year Students will demonstrate a 10% increase in self-confidence after one year Families report increased awareness of importance of literacy at home within first six months Parents spend 50% more time engaged in children's schoolwork after one year 25% increased parent participation at PTA meetings Tutors gain skills to help increase student reading abilities Sufficient program funding	50% reduction in reading gap after 3 years Standardized test scores improve by 25% after 3 years Students report 50% more time reading independently Sustained partnership between school, community, families 50% improved attendance over three years 25% reduction in behavioral issues over three years Teachers improve teaching of reading skills by 50% Reading materials relevant to students' experiences are utilized Outside funding supports additional student resources Fifty internships over four years	elimination of the opportunity gap between low and middle-income students, resulting in students better prepared to succeed as adults with increased high school graduation and college acceptance, resulting in greater career options.

Figure 6.5 Short and medium-term outcomes

Table 6.3 Teachers report 50% increase in confidence in OST

SPECIFIC	MEASURABLE	ACHIEVABLE	RELEVANT	TIMELY
Yes. Clearly states who will be impacted and what will change	Yes. Specifies the amount of increase to be sought, assuming a base line level can be established.	Yes, an increase of this amount is achievable	Yes, teacher skills are relevant to student success	Yes. As a short-term outcome, 1-3 years is reasonable

Table 6.4 50% of participants improve reading skills by one grade level

SPECIFIC	MEASURABLE	ACHIEVABLE	RELEVANT	TIMELY
Yes. Very clearly states who the target is and what the specific change will be.	Yes. Specifies the amount of change expected and who will experience the change.	Yes. A one grade level improvement is achievable. Note this outcome does not specify 100% of participants. Rarely do all participants achieve the same benefit.	Yes. Reading skills and the reading gap is what inspired the intervention.	Yes. A s a short-term outcome, 1-3 years is reasonable

Table 6.5 Students report increase of one hour weekly independent reading

SPECIFIC	MEASURABLE	ACHIEVABLE	RELEVANT	TIMELY
Yes. Clearly written, specifying what the change will be and who will experience it	Yes. Based upon student self-reporting with an established baseline.	Yes.	Yes.	Yes.

Table 6.6 Teachers improve teaching reading skills by 50%

SPECIFIC	MEASURABLE	ACHIEVABLE	RELEVANT	TIMELY
Yes. States who and what.	Yes. Gives a specific numerical measure of improvement.	Yes.	Yes.	Yes.

Checklist for SMART Objectives

SPECIFIC:

- The meaning is clear and unambiguous.
- It is stated in simple and direct terms.
- Specifies a change that will take place.

- Uses action-oriented verbs.
- Explains what will be done and for whom.
- Specifies by when it will be accomplished.
- Does not use jargon or nonspecific terms.
- The outcome includes clear indicators of success.

MEASURABLE:

- States how much change.
- How many will be impacted?
- How will we know when it is accomplished?
- Measure is clear and not open to interpretation.
- Uses numerical or standardized measures.

ACHIEVABLE:

- The outcome can be achieved within the time constraints.
- The needed resources are available.
- Responsible parties have the capabilities needed.
- There is evidence that the change can be accomplished.
- Factors beyond your control have been identified.

REALISTIC:

- Makes progress toward intended impact.
- Fits culture and structure of community.
- Important and worthwhile.
- Beneficial for the community.
- Effects desired impact.

TIMELY:

- Reasonable start and finish.
- Specifies time constraints.
- Will still be relevant when attained.

Process Objectives/Outputs

If we look at outcome objectives as the result or the ends, then we can see the outputs, or process objectives, are the means through which we get to the outcomes we are seeking. Outputs are considered process objectives because they provide the specific measures and keep track of the implementation or process of the program. Setting up process objectives allows us to determine if mid-course corrections need to be made to keep the program implementation on track. For example, if a short-term outcome is *tutors will gain skills to help students improve their reading abilities*, the process is how this happens, or the activities in which they will be engaged. For example, if one activity is tutor training, the process outcomes would be the measurable outputs of the activities related to training the tutors. These measures could include: the number of tutors recruited, the number of sessions included in the training module, and projected attendance and completion rates. Knowing these targets in advance provides the information needed to gauge whether or not the program implementation is on schedule, answering the following questions: Have sufficient tutors been recruited by the projected date? Is the program providing the required number of sessions? Are attendance rates sufficient? Knowing these expectations will allow for modifying activities to keep the program implementation on track. This will be discussed in greater detail in the next chapter and in Chapter 8 under evaluations.

The Importance of Collaboration

While the specifics outlined in this chapter may seem formulaic and a little daunting, these steps provide a guide that makes the task of program development easier. Only when you know where you want to go, can you find a path to get there. Program planning is a journey, and like any journey it has its challenges and its rewards. The reward is effective program planning, based upon social justice concepts. This is the result of a process based upon engaging communities in efforts to address social inequities and challenges resulting from opportunity gaps built into the system.

Chapter 2 discussed the value of collaboration in earning trust. It is also important to stress program planning as a collaborative process. Collaboration can be fun as you get to meet and work with new people while exploring a variety of insights and opinions. Unfortunately, some planners find collaboration to be tedious and challenging and prefer to come into the community as the experts with the answers. The collaborative nature of planning is dependent upon recognizing expertise comes in many forms. Community people who have lived with and know the inequities intimately bring with them expertise based upon experience and knowledge from an insider's perspective. Planners have as much to learn from the community about the issues as the community can learn from the planners about process.

Chapter Summary

Main Points

1. Strategy defines long-term goals, focusing on the end result to provide a path forward. In order to implement strategy plans and tactics must be specified.

2. Plans map out what will be done in order to achieve the goals, mapping out how resources will be used to support progress toward the goal, while tactics define the specific actions and concrete steps based upon the plan.
3. The theory of change logic model illustrates the strategy based upon the theory that has been developed; it does not specify steps or actions that will be taken.
4. Program logic models illustrate the specifics of the program implementation and the changes expected as a result.
5. Program logic models consist of six categories including: impact, short-term and medium-term outcomes, outputs, activities leading to the outcomes, and inputs or required resources.
6. Program outcomes are the changes resulting from participation in the program. To be effective, they should be specific, measurable, achievable, realistic and timely.
7. Outputs are the measurable products of the activities they do not measure change. Outputs are helpful measuring progress of the program implementation.
8. Measurable outcomes and outputs provide a way of determining if the program implementation SMART objectives are specific, measurable, achievable, relevant and timely.

Key Terms

Strategy
Plan
Tactics
Public value proposition
Theory of change logic model
Program logic model
Program outcomes
Process outcomes
SMART Objectives

Discussion Questions

1. What is the public value proposition and how is it to helpful to gain support for the program planning and implementation?
2. If your strategy is to earn a degree to finally get your dream job and begin a career, what are some of the plans and tactics you would need to follow in order to achieve this goal?
3. If you were tasked with developing a diversion program for youth entering the criminal legal system, what is the impact you would seek. Develop three to five short and medium-term objectives to help accomplish this impact.
4. For each of the objectives developed in question three, evaluate them according to the SMART rubric.
5. Develop one activity for each of the objectives developed in Question 3.

References

Allison, M. & Kaye, J. (2005) *Strategic planning for nonprofit organizations, 2nd ed.* Hoboken, NJ: John Wiley & Sons

Bryson, J.M. (2010) Strategic planning and the strategy change cycle. In D.O. Renz & Associates (eds.), *The Jossey-Bass handbook of nonprofit leadership and management* (pp. 230–261). San Francisco, CA: Jossey-Bass

Bryson, J.M. (2013) The strategy change cycle. In J.L. Perry (ed.), *The Jossey-Bass reader on nonprofit and public leadership* (pp. 202–221). San Francisco, CA: Jossey-Bass

Centers for Disease Control and Prevention (n.d.), Evaluation guide, writing smart objectives, https://www.cdc.gov/dhdsp/docs/smart_objectives.pdf, retrieved 2/17/21

Cels, S., Dejong, J. & Nauta, F. (2012) *Agents of change: Strategies and tactics for social innovation.* Washington, DC: Brookings Institution Press

Hickman, G.R. (2010) Organizational change practices. In G.R. Hickman (ed.) *Leading organizations: Perspectives for a new era* (pp. 510–524). San Francisco, CA: Jossey-Bass

Karsh, E. & Fox, A.S. (2009) *The only grantwriting book you will ever need, 3rd ed.* New York, NY: Basic Books

Kettner, P.M., Moroney, R.M. & Martin, L.L. (2017) *Designing and managing programs: An effectiveness-based approach, 5th ed.* Los Angeles, CA: SAGE Publications

Merriam-Webster Dictionary (n.d.) www.merriam-webster.com, retrieved 3/8/21

Phils, J.A. (2005) *Integrating mission and strategy for nonprofit organizations.* New York, NY: Oxford University Press

W. K. Kellogg Foundation (2004) Logic model development guide, https://www.wkkf.org/resource-directory/resources/2004/01/logic-model-development-guide, retrieved 3/8/21

University of Kansas (n.d.) Community tool box: Developing successful strategies – Planning to win,https://ctb.ku.edu/en/table-of-contents/structure/strategic-planning/developstrategies/main, retrieved 3/15/21

Waltz, C.F., Strickland, O.L. & Lenz, E.R. (2016) *Measurement in nursing and health research, 5th ed.* New York, NY: Springer Publishing

Weisenbach Keller, E. (2013) Nonprofit strategy and change. In W.G. Rowe & M.C. Dato-On (eds.) *Introduction to nonprofit management* (pp. 161–199). Los Angeles, CA: SAGE Publications

7 Developing the Program Logic Model

Learning Objectives

1. Articulate the steps to develop a program logic model.
2. Demonstrate an understanding of how activities lead to both outcomes and outputs.
3. Understand how to develop program activities informed by evidence.
4. Articulate how outputs are used to measure progress implementing the program intervention.
5. Demonstrate an understanding of why the program logic model is developed from the right to the left, beginning with the impact, but is read starting on the left through the right.
6. Understand how to develop and use a Gantt Chart to delineate implementation activities, responsibilities and time frames.

Chapter Overview

This chapter discusses how to complete the program logic model, filling in activities, outputs and inputs. Each section is discussed in detail showing how to develop activities, how these lead to the outcomes and outputs, and determining the resources, or inputs, needed.

Completing the Program Logic Model

Once the outcomes and impact have been identified, the next step is to develop the means to achieve these results. To accomplish this, the big plan is broken down into small steps, each one leading to an outcome. These are the activities or the services to engage participants and form the basis of the intervention. Indira Gandhi, former Indian Prime Minister, is quoted as saying "Have a bias towards action – let's see something happen now. You can break the big plan into small steps and take the first step right away."

Once the activities leading to the outcomes have been agreed upon, the next step is to determine the outputs, the numerical products of the activities. Advancing through the logic model development step by step, the

DOI: 10.4324/9781003148777-7

Logic Model Development Steps

1. Specify the impact, or the long-term results to be accomplished.
2. Determine short-term and medium-term outcomes, or the changes occurring as a result of participation in the program leading to the impact.
3. Develop the activities leading to the outcomes.
4. Enumerate the outputs, or products of the activities.
5. Determine the inputs, or resources needed to successfully implement the program intervention.

final step is to determine the inputs, or the resources needed to support the proposed activities. Previously, it was specified that the logic model is read from left to right, but is developed from right to left, with one exception. We skip over the outputs column because we cannot reasonably predict the products of the activities until we have developed these activities.

Activities

> Activities are the specific actions that make up the program. They reflect tools, processes, events, technology and other devices that are intentional in the program. Activities are synonymous with interventions deployed to secure the desired change or results.
>
> (Knowlton & Phillips, 2013, p. 36)

The activities and the products they produce, or the outputs, are the elements that fill out the strategy. The activities to be provided to participants represent the plan of how to achieve the outcomes and the impact.

Clearly written program activities demonstrate the planners have developed a thoughtful and impactful plan to address the identified inequities. The plan details (the interventions) are developed in a close ongoing partnership with community representatives who understand the population to be served and the community needs. The program intervention clearly outlines what is intended to be provided, what is to be achieved, and how the different components impact the inequity. Without linking program components directly to the proposed outcomes, the plan can go off track. Therefore it is critical program planners carefully and repeatedly review the objectives as each activity is planned (Karsh & Fox, 2009).

Evidence-Informed Activities

Planning activities that relate directly to the objectives helps to keep the intervention on track and ensures they target and address the identified community needs successfully. When program planners attempt to do too much and provide too large a menu of services, they risk diffusion of resources and diluting the effectiveness of the program intervention. Trying to do too much and failing to address the inequities can prove to be a fatal setback to the success of the program by risking losing supporters and community trust.

Program interventions – the activities designed to engage participants to help reach the stated outcomes – are informed by research, practice experience and community input to develop an understanding of how to address the underlying inequities. This is best accomplished through evidence-informed practice as discussed earlier. It is helpful for human services program planners and community members working to address the identified issues to familiarize themselves with other programs and interventions developed to address these or similar issues. A great deal can be learned, and insights gained, from understanding what has been done by others before designing new interventions.

If there are successful interventions developed by others, then there is no need to reinvent the wheel. By learning about the success of others, and building upon these successes, the possibility of success is greatly improved. However, merely duplicating the success of others does not guarantee the same level of success again. People and communities are different. This is not to place a value judgment on this difference, but just because an intervention works in one community or under other circumstances does not suggest it will work in another community or under different circumstances. This is the crux of evidence-informed practice. By investigating other successful programs, it is possible to find ideas and activities that can be applied in another community. However, this is not a given. "Evidence-informed" simply means you have done your due diligence and the work is informed by the experiences or research of others and by the experience and knowledge of community members. The more information collected prior to determining the specific interventions the better the chances of success.

Gathering evidence is a two-tailed process. The work of planning can also be informed by learning about interventions that did not realize their potential. Too often we tend to think if we can find a successful model then all we have to do is replicate it. There is no questioning about how or why it worked, the fact it worked is sometimes used as the only justification needed to replicate. So, there is nothing learned, other than how to replicate. However, there is much to be learned as well, from interventions that have not succeeded in achieving their stated goals. The focus then becomes trying to understand where these programs went wrong – why did they not succeed? Armed with the understanding of programs that did not meet their goals, program planners can enter into the planning process with knowledge of what to avoid. Replication does not lead to innovation. Nor is replication a bad thing. Knowledge of what works and what does not work is the foundation for developing successful program interventions.

Building the OurKids AfterSchool intervention on some of the precepts of positive youth development (PYD) leads to the case study intervention based upon an afterschool or out of school time (OST) program model and a summer learning program to develop academic and social-emotional skills. Eccles and Barber (1999) identified the link between adolescents' OST activities and their educational and occupational attainment as adults and a reduction in risky behaviors. Approaching the program intervention through a social justice lens, the focus is not solely on the students but also addresses teachers' abilities and skill levels and community and family involvement. Through this perspective the program incorporates parts of the PYD approach. A comprehensive needs assessment would have uncovered and researched PYD and OST program interventions. Including parents, students, teachers, school administrators and other community members in the needs assessment supports the importance of structured out of school time activities for youth in the community. There are a large number of families where parents work one or more low wage jobs and are unable to provide structure for their children during their out of school hours. Based upon the research and input from the community, it was determined an afterschool and summer program best serves the needs of community youth and families.

Based upon the concepts of evidence-informed practice, a foundation in social justice, and input from students, families and school staff, the OurKids AfterSchool case study now focuses on the amended issue and impact statements, utilizing a three-pronged approach: an OST program for the youth, teacher training and support, and family outreach and support. The program design is not focused solely on the students who are being disadvantaged as a result of the opportunity gap, so they are not singled out as the locus of the "problem." This intervention recognizes students need positive supports and structured out of school time, teachers can use training and support to be more effective in helping to reduce the opportunity gap, and, by involving parents and the community, it is a larger effort with a broad range of inputs and responsibilities.

Activities Lead to Outcomes

The program design for OurKids AfterSchool addresses the "5-Cs" of positive youth development with interventions focusing on student confidence and competence, creating connections and helping to increase the students' ability for caring, compassion and character. Additionally, the program will help to develop social capital for the students and their families. Scrivens and Smith (2013) have developed three foci of building social capital: 1) bonds, or links to people with common identity, 2) bridges, or extending to larger circles, and 3) linkages to people who possess more social capital.

Activity	Outcome
Develop teacher training module Teacher training	Increase in teacher self-confidence Teachers improve skills
Enroll students in tutoring Weekly tutoring Homework help Summer reading group Gardening club	Improved reading skills Reduction in reading gap Improved reading scores Improved standardized test scores Increased self-confidence
Weekly tutoring sessions Daily homework help groups After-school program activities Team sports, Tutoring, Performing arts, Chess club, Gardening club, Group games, Arts and Crafts, Drawing and Cartooning Street photography	Reduce reading gap Improved reading scores Improved standardized test scores Increased self-confidence Improved attendance Reduced behavioral issues
Parent newsletter Parent workshops	Families aware of importance of literacy Parents spend more time Increase in PTA participation School/family partnership
Recruit tutors Tutor training Ongoing tutoring support/workshops	Tutors gain skills Improved reading skills Increased self-confidence Reduction in reading gap Improved standardized test scores
Purchase relevant reading materials Lending library Tutoring Homework help	Increase in independent reading Improved reading scores Improved standardized test scores
Tutoring Homework help	Increased social capital
Gardening group	Increased self-confidence Reduced behavioral issues
Summer program: Academic supports Gardening Soccer Arts and Crafts Field trips Lending library	Increase in independent reading Improved reading scores Improved standardized test scores Reduce reading gap Increased self-confidence Increased self-confidence

Figure 7.1 Activities and outcomes

Activities in the proposed program are designed to address these building blocks of social capital. With this in mind, the program activities address and lead to each of the projected outcomes. As described in Figure 7.1, specific activities can serve more than one outcome. The activities in the chart are a sampling of the possible activities that can be established to realize the projected outcomes. None of these examples are to be taken as suggestive of the only way to achieve any of the stated outcomes. These are only examples of how activities lead directly to desired outcomes.

Filling in the Logic Model

Once the outline of the program has been developed, it is time to continue to fill in the logic model. The key point to remember here is the logic model is a graphic representation of the program, it is not meant to fill in all the details. As a representation it shows how the components fit together logically and provides an overview of the intervention and the thinking behind the design. The program detail is provided in the program narrative. This is a prose description of the program filling in the information to support the logic model. The program narrative is reviewed in Chapter 8.

Figure 7.1 illustrates the next step in building the logic model, enumerating the activities that will lead to the short- and medium-term outcomes that have been delineated.

Issue or inequity to be addressed: **Opportunity Gap Between Low and Middle-Income Students**

Inputs Resources that will be devoted to or invested in the intervention. What you will need to make the planned change effort work.	**Activities** What you will be doing in the program. What actions, steps or tasks are essential to the intervention	**Outputs** What the program will produce as a result of the activities. The services offered, how frequently, to whom and the products that will be produced as a result	**Short-term outcomes** The results that you expect to occur immediately due to intervention	**Medium-term outcomes** The results that will occur next due to the intervention	**Impact** The long-term changes to larger systems resulting from the planned change effort
	Design and implement fundraising plan, write and submit proposals Recruit, hire & orient staff Design training curriculum for teachers, tutors & homework helpers Bi-weekly teacher training & support sessions Recruit & train adult & college student tutors Weekly tutoring Recruit college student volunteers as homework helpers After-school activities Team sports, Homework help, Tutoring, Performing arts, Chess club, Group games, Arts & Crafts, Dance, Drawing & Cartooning, Street Photography Parent outreach, Newsletter & Workshops Purchase relevant reading materials Enroll parents in advisory board Summer program: Gardening Club, academic support, reading group, lending library, soccer, arts & crafts, field trips, street photography		Teachers self-report a 50% increase in confidence in OST programming 85% of participants improve reading skills at least one grade level by end of first program year Students will demonstrate a 10% increase in self-confidence after one year Families report increased awareness of importance of literacy at home in first six months Parents spend 50% more time engaged in children's schoolwork after one year 25% increased parent participation at PTA meetings Tutors gain skills to help increase student reading abilities Sufficient program funding Advisory board meets monthly engaging parents in program & advocacy	50% reduction in reading gap after 3 years Standardized test scores improve by 25% after 3 years Students report 50% more time reading independently Sustained partnership between school, community, families 50% improved attendance over three years 25% reduction in behavioral issues over three years Teachers improve teaching of reading skills by 50% Reading materials relevant to students' experiences are utilized Outside funding supports additional student resources	elimination of the opportunity gap between low and middle-income students, resulting in students better prepared to succeed as adults with increased high school graduation and college acceptance, resulting in greater career options.

Figure 7.2 Activities in the logic model

Outputs

Once the activities have been decided upon and specified, and it is determined each activity leads directly to one or more outcomes, the next step in developing the logic model is to specify the outputs resulting from each of the activities. It is necessary to stress again outputs are the measures of the services offered or the products produced as a result of the activities. These measures can include how frequently, how many, and to whom. Unlike outcomes, outputs do not measure change. For example, the outputs of a group experience could include how often the group meets, how many people are registered and how often they attend, but not what they have learned or gained from the group experience.

Specifying this information helps program implementers and managers determine if the intervention is on track to provide the projected services and engage the projected number of participants.

Through specifying outputs, program managers have the measures necessary to evaluate the process of the intervention and help determine whether program modifications are needed along the way. For example, a red flag is raised if it is projected that twenty-five tutors are recruited and trained within the first three months, but after two months only ten have been recruited, suggesting the target will not be met. Armed with this knowledge, program managers can reevaluate their recruitment efforts or modify the plan to achieve the projected target number of tutors.

Developing Outputs

Developing and specifying outputs helps program planners to determine time frames and targets for program implementation. The process of developing specific targets helps program planners think through what

Program outputs can include, but are not limited to:

1. number of students enrolled;
2. average attendance;
3. number of volunteers recruited;
4. the number of classes taught;
5. workshops held;
6. newsletters distributed;
7. meetings held;
8. hours of service delivered;
9. training sessions held;
10. parents or community members outreached to;
11. funding proposals submitted;
12. grants received.

is possible, such as how many sessions to offer, how many groups are reasonable with the resources and number of participants to be served. These specific measures then serve as targets to be achieved and measures of progress. Specifying outputs helps to determine the number of units of services to be provided, helping possible funders to determine if the program is both cost efficient and effective. Funders want to know what the program hopes to achieve, as well as how many people will be served by the program and the number and frequency of services offered. Specifying these numbers is both an art form and a science, projecting what is both possible and reasonable within the confines of the available and proposed resources. When program planners project high numbers of outputs to impress possible funders, the risk of falling short of projections and forfeiting a portion of the grant or government contract is introduced. When the proposed numbers are too low, funders can determine the program is too expensive or not worth the effort.

There are no hard and fast rules or formulas for determining the level of outputs projected. These levels can only be developed through determining what is possible with the projected resources and within the time limits and any other limiting constraints. When choosing activities and outputs, there are a number of intervening factors to be considered. Failure to do this can result in a program too small to achieve its stated goals or one too ambitious and doomed to failure as a result. Therefore, determining activities and outputs requires careful attention to what is possible. Be careful not to let the zeal of accomplishing big things get in the way of the need for change. New programs must be very realistic in the projected achievements. It is better to set a moderate, achievable course of action and then build upon the success and then seek additional funding or resources to expand and continue services. In order to successfully receive additional grants or contracts, or renewals, success is one of the measures used. Funders prefer to support successful programs and interventions.

Figure 7.3 illustrates some examples of outputs that can result from the listed activities. As noted, each activity has at least one output attached to it. Reviewing these, we see the funding cycle is the first five months of the project. During this time, staff will submit a minimum of six proposals. While this is an illustration of how to develop a program through a logic model, in reality it takes more than five months to establish funding to start-up a new program. The funding stage can take up to one year before the program is actually kicked off. It is included here merely as an example of all of the activities and outputs, and to illustrate the importance of factoring in the need for funding. Following this one item through shows the activity is to write and submit proposals, the output is the number of proposals submitted in a specified time frame and the outcome is sufficient program funding. Reading from left to right each activity leads to an output and at least one outcome, presenting a logical flow of the program.

While recruiting and hiring staff may not be thought of as a program activity, unless there is sufficient staff already on hand to run a new program, this is factored into the program activities and outputs. In this example, the activity is to recruit, hire and orient staff. The output column delineates how many staff and indicates time frames for recruiting and hiring. The activity column also indicates a staff orientation. To address this there must be a product of this activity. This is listed as one week of orientation for new staff.

While the logic model does not indicate issues such as positive youth development or social capital development, these are discussed in the program narrative. This is the distinction between the program narrative and the program logic model. The logic model is a representation of the program, the details and specifics of the logic model are explained and detailed in the narrative. The narrative also includes the rationale and support for the decisions that have been made in the design of the program. Once the program logic model has been completed, then it is time to write the program narrative. However, there is one more step in completing the logic model before moving on to the program narrative; determining the inputs, or resources needed to implement and sponsor the program.

Inputs

Inputs are the resources necessary to successfully carry out the program intervention. These resources, or inputs, are the last step in developing the program logic model. In order to determine the resources needed, the intervention activities and the outputs of each activity are specified. It is difficult to quantify the resources needed without specifying the activities and quantifying the outputs. Each activity or output requires an input, or resource, to support it. For example, for an activity such as parent support groups, the minimum input required is a staff person to facilitate these groups. Proposing an arts and crafts activity group requires sufficient supplies appropriate to support this activity in addition to staffing the activity. Knowing how many arts and crafts groups are provided, how often the groups meet and the target registration helps to determine how many and the types of supplies needed.

Then, reading the logic model from left to right begins with "w" resources needed to provide "x" activities, producing "y" outputs leading to "z" outcomes. This order presents a logical way of looking at and understanding the program proposal. Reviewing the inputs informs the program planners about new resources needed and existing resources that can be utilized for the new program intervention.

Figure 7.4 shows the relationship between inputs, activities and outputs as illustrated in the program logic model. The inputs listed here are meant to be illustrative of the types of inputs required to support a program of this type. The input funding leads to the activity of designing

Issue or inequity to be addressed: **Opportunity Gap Between Low and Middle-Income Students**

Inputs Resources that will be devoted to or invested in the intervention. What you will need to make the planned change effort work.	**Activities** What you will be doing in the program. What actions, steps or tasks are essential to the intervention	**Outputs** What the program will produce as a result of the activities. The services offered, how frequently, to whom and the products that will be produced as a result	**Short-term outcomes** The results that you expect to occur immediately due to intervention	**Medium-term outcomes** The results that will occur next due to the intervention	**Impact** The long-term changes to larger systems resulting from the planned change effort
	Design and implement fundraising plan, write and submit proposals Recruit, hire & orient staff Design training curriculum for teachers, tutors & homework helpers Bi-weekly teacher training & support sessions Recruit & train adult & college student tutors Weekly tutoring Recruit college student volunteers as homework helpers After-school activities Team sports Homework help Tutoring Performing arts Chess club Group games Arts & Crafts Cartooning Parent outreach Parent Newsletter Parent workshops Purchase relevant reading materials Enroll parents in advisory board Summer program: Gardening Club, academic support, reading group, lending library, soccer, arts & crafts, field trips	Submit 6 proposals in first 5 months 6 staff recruited & hired in 2months provided one week orientation Teacher training module 25 tutors recruited with 6 hours training 1 ½ hours of tutoring for 25 students weekly 15 college homework helpers recruited & trained Daily homework help for 25 students 120 enrolled students in after school activities 10 group activities daily serving 100 students Every parent outreached to at least once 6 parent workshops for 60 parents 100 books purchased for lending library 10-15 parents recruited for advisory board monthly meetings 50 students participating in summer activities	Teachers will self-report a 50% increase in confidence in OST programming at completion of training 85% of participants will improve reading skills by at least one grade level by end of school year Students will demonstrate a 10% increase in self-confidence after one year Families report increased awareness of importance of literacy at home within first six months Parents spend 50% more time engaged in children's schoolwork after one year 25% increased parent participation at PTA meetings Tutors gain skills to help increase student reading abilities Sufficient program funding Advisory board meets monthly engaging parents in program and advocacy	50% reduction in reading gap after 3 years Standardized test scores improve by 25% after 3 years Students report 50% more time reading independently Sustained partnership between school, community, families 50% improved attendance over three years 25% reduction in behavioral issues over three years Teachers improve teaching of reading skills by 50% Reading materials relevant to students' experiences are utilized Outside funding supports additional student resources	elimination of the opportunity gap between low and middle-income students, resulting in students better prepared to succeed as adults with increased high school graduation and college acceptance, resulting in greater career options.

Figure 7.3 Outputs in the logic model

and implementing a fundraising plan, writing and submitting proposals. This activity then leads to the output of a minimum of six proposals submitted in the first three months. The short-term outcome of this activity is sufficient program funding. Realistically, it is crucial to secure funding for any new program prior to implementation. This can often require a year or more search for funding as both philanthropic foundations and government funders do not move quickly.

Once the logic model is completed it is time to review the plan to ensure it is "logical." This review can be done by testing the "if–then" relationships of the components. This is accomplished by determining if the resources are available or achievable to support the listed activities, logically leading to the short-term outcomes. When the outcomes are

Inputs can consist of a variety of resources, these can include:

1. **Human resources**: Personnel and volunteers;
2. **Financial resources**: Funds needed to support the cost of proposed activities;
3. **Space**: Facilities needed for activities;
4. **Technology/equipment**: Technology and/or equipment required (e.g., computer hardware, software, printers, and copiers, office furniture, telephones, etc.);
5. **Materials**: Consumable supplies or materials required for activities (e.g., office supplies, training materials, arts and crafts supplies, books, etc.);
6. **Constraints**: Program planners must also consider state regulations or requirements on use of program funds imposed by funders;
7. **Other resources**: such as transportation if needed for program activities;
8. **Agreements**: Cooperative arrangements with other programs or organizations, such as referral agreements, endorsements, shared staff, facilities, etc.

achieved, and the proposed activities are continued, does this logically lead to achieving the medium-term outcomes as well? Each activity is reviewed to determine if it is necessary and leads to one or more outcomes. Are there any gaps in the logic of this plan? Once this review has been completed, and you are satisfied the plan is logical, the next step is to write a narrative description of the program. Remember, the logic model is a one-page illustration of the program, but there are many details it leaves out. It is the job of the program narrative to fill in all the details necessary to understand the logic behind the program, how it is expected to work, and to demonstrate the proposal is achievable.

Program Implementation

Once you have the funds in place it is time to take the leap from planning to implementation. The steps for implementation are already laid out when the logic model and program narrative are complete and address all aspects of the program. There are tools available to help ensure program implementation is on track and follows the logical progression laid out in the logic model and narrative. One example of such tools is the Gantt Chart, which is a horizontal bar chart illustrating the project schedule. In addition to illustrating time frames for implementation of each program component, it also demonstrates the relationships between activities, showing the order implementation activities occur and whether an

Issue or inequity to be addressed: **Opportunity Gap Between Low and Middle-Income Students**

Inputs Resources that will be devoted to or invested in the intervention. What you will need to make the planned change effort work.	**Activities** What you will be doing in the program. What actions, steps or tasks are essential to the intervention	**Outputs** What the program will produce as a result of the activities. The services offered, how frequently, to whom and the products that will be produced as a result	**Short-term outcomes** The results that you expect to occur immediately due to intervention	**Medium-term outcomes** The results that will occur next due to the intervention	**Impact** The long-term changes to larger systems resulting from the planned change effort
Funding OST staff (coordinator, trainer, outreach worker, 7 activity leaders) Summer staff (coordinator, 5 activity leaders, outreach worker) Teacher stipends for training Tutors Homework helpers Literacy supplies Training curricula for Teachers Tutors Homework helpers Parent workshops Books for lending library and summer reading group Office supplies Arts and crafts materials Games Chess sets Snacks Gardening supplies Plants	Design and implement fundraising plan, write and submit proposals Recruit, hire & orient staff Design training curriculum for teachers, tutors & homework helpers Bi-weekly teacher training & support sessions Recruit & train adult & college student tutors Weekly tutoring Recruit college student volunteers as homework helpers After-school activities Team sports, Homework help, Tutoring, Performing arts, Chess club, Group games, Arts & Crafts, Dance, and Cartooning Parent outreach Parent Newsletter Parent workshops Purchase relevant reading materials Enroll parents in advisory board Summer program: Gardening Club, academic support, reading group, lending library, soccer, arts & crafts, field trips	Submit 6 proposals in first 5 months 6 staff recruited & hired in 2months provided one week orientation Teacher training module 25 tutors recruited with 6 hours training 1 ½ hours of tutoring for 25 students weekly 15 college homework helpers recruited & trained Daily homework help for 25 students 120 enrolled students in after school activities 10 group activities daily serving 100 students Every parent outreached to at least once 6 parent workshops for 60 parents 100 books purchased for lending library 10-15 parents recruited for advisory board monthly meetings 100 students participating in summer activities	Teachers will self-report a 50% increase in confidence in OST programming at completion of training 85% of participants will improve reading skills by at least one grade level by end of school year Students will demonstrate a 10% increase in self-confidence after one year Families report increased awareness of importance of literacy at home within first six months Parents spend 50% more time engaged in children's schoolwork after one year 25% increased parent participation at PTA meetings Tutors gain skills to help increase student reading abilities Sufficient program funding Advisory board meets monthly engaging parents in program	75% reduction in reading gap after 3 years Standardized test scores improve by 30% after 3 years Students report 50% more time reading independently Sustained partnership between school, community, families 50% improved attendance over three years 25% reduction in behavioral issues over three years Teachers improve teaching of reading skills by 50% Reading materials relevant to students' experiences are utilized Outside funding supports additional student resources	elimination of the opportunity gap between low and middle-income students, resulting in students better prepared to succeed as adults with increased high school graduation and college acceptance, resulting in greater career options.

Figure 7.4 Completing the logic model

activity is dependent upon the completion of a previous activity. Each activity is represented by a horizontal bar showing the start and end date, the responsible party or parties for each task and the dependency on the start or completion of other tasks.

As a visual representation of the tasks to be accomplished, a Gantt Chart illustrates:

1. The various activities;
2. Start and end dates for each activity;
3. The length of time each activity is scheduled to last;

4. How activities overlap with other activities, and the period of time for this overlap;
5. The project start and end dates.

While there are a number of software programs to help create Gantt Charts and templates available online, a chart can be created using Microsoft Excel without charge. Figure 7.5 is an illustration of one possible Gantt Chart for the implementation of the OurKids AfterSchool program. The time frames illustrated in this chart are for example only and not to be taken as indicative of actual time frames for implementing a program such as this.

Figure 7.5 illustrates an example of a Gantt Chart for OurKids AfterSchool using Excel. The activities listed in the left-hand column are reflective of the activities listed in the logic model. This chart illustrates the first year of the program. Activities taking place in July through December are required to start the program in January. The provision of services cannot start on day one, as there are preliminary activities to be accomplished and resources to be obtained before kicking off a new program.

The first activity, beginning in July, is soliciting funding. As this chart shows, it is projected to take five months. While in reality this is too short a period of time to secure adequate funding, this time frame is used here purely for illustrative purposes. The next activity is recruiting the parent advisory board. This is projected to take three months and is scheduled to begin simultaneously as staff are recruited and hired. This allows parents to be represented in the hiring process. This represents a social justice consideration. If you want the community to be involved in the program, it is necessary they have input to all critical decisions. When the program planner picks and chooses the decisions community members are involved in, the planner runs the risk of losing necessary input as parents could begin to feel disenfranchised.

The chart projects staff hiring and orientation to be completed by the end of October, with staff to begin working on setting up the program in November. There are eight activities taking place during November and December, these include developing the curricula for the teacher, tutor and homework helper training. Also planned to take place in November and December are purchasing supplies and books for the lending library, and the monthly parent advisory board meetings, beginning in November and continuing throughout the end of the school year.

Next the chart shows four activities beginning in December, these include teacher training continuing through the end of May. During December students are enrolled in the OST and tutoring programs. Parent outreach also begin in December, continuing through the end of the school year and into the summer school vacation. The chart then illustrates that the remainder of the activities begin in January, the official

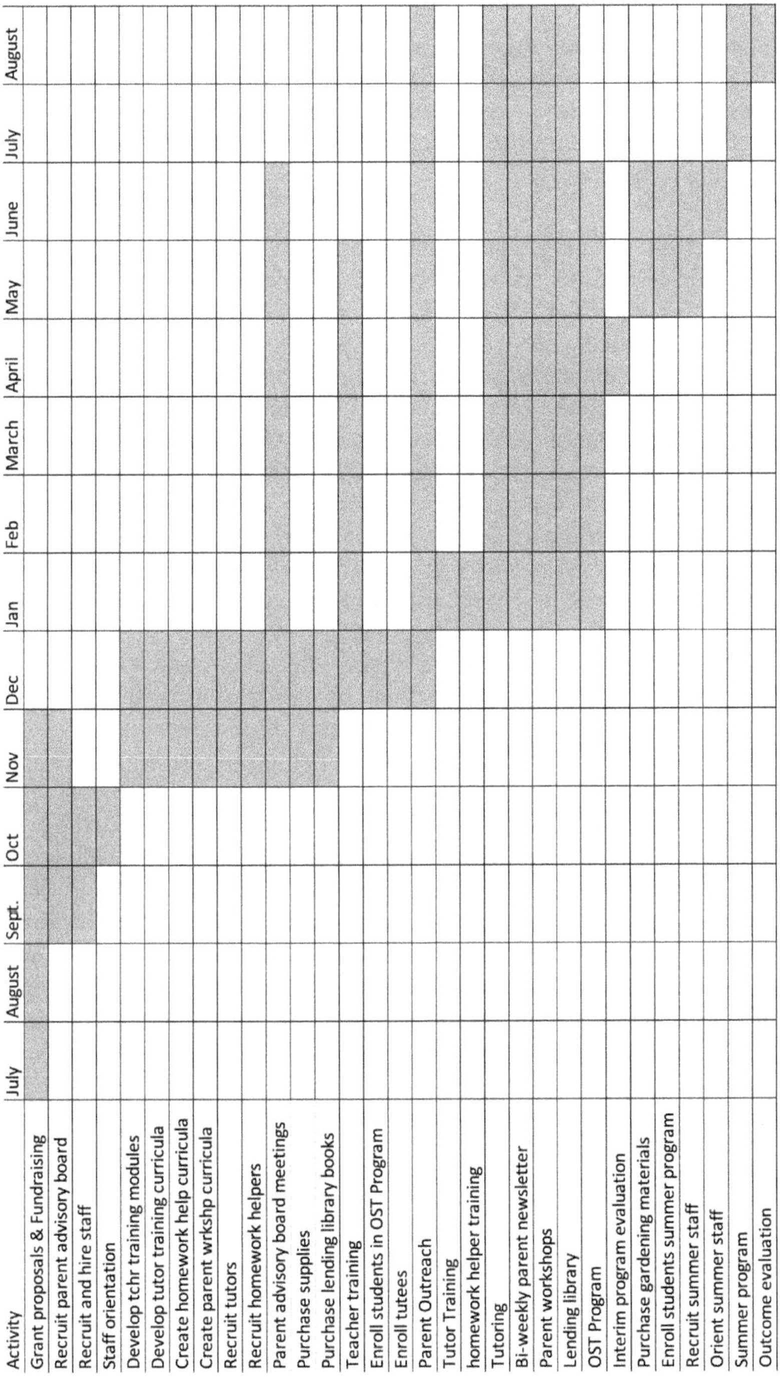

Activity	July	August	Sept.	Oct	Nov	Dec	Jan	Feb	March	April	May	June	July	August
Grant proposals & Fundraising														
Recruit parent advisory board														
Recruit and hire staff														
Staff orientation														
Develop tchr training modules														
Develop tutor training curricula														
Create homework help curricula														
Create parent wrkshp curricula														
Recruit tutors														
Recruit homework helpers														
Parent advisory board meetings														
Purchase supplies														
Purchase lending library books														
Teacher training														
Enroll students in OST Program														
Enroll tutees														
Parent Outreach														
Tutor Training														
homework helper training														
Tutoring														
Bi-weekly parent newsletter														
Parent workshops														
Lending library														
OST Program														
Interim program evaluation														
Purchase gardening materials														
Enroll students summer program														
Recruit summer staff														
Orient summer staff														
Summer program														
Outcome evaluation														

Figure 7.5 Gantt Chart

start of the OST program. In an actual Gantt Chart, each bar depicting an activity has a name or names attached to it showing who is responsible for ensuring the activity takes place and is on schedule.

Once the relative order of the implementation steps are established, it is time to agree upon how to proceed. The following discussion uses some of these planned activities to illustrate the thinking and steps necessary to implement the plan.

1. *Recruit and hire staff.* The first steps are to determine how many staff are needed and the specifics of the types of staff you are seeking in order to achieve the best possible outcomes. Are there specific education requirements needed? Would it be most helpful for prospective staff to have experience with the population? Do they have experience with the issues of concern, and are they reflective of the race, culture or gender of the target population? Additionally, what are the personal characteristics you are looking for. Can you determine they are credible and caring, do they have the ability to connect personally with program participants and parents? Do they have the ability to show respect for participants regardless of life situations, and perhaps most crucial, a strong desire to help people and show compassion and empathy (Department of Health and Human Services, n.d.). Maintaining the focus on social justice, it is essential to choose staff who believe in and support participant self-determination, allowing people to make decisions for themselves.
2. *Recruit parent advisory board.* The first step in recruiting the advisory board is to determine the goals of such a board. Typically, the goals of a parent advisory board are to increase awareness of the program and attract families to support and participate; provide input on specific aspects of the program; provide feedback about how people seeking services and participating are experiencing the program; help shape the strategic direction of the program; provide feedback for evaluation purposes; and, become involved in advocacy for their children, the community, and the school. Before beginning to recruit the advisory board, there are a number of steps to complete, some of these include:

    1. How many parent members?
    2. Types of people to recruit, are they representative of the diversity of the community?
    3. How are new members oriented?
    4. How will feedback be utilized?
    5. How are meetings structured?
    6. How often and when does the board meet?
    7. Who is the facilitator? (National Child Traumatic Stress Network, n.d.)

3. *Develop training modules and curricula.* For each of these curricula and training modules, the first decision is whether to employ or modify existing training materials or to create new curricula. Creating new curricula requires recruiting a professional with the expertise within the budget constraints. When implementing training curricula there are generally many examples of successful curricula and training modules that can be researched and used without cost. It is not always best to create new material if existing materials can be used and serve the program purposes. As a social justice focused program, the tutor and homework helper roles serve more than a singular purpose. Through these relationships the students will have role models who can show them what is possible, expanding their horizons and creating the possibility of increasing their social capital.
4. *Recruit tutors and homework helpers.* Prior to recruiting tutors and homework helpers, a number of decisions are taken into consideration. These include, deciding if the positions are volunteer or stipended; who, where and how you will recruit; determining responsibilities and creating job descriptions; and developing a volunteer agreement. Other necessary decisions include enumerating the necessary qualities required of tutors and homework helpers, such as patience, flexibility, strong communication skills, self-discipline, empathy and commitment to the goals of the program. Recruiting people from the community or people who have experience and/or knowledge that can be shared with the students is as important as their ability as tutors or homework helpers, thereby creating the opportunities to increase the students' social capital as well. College students or recent grads can help students understand the importance of completing their education and the advantages of a college education. They can also help students understand how to prepare themselves for college and how to persevere over the challenges faced along their path. Having regular contact with young adults who look like them and come from their community can help to demystify the challenges of preparing for college. This holds true as well for adults serving as tutors who share similar backgrounds to the students they are tutoring.
5. *Out of school time program.* There are many decisions to be made here. The logic model example illustrates some of the types of activities that could be included. Decisions include the types of activities to further the objectives of the program and engage the youth. The overarching task is to design a program attractive enough, so young people want to participate. Additionally, activities furthering positive youth development and increasing the possibilities of school success are necessary ingredients. To do this, it is essential that an afterschool program provides a variety of activities to develop necessary skills in fun and engaging ways. If the young people do not come

to the program, then the program cannot achieve the goals of helping them to succeed. The range of activities are most effective when based on an understanding of the skills and characteristics needed to succeed. This also requires staff who bring with them the skills and perspectives to achieve these goals.

These are just a sampling of the decisions human services program planners have to consider when developing a program of this type. There are many more, in fact the number of decisions is countless. The critical ingredient here is involving parents and youth in as many of these decisions and determinations as is feasibly possible. Decisions to include parents and young people should not be made based upon expediency. When you decide to leave them out of specific decisions you run the risk of alienating them from the program. Once you have made the decision to involve the parents and the youth, it is crucial to include them as equal partners. Developing a program through a social justice lens is not easy, if it was, it would be the standard rather than an ideal.

Chapter Summary

Main Points

1. Activities are the specific actions making up the program.
2. Activities are best when they are evidence-informed utilizing research, practice experience and community input.
3. Each proposed activity leads directly to one or more outcomes.
4. Outputs are the measures of services offered. They are the products produced ss a result of the activities.
5. Inputs are the resources necessary to successfully carry out the intervention.
6. The Gantt Chart delineates time frames for the implementation of each program component, demonstrating the relationship between activities and when implementation activities occur.

Key Terms

Logic model
Positive youth development
Activities
Outputs
Inputs
Gantt Chart

Discussion Questions

1. If you were designing an intervention to assist people who have lost their homes through eviction, what evidence would you seek to inform the intervention design?

2. How can developing specific and attainable outputs help to keep the program implementation on track?
3. What is the value of a Gantt Chart in specifying the steps and time frames to implement a program intervention?
4. How do activities lead to both outcomes and outputs?
5. Why is the program logic model developed from right to left, beginning with the end result sought?

References

Department of Health and Human Services, Office of Family Assistance (n.d.) Implementation resource guide for social service programs: An introduction to evidence-based programming, https://www.healthymarriageinfo.org/wp-content/uploads/2017/12/ Implementation-Resource-Guide.pdf, retrieved 4/14/21

Eccles, J. & Barber, B. (1999) Student council, volunteering, basketball, or marching band: What kind of extracurricular activity matters? *Journal of Adolescent Research*, 14, 10–43

Karsh, E. & Fox, A.S. (2009) *The only grantwriting book you'll ever need, 3rd ed.* New York, NY: Basic Books

Knowlton, L.W. & Phillips, C.C. (2013) *The logic model guidebook*. Los Angeles, CA: SAGE Publications

National Child Traumatic Stress Network (n.d.) A guide to forming advisory boards for family- serving organizations, https://www.nctsn.org/sites/default/files/resources/resource-guide/ a_guide_to_forming_advosiry_boards_for_family_serving_organizations.pdf, retrieved 4/15/21

Scrivens, K. & Smith, C. (2013) Four interpretations of social capital: An agenda for measurement, OECD Statistics Working papers, No.2013/06, OECD Publishing, Paris, https://doi.org/10.1787/5jzbcx010wmt-en, retrieved 6/2/20

8 The Program Narrative

Learning Objectives

1. Summarize the sections of a funding proposal and the information included in each.
2. Understand the importance of writing a funding proposal in clear language, including the active voice, avoiding professional jargon and writing in the third person.
3. Describe what is meant by "show me, don't tell me."
4. Understand how to write measurable program outcomes.

Chapter Overview

This chapter provides an overview of each section of a typical fundraising proposal, focusing on the program narrative. The detailed discussion of the program narrative reviews each content area with an explanation of the information to be included. Utilizing the OurKids AfterSchool case study as an example, the program narrative is filled in, detailing what is to be addressed.

The Program Funding Proposal

The program narrative serves two purposes. First it is a complete description of the intervention that is being planned so that all involved in the planning process can clearly understand and agree upon the details. Once this agreement is reached, then the program narrative becomes an integral part of a funding proposal. In the poem "Wind-Wafted Flowers," the poet Muriel Strode (1903) wrote, "I will not follow where the path may lead, but I will go where there is no path, and I will leave a trail." The act of developing a social justice program intervention is the equivalent of going where there is no path, and the narrative describing the intervention is the trail to leave so others can follow.

DOI: 10.4324/9781003148777-8

Proposal Sections

The typical funding proposal consists of seven sections:

1. Summary: The summary is a brief paragraph summarizing the proposed intervention specifying the amount being requested. Also called an executive summary, this summary serves as the case statement and is a key component of the proposal, designed to interest the grantee to read more and to consider the proposal for funding. An example of such a summary for the OurKids AfterSchool program can read similar to the following:

   > OurKids AfterSchool is requesting $100,000 to support the Yes We Can program, a two-year Out of School Time and Summer Youth Program designed to address the opportunity gap experienced by low-income and immigrant children in our community. Low-income children begin school behind their middle-income peers in reading skills. This gap continues to grow as the children progress through school, widening each summer. While seen by many as an achievement gap, research has shown that this can also be viewed as an opportunity gap. Viewing it as an achievement gap places the onus on the children, while an opportunity gap recognizes that there are structural challenges to be overcome.

   The Yes We Can program will provide afterschool and summer enrichment designed to close the opportunity gap with programs such as tutoring, homework help, STEM activities, a lending library, arts programming and other activities to increase self-confidence and self-esteem and improve academic achievement. The program design incorporates positive youth development aspects while involving teachers and parents in addressing this opportunity gap and helping students succeed in their schoolwork and into adulthood.

   Additional training and support is offered to teachers to learn ways to address the opportunity gap and provide the supportive atmosphere needed to help students succeed. The parent advisory board will give input and feedback on the program, providing support and information for continual quality improvement. Training and support is provided to parents to help identify and advocate for policy and systems changes impacting their children and the community.

   Resulting from participation in this program students will improve their reading scores and increase school attendance, and teachers will experience a measurable improvement in classroom behavior among students. Parents will develop the necessary skills to advocate for their children and put these skills to work to increase resources allocated to education in the community. Parents will also increase the amount of time they spend supporting their children's schoolwork at home. Additionally, teachers will gain skills and insights in how they can improve the classroom environment to support student growth and reduce the existing opportunity gap, providing a more robust and equitable education for all students, regardless of their economic or immigration status.

2. Organizational Information: This next section is a brief description of the organization that is seeking support. In no more than three to five paragraphs describe the organization, its mission and track record in providing services. The organizational description demonstrates the credibility of the organization and builds confidence that it has the capacity to accomplish what is being proposed and to responsibly use the funds requested.
3. Description of Need: The first step in developing the description of need is to frame it in such a way that the person reading understands and appreciates the need, even though they may have no prior knowledge of the issue. This section provides facts and figures supporting the importance of the inequity, but not so many facts and statistics that it takes away the human element. Unless this is a national program, the focus remains on the community or communities that are impacted. It is essential to balance deficits with community and individual assets and not present an image of the community that is too dark or negative. The description of need clearly and concisely demonstrates a compelling need in a way that it is of interest to the grant maker. Finally, remember not to write this description in terms of "lack of." The fact that specific services do not exist, or are insufficient to meet the need, does not make a case for an intervention. The real issue is that the need exists, that it may be increasing and the impact it has on people and the community.
4. Program Description: This is a narrative description of the theory of change and the program logic model that is being presented. Describe all program activities, interventions and the work plan in detail, followed by the proposed outcomes resulting from these activities and the impact that the program will have. In clear, distinct language describe proposed outcomes and accomplishments in measurable terms. Be specific about how the proposed activities meet the project goals and objectives. Included in this discussion is a description of how the proposed program achieves the outcomes and accomplishments, including the actions to accomplish the objectives and how these benefit the community. Finally, this section includes information on who will carry out the activities and oversee the time frames for the program.
5. Additional Support and Future Funding: Discuss whether or not other funders have committed support to the project or if other

requests have been submitted and are pending. Most funders want to know that there are other supporters and do not want to be the sole support of a project. Many philanthropic foundations prefer to fund innovation and shy away from continuing support for ongoing programs. Funders want to see a statement of how the program projects to continue after the requested grant is completed.

6. Budget: This section presents a clear and detailed budget for the program. The budget information demonstrates all sources of funding for the program. One source that many funders look for is "in-kind" support. This represents support for the program by the organization and can be in cash, personnel, equipment, technology, physical space, etc.
7. Evaluation Plan: A detailed evaluation plan demonstrating it will be determined the program has been successful meeting the outcomes and goals proposed.

There are numerous books and online resources providing detailed information and guidelines for effective proposal writing. This chapter focuses on the program description as it is an integral part of the planning process. While budgeting is also a necessary planning consideration, there are equally as many resources for developing program budgets.

Know Your Audience

The key to a successful program description with impact is writing to engage and inspire the audience. As with most program proposals, OurKids AfterSchool is writing for two audiences – potential funders and the community. This does not require two different program descriptions, rather one that meets both their needs and expectations. Writing for a potential funder requires clear language detailing the program, the expected results and the plan to accomplish these. There are rules and considerations to help writing a program description that meets the needs of both.

There are many factors to consider when writing a program description or a funding proposal. These are the same regardless of the audience you are writing for, these include:

1. **Write to be understood without being overly formal or pretentious**. Do not use slang, unless it is a direct quote that is being used to make a point or illustrate an idea.
2. **Avoid professional jargon, abbreviations, and acronyms**. Do not assume that the reader has the educational or professional background as you. If you are abbreviating an organization's name, spell out the full name (followed by the abbreviation or acronym) the first time it is referred to, then the abbreviation can be used again on the same

page. If the organization is referred to later on, it is be spelled out again, so that the reader is not forced to search the document to identify the full name. Even though there are abbreviations or words used that are common in the profession or in the specialty area served, do not assume the reader is familiar with these terms. Spell out all abbreviations and acronyms. The goal is to make the reader as comfortable as possible while reviewing the proposal.

3. **Write in the active voice, conveying a stronger and clearer message**. Without getting into a grammar lesson, when writing in the active voice the subject of the sentence acts upon the verb. An example of passive voice is "Students will be recruited by OurKids AfterSchool to participate in the afterschool program." Written in the active voice, this reads "OurKids AfterSchool staff will recruit students to participate in the afterschool program." A small change, but one that gives more strength and action to the description.
4. **Show me, don't tell me**. Avoid superlatives and adjectives such as: "this unique, high quality program...," or "will provide the highest quality and most effective programming..." These terms are all subjective; what is unique or most effective to one reader may not be seen that way by another reader. Instead, describe the program with specifics that demonstrate its unique approach, quality and effectiveness. Tell the reader what makes this program unique, giving specific examples of its effectiveness and quality.
5. **Write in the third person, avoid using "I," "we," or "our."** Name the organization or the individuals and what they will do. Writing in the first person, using the pronouns "I" or "we" makes it about individuals and not about the organization. It is the organization that is applying for funding, not the individual planner or proposal writer.
6. **Do not assume the reader is familiar with or understands the concepts or interventions being proposed**. Effective proposals are written in plain language with all ideas, concepts and interventions clearly and plainly described as if the reader has no prior knowledge of the program or the issue that is being addressed. One way to ensure you have done this, is to have someone who has little to no knowledge of the issues you are addressing. If the proposal is clear to them, you have succeeded. If this person has too many questions, or needs things explained to them, you have not presented the information clearly enough.

A critical aspect of knowing your audience is writing to their priorities. Working with and studying the community helps to develop familiarity with their concerns and priorities. Hopefully these have been addressed in the program plan. The same is true for potential funders. If you are seeking philanthropic support, study the foundation or corporation and identify their priorities to be sure it is a good fit before writing or submitting a funding request. Once you have determined the program is within the priorities of the funder, make sure these are addressed in your proposal. Use some of their language in your program description so that you underscore this is a good fit. This does not mean copying phrases or sentences from their website, instead incorporate their priorities in your program description. For example, a philanthropic foundation that focuses on child development has this phrase on its website describing one if its priority approaches: "A community development strategy promoting healthy development and academic success for kids." This can be addressed by OurKids AfterSchool in this manner:

> OurKids AfterSchool is proposing the Yes We Can afterschool and summer program, a comprehensive strategy to reduce the opportunity gap among public school children in the community. The proposed program incorporates strategies to promote healthy development and academic success through engaging young people in academic and skill building activities in their out of school time, while also engaging parents in leadership and advocacy development.

The Program Description

All aspects of organizing the program and implementing the program are described in detail in the program description also referred to as the methods. The program description includes:

- **Staffing pattern**: how many staff, job titles, qualifications and their roles in the program. Show how staff are recruited, hired and trained or oriented.
- **Project outcomes/objectives**: Clearly detail the outcomes to be achieved as a result of the program.
- **Activities**: Detail each activity, how it will be run, who will be served, how often it meets, and specifics about the content of each activity. Each activity has a direct impact on at least one of the proposed outcomes. This is where the Gantt Chart helps to show the thinking that has gone into organizing and getting the program up and running.
- **Recruitment**: Be clear about your plans for recruiting program participants and in this case the parent advisory board.

Provide Supportive Documentation

While a program description is not an academic thesis or a research paper, it is important to provide support for the interventions being proposed and the outcomes sought. It is written in positive language, demonstrating the path forward has been determined and it is one the proposer is confident about. An effective program description demonstrates a high level of confidence in the program being proposed. Oftentimes, proposers demonstrate their lack of confidence in their own program by using terms such as "we hope that …," or "if the program is successful it will…" Positive language demonstrates that there is a high degree of confidence in the interventions being proposed, telling potential funders and the community partners this is the best way forward. The following paragraph is one example of how research can be incorporated into the program narrative for OurKids AfterSchool program.

> The Yes We Can program is built upon positive youth development (PYD) principles and interventions. According to Taylor et al. (2017), the focus of PYD is on "building young people's positive personal competencies, social skills and attitudes (i.e. asset development) through increased positive relationships, social supports and opportunities that strengthen assets and help youth flourish within their environments" (p. 1156). PYD interventions focus on developing the so-called Five Cs; confidence, competence, connection, caring/compassion and character. Yes We Can afterschool and summer program activities are each designed to foster these principles and are supported by the research of Roth and Brooks-Gunn (2000), who report that engagement in PYD activities promotes the growth of the whole person advancing their chances for life success. This is further supported by Quinn's (1999) research findings that programs with demonstrated successful youth outcomes include hands-on education, promote pro-social values, build leadership, decision-making and problem-solving skills. Additionally, Zarrett and Lerner (2008) found the number of OST activities was predictive of adolescent functioning. Students who participated in one to four activities each week were found to score higher on established scales of positive youth development. These findings have informed the design of the OurKids AfterSchool program – Yes We Can.

Now that the program has been introduced with supportive documentation of the proposed approach, the next step is to enumerate and specify the outcomes and impact that the program is designed to achieve

Outcomes and Impact

The Yes We Can program is designed to engage students, parents and teachers working together to help achieve the impact of eliminating the opportunity gap between low- and middle-income students, thereby better preparing students to succeed as adults. This will be accomplished through increased high school graduation and college acceptance rates resulting in greater career options for these students.

While an actual program description enumerates and specifies each proposed outcome, following are six examples of how outcomes can be presented including how they are measured:

- **Outcome 1**: 85% of participants will improve their reading by at least one grade level in one year, measured by the Massachusetts Comprehensive Assessment System that is administered to all students from third grade through to eighth grade. (Note: Specifically naming the way in which progress or change is measured shows that you are aware of the importance of measuring and documenting progress and the methods to measure).
- **Outcome 2**: 75% of participants will report increased self-confidence at the end of the first year of participation as measured by the Adolescent Self-Esteem Questionnaire (ASQ) administered to all participants at the beginning and again at the end of the program year.
- **Outcome 3**: Teachers will report a 50% increase in skills and knowledge of OST programming and PYD concepts at the end of training. This will be measured by a pre- and post-test. (It is not always necessary to use existing or standardized measures to determine growth and change. Note: In this case, a brief questionnaire can be developed to determine a teacher's knowledge of PYD concepts prior to training and after training is completed).
- **Outcome 4**: Parents will report spending an average of 50% more time engaging with their children's schoolwork at the end of the first year. Parents will be interviewed by the Outreach Worker at the beginning of the program and a sample of parents at the end of the program. This measure will be based upon self-reporting by participants.
- **Outcome 5**: Program participants will show at least a 50% improvement in attendance rates at the end of three years, as determined by school attendance records.
- **Outcome 6**: Parents will become engaged in advocacy for increased school resources. This outcome will be measured by the number of parents involved in activities such as letter writing, petitioning and advocacy meetings with school board members and elected officials.

The next step is delineating the specifics of each of the activities that are enumerated in the logic model. Every activity leads to at least one outcome, and every outcome has at least one activity designed to achieve that outcome.

Methods or Program Activities

Having detailed the proposed outcomes, or what you hope to achieve, now the task is to detail how these are to be achieved. These are the activities that are being proposed, or they can be referred to as the methods through which the outcomes and impact are realized. The methods are presented in sufficient detail making it possible for the reader to visualize the program being presented. When deciding which details to include, ask yourself what is most compelling about the program, and which parts would appeal most to the reader (Barbato & Furlich, 2000). This is the section where you describe what you are going to *do* and how you plan to *do* it. The action word "do" is stressed here because strong action verbs and adverbs demonstrate confidence in the plan being proposed. "The methods section of a proposal systematically walks funders through the strategies the organization proposes to carry out in order to accomplish its objectives. Methods answers this key question: how will an organization actually accomplish its work?" (O'Neal-McElrath, 2013, p. 49).

Karsh and Fox (2009) point out that the proposal is also a marketing tool. The product that is being sold is the importance of the inequity that you are proposing to address and the wisdom of the proposed approach. Phrases such as "we hope to" or "we are planning to" do not convey a sense of confidence. The purpose of this section is not only to be clear describing the program that is being proposed, but also to convey confidence in the program. This is where you have the opportunity to sell the program to potential funders and supporters. Human services workers do not like to think of the work they are doing in business terms. However, it is essential to understand it is indeed a competitive business when it comes to soliciting support. While you are fully committed to the value of your program, do not assume because you believe you have designed a strong intervention it will automatically be seen as such by potential supporters needed to move the program idea forward. Selling the program to gain support is no different than marketing a product or service.

The program description clearly demonstrates a direct connection between the program activities, or methods, being proposed and the outcomes. An effective description includes sufficient detail

> to demonstrate that the planned activities, the number and types of staff, the number and type of persons that are to receive services and the timeframes for accomplishing your objectives are realistic and that the program you have designed has a good chance of succeeding in achieving those objectives.
>
> (Karsh & Fox, 2009, p. 171)

The methods section clearly describes what you plan to do and how you plan to do it. The description demonstrates that the intervention choices are informed by evidence such as research findings, best practices, expert opinion, community input or past experience. Asking yourself the following questions can be helpful when preparing this section:

1. Is there a direct and logical link between the statement of the issue being addressed and the methods being proposed?

2. Are the specific program activities being presented in a clear and concise manner?
3. Is there justification for the chosen interventions?
4. Are all proposed activities feasible within the resources to be allocated or available?

Once you have asked and answered these questions, and have located supportive documentation for your choices, then you are ready to begin writing the methods or program description. The following is an example of a brief paragraph, in active voice, introducing the methods section:

> The participant outcomes enumerated above will be achieved through a comprehensive program involving students, parents and teachers. Students will participate in afterschool and summer enrichment activities designed to develop academic and social skills, and teachers will participate in training to help develop their skills to promote student objectives. Recognizing the importance of involving parents, the program includes a parent advisory board and workshops designed to help parents develop skills to support their child's academic achievement and become involved in advocacy to increase academic supports and resources for their children.

While an actual program description enumerates and specifies each of the proposed activities, following are two examples of how activities can be presented. The description of the program activities demonstrates details that have been thought through and those possible with the funds requested and the proposed staffing pattern.

Activity 1: Afterschool program. The afterschool program will enroll 120 students in a range of activities designed to support their academic achievement and personal growth. The afterschool program meets five afternoons per week from 3 p.m. to 6 p.m. each day. The program will run from the beginning of the school year through June following the school calendar. The daily schedule will be divided into two one-and-a-half hour sessions. All students will be enrolled in tutoring for a minimum of three hours per week and homework help for an additional three hours per week. Other activities that students can participate in include basketball, soccer, performing arts, chess club, arts and crafts, tinkering, dance, and drawing, street photography and cartooning.

Table 8.1 is a chart of the activity schedule for the afterschool program.

The Youth.gov (n.d.) website has summarized research on the benefits of afterschool programming for school age youth. They found that "afterschool programs also provide a significant return-on-investment, with every $1 invested saving at least $3 through increasing youth's earning

Table 8.1.

	MONDAY	*TUESDAY*	*WEDNESDAY*	*THURSDAY*	*FRIDAY*
3:00-4:30	Tutoring	Tutoring	Tutoring	Tutoring	Tutoring
	Homework Help	Homework Help	Homework Help	Homework Help	Homework Help
	Basketball	Soccer	Basketball	Soccer	Basketball
	Dance	Performing Arts	Dance	Performing Arts	Dance
	Drawing & Cartooning	Arts & Crafts	Drawing & Cartooning	Arts & Crafts	Drawing & Cartooning
	Tinkering	Chess club	Tinkering	Chess club	
		Street photography		Street photography	
4:30-6:00	Tutoring	Tutoring	Tutoring	Tutoring	Tutoring
	Homework Help	Homework Help	Homework Help	Homework Help	Homework Help
	Soccer	Basketball	Soccer	Basketball	Soccer
	Performing Arts	Dance	Performing Arts	Dance	Performing Arts
	Arts & Crafts	Drawing & Cartooning	Arts & Crafts	Drawing & Cartooning	Arts & Crafts
	Tinkering		Tinkering		
	Street photography		Street photography		

potential, improving their performance at school, and reducing crime and juvenile delinquency." This research also found additional benefits including:

1. improved social and emotional competencies, including pro-social behavior, intrinsic motivation, better concentration efforts and higher sense of self-worth,
2. students improved their reading and math grades, and those who attended more regularly were more likely to make gains,
3. improved in class participation,
4. better adjustment as young people move to the next phase of schooling,
5. increased school day attendance and participation, and reduced school dropout rates,
6. increased adult supervision making youth feel safer and reduced instances of unsupervised time with peers out of school, and
7. benefits to working families and businesses from afterschool programs ensuring that youth have a safe place while parents or guardians are at work.

Arts programming, too often cut from school budgets, is an integral component of the Yes We Can afterschool program. Research by the Brookings Institute found

> that increases in arts learning positively and significantly affect students' school engagement, college aspirations, and their inclinations to draw upon works of art as a means for empathizing with others. In terms of school engagement, students in the treatment group were more likely to agree that schoolwork is enjoyable, makes them think about things in new ways, and that their school offers programs, classes, and activities that keep them interested in school.
>
> (Kisida & Bowen, 2019)

The afterschool program includes a special group activity titled "Tinkering." This STEM program is based upon curriculum and research from the California Tinkering Afterschool Network (n.d.) that found "tinkering in afterschool can make STEM more accessible to youth from low-income, historically marginalized communities" by:

1. building generous learning environments that emphasize shared activity, process and iteration,
2. cultivating play and creativity,
3. widening definitions of intelligence and science, and
4. treating learning as purposeful and a social endeavor.

The tinkering program will be available twice per week for three hours each day. Each tinkering group will enroll up to fifteen young people for a total of thirty youth engaging in STEM learning activities. The tinkering groups are intentionally designed to build upon youth knowledge and prior interests. Activities are be based on curriculum developed by the Tinkering Studio including experiments and projects with science, art, technology and other ideas.

In addition to tinkering, another activity to help increase creativity is street photography. Students will learn the basics of digital photography and then develop photo essays about their community. In addition to nurturing creativity, this program helps students to learn about their community. At the end of the semester, the street photography participants will present their photographic essays at a special program for parents and community members. Each week students will have the opportunity to photograph and capture aspects of community life. Enabling young people to explore and use their environment

> as an arena for critical learning has multiple benefits: It aids their political socialization, understanding of cultural differences, and knowledge of local history, social issues and public affairs. It also allows them to become active observers and participants in the urban landscape, while also benefitting the community and the civic culture at large.
>
> (Gerodimos, 2018, p. 84)

The afterschool program will be staffed by a part-time coordinator, working twenty hours per week, and eight activity leaders, each working seven-and-a-half or fifteen hours per week, depending upon their area of expertise. The homework help and tutoring activities will be staffed by volunteers who receive training and ongoing supervision.

Activity 2: Parent Advisory Board. The OurKids AfterSchool outreach worker will reach out to parents to recruit a minimum of ten advisory board members. The advisory board will be constituted prior to hiring staff so that parents can be involved in choosing staff for the program. The advisory board will meet twice a month to review program progress and to develop leadership and advocacy skills. Board members will utilize these skills to engage other parents, meet with school administrators and lead an advocacy campaign reaching out to the school committee and other elected representatives to increase school resources. During the course of the year, additional parents will become engaged as advisory board members and in advocacy efforts. The advisory board offers a forum for parents, as program stakeholders, to communicate their opinions, and to share their expertise.

The parent advisory board will help to:

1. increase awareness of the program and attract families;
2. receive input on specific aspects of the program;
3. collect feedback about how people experience the program;
4. shape the strategic direction of the program;
5. gather qualitative data on the experience of program participants;
6. provide advocacy for increased school resources.

According to Community Organizing and Family Issues (COFI, n.d.) an organization located in Chicago created to "strengthen the power and voice of low-income and working families," parents can become involved in policy advocacy through building trusting relationships among themselves. Work with the parent advisory board follows the three-step process developed by COFI (n.d.). These are:

1. Getting to know each other on a one-to-one bases by sharing their personal and family stories and sharing their hopes and dreams. Developing trust in this way helps to sow the seeds of common ground across the differences that are so often used to divide people.
2. Through their shared stories parents identify common struggles and challenges, identifying the changes they believe need to happen and how they can act to make a difference in their community and in their lives and the lives of their children. Through dialogue in a safe and supportive environment parents work to build a vision for positive change.
3. Over the course of the advisory board meetings parents will be able to articulate desired changes in systems and policies to have a positive impact on their children and their community.

Once members have determined the changes and progress they would like to see, the outreach worker will assist parents in reaching out to elected officials to advocate for these changes. Additionally, advisory board members will reach out to friends, family and neighbors to engage them in advocacy efforts including petitions and letter writing campaigns. Parents shall also learn how to write effective letters to local newspapers and elected officials.

Pulling It All Together

These two examples – the afterschool program and the parent advisory board – illustrate the information included in the description of the program activities. As these examples illustrate, it is not only important to describe each of the proposed activities but also to provide support for the choices that have been made. References are made to research, programs and best practices to demonstrate the efficacy of the choices that have been made. While it is necessary to provide support for the methods being proposed, there is a fine balance between too much detail and not enough. The art form here is to determine how much detail is needed to provide a clear picture of the activity, why it was chosen and support for the choices made. If the writer provides too much detail, the reader can get lost in the detail and not fully understand the "why" of the program interventions. Too little detail and you may not be providing enough information for the reader to grasp the "why" of the chosen interventions or take away that you are not sufficiently informed about the issue.

The examples above show that every activity does not have to be described in a lot of detail. These two are highlighted because they are unique activities that might help to make this program proposal stand out. There is no need to describe arts and crafts, basketball or the other OST activities listed because they are well known and are often included in OST programs. That is true, unless you are proposing a different approach or seeking special outcomes that help to make this program unique. These activities are included in the schedule, demonstrating that the program details have been thought out while giving an overview of the entire program.

Unfortunately, there is no formula for how much or how little information to provide. This is where it is crucial to have a second reader who is not as informed about the project and the issues as you are. If this reader sufficiently understands what you are proposing, and why, without getting lost in detail, then it is a good bet the right balance has been achieved.

Chapter Summary

Main Points

1. When soliciting funds and support from philanthropic or government sources the program description usually consists of seven sections: 1) summary, 2) organizational information, 3) description of need, 4) program description, 5) additional support/future funding, 6) budget, and 7) evaluation plan.
2. The description of need provides facts and figures supporting the importance of the inequity, clearly and concisely demonstrating a compelling need.
3. The program description is a narrative presentation of the program logic model, describing program activities, interventions and the work plan in detail, followed by the proposed outcomes resulting from these activities and the program's impact.

4. Additional support and future funding informs potential funders whether or not other funders have committed support to the project or if other requests have been submitted and are pending and how the program will be supported after the initial grant expires.
5. The budget provides information detailing all sources of funding for the program, including in-kind resources, and how these funds are to be spent.
6. Finally, the evaluation plan demonstrates how to determine if the program has been successful, meeting the outcomes and goals proposed.

Key terms

Active voice	Show me, don't tell me
Passive voice	Methods

Discussion Questions

1. What does it mean to write in the active voice, and why is this important in presenting the program?
2. What is meant by "show me, don't tell me" when writing the program description and about the organization proposing the program?
3. How do action verbs demonstrate confidence in the details of the program pan being presented?
4. Why is it necessary to think in marketing terms when presenting the program to potential funders and supporters?
5. How do you determine how much, or how little information to present to make an effective case for the intervention?

References

Barbato, J. & Furlich, D.S. (2000) *Writing for a good cause.* New York, NY: Fireside

California Tinkering Afterschool Network (n.d.) www.exploratotium.edu/california-tinkering- afterschool-network, retrieved 5/15/21

Community Organizing and Family Issues (COFI) (n.d.) The COFI way: Policy and systems change, https://cofionline.org/COFI/cofi-reports/the-cofi-way-policy-systems-change/, retrieved 5/19/2021

Gerodimos, R. (2018) Youth and the city: Reflective photography as a tool for urban voice. *Journal of Media and Literacy*, 10(1), 81–102, http://eprints.bournemouth.ac.uk/30695/2/Gerodimos%20templated%20FINAL%20JMLE%20 10.1%20-%20with%20changes%20accepted.pdf, retrieved 8/23/21

Karsh, E. & Fox, A.S. (2009) *The only grantwriting book you'll ever need.* New York, NY: Basic Books

Kisida, B. & Bowen, D.H. (2019) New evidence of the benefits of arts education, Brookings Institute Brown Center Chalkboard, 2/12/19, https://www.brookings.edu/blog/brown-center-chalkboard/2019/02/12/new-evidence-of-the-benefits-of-arts-education/, retrieved 5/11/21

O'Neal-McElrath, T. (2013) *Winning grants step by step.* San Francisco, CA: Jossey-Bass

Quinn, J. (1999) Where need meets opportunity: Youth development programs for early teens. *The Future of Children*, 9(2), 96–116

Roth, J.L. & Brooks-Gunn, J. (2000) What do adolescents need for healthy development? Implications for youth policy. *Social Policy Report*, 14(1), https://srcd.onlinelibrary.wiley.com/doi/pdf/10.1002/j.2379-3988.2000.tb00012.x, retrieved 3/10/21

Strode, M (1903) The open court. No. 8, Article 5, https://opensiuc.lib.siu.edu/ocj/ vol1903/iss8/5

Taylor, R.D., Oberele, E., Durlak, J.A. & Weissberg, R.P. (2017) Promoting positive youth development through school-based and social emotional learning interventions: A meta-analysis of follow-up effects. *Child Development*, July/August, 88(4), 1156–1171

Youth.gov (n.d.) Benefits for youth, families and communities, https://youth.gov/youth-topics/afterschool-programs/benefits-youth-families-and-communities

Zarrett, N. & Lerner, R.M. (2008) Ways to promote positive development of children and youth, Research to Results, Childtrends.org, 2/11/08, https://childtrends.org/wp-content/uploads/2014/05/2008-11PositiveYouthDev.pdf, retrieved 4/6/21

9 Program Evaluation

> Always ask yourself if what you are doing today is getting you closer to where you want to be tomorrow.
>
> Paulo Coelho (2017), Brazilian novelist

Learning Objectives

1. Articulate the difference between the "process evaluation" and "outcome evaluation."
2. Understand how a well-developed program logic model informs the evaluation process.
3. Recognize the value of process evaluation for program implementation.
4. Develop an evaluation plan.
5. Articulate the role of the pre- and post-test to determine progress meeting the proposed outcomes.

Chapter Overview

The program evaluation is a critical tool to determine if the intervention is being implemented as planned and whether or not the program has achieved the projected outcomes. There are two types of program evaluations: the process or formative evaluation and the outcome or summative evaluation. The appropriate framework for the evaluation process is the logic model developed to guide the program design and implementation. The program evaluation is not the final step in program planning and implementation, rather it is part of a continuous loop providing feedback for further planning and improvement.

The Why of Program Evaluation

You have worked with the community to develop the best possible intervention to address the identified inequity. The logic model informed the thinking and planning to develop the intervention, providing the road map to move forward on the journey. The program is up and running

DOI: 10.4324/9781003148777-9

and the services that were planned are functional. At this point, why take the time and effort to look back and see if you accomplished what you set out to do? You believe the program, as designed and implemented, is the most effective intervention possible. Why spend time and additional resources evaluating the program? Right? Wrong! Program evaluation is an important and useful tool for social justice program planners.

Program evaluation should not be seen as an exercise merely to satisfy the requirements of the funder. It is a necessary function of any program intervention, providing information to determine if the intervention has worked and implemented as proposed. When you believe all the appropriate steps have been followed planning and implementing the program, the community was involved, and all agree this was the best planned intervention to implement, is it possible to know this is true without engaging in a program evaluation? "Evaluation is a structured process intended to reduce the level of uncertainty for decision makers and stakeholders about a given program or policy. It is usually intended to answer questions or test hypotheses the result of which are then incorporated into the information base used by those who have a stake in the program or policy" (McDavid et al., 2019, p. 3).

Testing Assumptions

The program evaluation is used to test assumptions made about the efficacy and effectiveness of the interventions planned, and whether or not the intervention hypothesis is valid. While many planners see the evaluation coming at the end of the program, it is not the final stage of program planning. The feedback and information gained through evaluation is best used when it is cycled back into the program for continuous improvement and learning. In this way, evaluation helps answer the questions: Did the program accomplish what it was designed to do? Are there ways the intervention could have been improved? Was the program implemented as planned? Is this an effective intervention that is worth institutionalizing? Is it a successful enough model for replication? These important questions can only be answered through a rigorous program evaluation. There is no way to know if an intervention is effective without performing an evaluation. Therefore, the program evaluation is a tool for social justice planners to remain focused on planning and implementing effective program interventions.

Building an Evaluation Based Upon the Logic Model

The appropriate framework for the evaluation process is the logic model that was developed to guide the program design and implementation. The program evaluation is part of a continuous loop providing feedback for further planning and improvement.

Figure 9.1 demonstrates the continuous relationship of each element of program planning, the needs assessment leads to the program design, which leads to the program launch, followed by implementation which

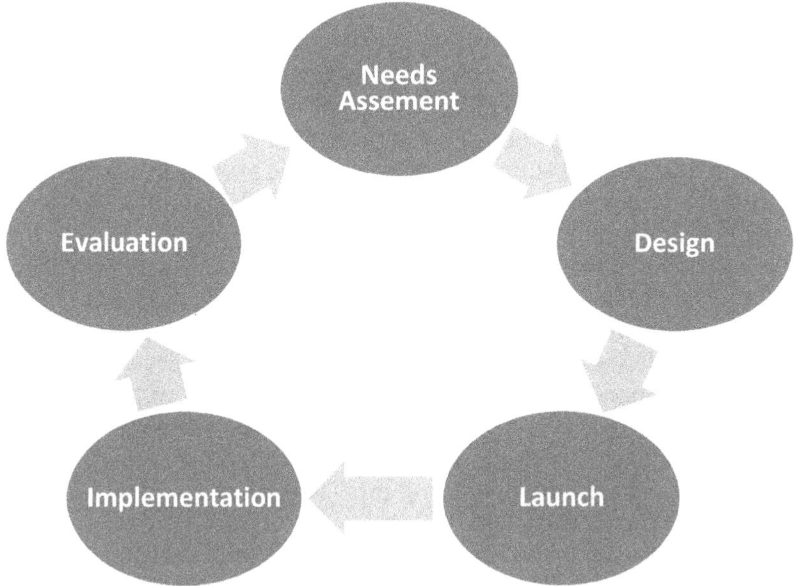

Figure 9.1 Program planning flow chart

then leads to evaluation. But this is not the end of the cycle. The information discovered in evaluation informs the needs assessment which is then used to improve the design of the program, and the cycle continues with the launch and implementation of an improved program.

The information gathered through the program evaluation helps to inform program improvement. Never think that since you have followed all the steps correctly, you will have developed the perfect program. There are always tweaks and improvements to be made making a good program better and more effective.

Process/Formative and Outcome/Summative Evaluation

"Evaluation is a process that determines the impact, effectiveness and efficiency of a program. It reveals what worked – and equally important – what did not work" (O'Neal-McElrath, 2013, p. 56). Program evaluation does not only take place at the end of the program where you look back to determine if you have achieved what you set out to accomplish. If you wait to the end of the program to see whether or not you accomplished what you set out to, you are not in a position to change the outcome, and you have missed opportunities to fine tune the program and your assumptions along the way. Therefore, it is important to assess the program as it is implemented and at the end.

Program evaluation is used to provide information on program performance, monitoring and assessment. To do this, two types of program evaluations are conducted. The *formative* or *process* evaluation, conducted during the program implementation, helps you to gather information for program improvement. The *summative* or *outcome* evaluation, conducted at the end of the program implementation, provides information to help determine whether the program worked the way as planned. Both evaluations provide information to help determine the extent to which the program has achieved the projected success and provide information for sharing the successes and lessons learned from your program.

Evaluating the implementation assesses whether or not the activities were executed as planned. The program's ability to deliver the desired results depends on quality and quantity of the projected outputs. "They tell the story of your program in terms of what happened and why." The outcomes evaluation measures the desired changes that occur in individuals, organizations, communities or systems as a result of the program. The evaluation, when done correctly, generates "answers about the effectiveness of activities in producing changes in magnitude or satisfaction with changes related to the issues central to your program" (W.K. Kellogg Foundation, 2004, p. 36).

When the cook tastes the soup that is formative, when the guests taste the soup that's summative. This statement illustrating the distinction between formative and summative assessment has been attributed to several authors. Regardless of who originally said this, it clearly illustrates the distinction between these two types of assessment. When the cook tastes the soup, before serving it, there is still time to make adjustments. When the soup is served and the guests taste it, the cook determines if it was a success by their reactions to the finished product.

The Evaluation Plan

Developing the evaluation plan does not have to be complicated. The plan requires giving thought to the program evaluation: what will be

	Process/Formative Evaluation	Outcome/Summative Evaluation
Purpose	Provides information improve the program during implementation to monitor progress and make corrections and improvements as needed.	Provides information to determine if the program was effective meeting proposed outcomes and impact, to evaluate the worth and value of program based upon the results achieved.
When	Periodically throughout the implementation phase	Engaged in at the completion of the program. Data is gathered throughout the program, but the evaluation takes place at the end.
Focus	Focuses on activities, outputs and short-term outcomes	Focuses on long-term outcomes and impact

Figure 9.2 Process and outcome evaluation

evaluated? When will the evaluation takes place? Who is responsible for the evaluation? And how will it be reported and used?

> The process alone of thinking through the evaluation design can strengthen the program before it's even implemented. From there, the organization can take the knowledge gained through an actual evaluation and share it with staff and volunteers to improve programs as they are being implemented.
>
> (O'Neal-McElrath, 2013, p. 57)

For social justice program planners and administrators there are two more constituencies in this equation – program participants and the community – who also have a voice using the evaluation to help improve programs.

Figure 9.3 illustrates the steps to develop an evaluation plan. The first question to address is who is responsible for conducting the evaluation. The determination here is whether or not there is someone on staff who has the capacity and the time to oversee the evaluation. When there is no one on staff who can take on this assignment, are the resources available to engage an outside evaluator to oversee the evaluation? When it is determined an outside evaluator is required, be sure to build the cost of the evaluation into the budget for the program.

The next step is to determine when the evaluation will take place. There are two types of evaluations as described above: process or formative and outcome or summative. Therefore, there are two time frames to be factored into the plan. The process evaluation requires intervals during the program implementation to evaluate if the program

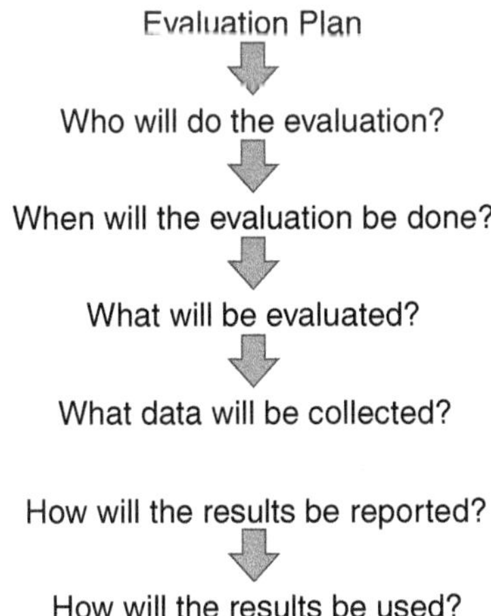

Figure 9.3 Evaluation plan

is on track as planned. This is done at regular intervals such as monthly, every three months or at six months. These time frames are determined by how closely administrators wish to monitor the program. The more closely it is monitored, or the more frequently data is collected, the greater the ability to engage in a process of continuous improvement. However, this evaluation should not be performed before there is significant progress implementing the program, so that data exists to help the decision-making process. The outcome, or summative evaluation, is performed at the end of the program. While data is collected throughout the program, the success in achieving the outcomes is measured at the end.

The logic model serves as the guide to determining what will be evaluated. The process evaluation relies on the activities and outputs to determine if the program is being implemented as planned. To accomplish this level of measurement, the logic model includes measurable benchmarks attached to all activities and outputs. The process evaluation also measures progress to the short-term outcomes. Therefore, in order to determine the outcomes have been achieved, they are written to be specific and measurable (the first two letters of SMART objectives).

The type of data to be collected in the evaluation must also be determined. In a process evaluation the evaluator collects attendance and registration materials as part of the data collected. Pre- and post-tests can be used to determine some of the outcomes as well as interviews with participants to gather additional information. Finally, the evaluation plan includes a statement clarifying how and to whom the data is reported. The worst thing that can happen with a program assessment, besides not doing one, is going through the motions and expense of completing an evaluation and then not using the results to improve or replicate the program.

When considering the data collected during the evaluation and the purpose of this data, there needs to be a determination of the points in time when data is collected:

- Before the program implementation
  - Pretest
  - Provides baseline date
- During the program
  - Monitors progress
  - Provides interim outcomes
- After program completion
  - Post-test
  - Shows change over time
- Follow-up
  - Post program completion
  - Determines long-term benefits (impact)

Now that you have determined what is included in the evaluation, it is time to write up the plan, with the specifics of how and what will be done.

Writing the evaluation plan:

1. Identify evaluation goals
2. Describe the evaluation design
3. Identify what will be measured
4. Describe the data collection plan
    a. Indicators or types of data
    b. Sources of data
    c. Data collection procedures
    d. Timetable
5. Discuss data analysis techniques
6. Specify confidentiality and cultural issues or concerns
7. Responsible party
8. Reporting procedures
9. Proposed evaluation budget

Process or Formative Evaluation

Revisiting the cooking metaphor above, tasting the soup while it is still being prepared allows the cook to adjust the taste, add salt, more garlic or whatever is needed to get the taste right. This is the value of a process evaluation does, helping to determine if the program implementation is on track or adjustments are needed along the way. The process evaluation is done at periodic intervals during program implementation. Utilizing the activities, outputs and short-term outcomes columns of the logic model as a guide, it is designed to measure the extent to which the program is being implemented as designed. The process evaluation is essential to helping obtain a greater understanding of what occurred in the program, providing insight into whether or not expected outcomes have been achieved, and where program adaptations or improvements need to occur (Royse et al., 2001).

The process evaluation focuses on three areas: 1) measuring actual service delivery to planned service delivery, 2) measures the extent to which program implementation is keeping to the established schedule, and 3) determining if the activities are producing the short-term outcomes that are projected. Focusing on the logic model components, including resources, activities, and operations of a program, this type of evaluation provides documentation of how it is functioning. The process evaluation provides information about whether the program is being implemented as intended in the design and planning process, and can help to illuminate programmatic strengths and weaknesses (Rossi et al., 2004).

Curry (2008) developed a series of questions the process or formative evaluation is designed to answer:

- Are necessary program functions being performed adequately?
- Are participants receiving the proper amount, type, and quality of services?
- What are strengths and weaknesses of day-to-day operations?
- How can these processes be improved?
- How do participants experience and perceive the program?
- Are participants satisfied with program personnel and procedures?
- How are staff members trained, and how effective are they?
- Is performance at some program sites or locales significantly better or poorer than at others?
- Are resources, facilities and funding adequate to support program functions?
- Are the objectives of the program being met?

(p. 13)

For example, looking at the OurKids AfterSchool logic model we see one activity is to recruit and hire twenty-five tutors and provide six hours of training. The logic model also tells us the program will provide one-and-a-half hours of tutoring for twenty-five students weekly. By regularly evaluating the progress toward meeting these numbers, the program administrators can tell whether this mark is on track to be met.

Figure 9.4 provides a few examples of how the information for the evaluation is taken directly from the logic model. The evaluation questions and the data collected are in direct response to the activities, outputs and short-term outcomes columns of the logic model. Two examples of how this works follow:

- *Are we serving the number of students projected?* This question is in direct response to information in the activities and outputs columns where the logic model specifies the number and frequency of after-school and summer activities and the outputs projects the number of students to be enrolled and participating. The short-term outcomes column provides specific changes projected in the short-term. The measure here is very specific, 85% of students participating will achieve a one grade improvement in their reading level by the end of the first year and 10% will demonstrate increased self-confidence after one school year. The data to be collected reflects these measures. These include registration materials, number of sessions held, attendance records, and pre- and post-tests as delineated in the program narrative to determine growth in self-esteem and self-confidence. The timelines are based upon the specific data being collected. Attendance records will be collected monthly and the pre- and post-tests

Evaluation Question	Data	Data Collection	Timeline	Person Responsible for Data Collection
Are we providing the proposed activities and serving the number of students projected?	Number of students registered Number of students attending regularly	Registration materials Number of sessions held Attendance sheets Pre and post tests	Monthly Beginning and end of each semester	Group leaders Program Coord. Evaluator
Is the homework help program serving the number of students expected? Are homework helpers feeling confident about their skill level? Are students improving their academic work?	Number of students registered Number of students attending regularly Number of homework helpers recruited Academic improvement Homework helper satisfaction	Registration materials Attendance sheets Number of homework help sessions Teacher responses to questionnaires Student grades Homework helper interviews and group meetings Pre and posttests	Monthly Midterm and end of fall and spring semesters	Program Coord. Homework helpers Evaluator
Are teachers feeling increased self-confidence in OST programming?	OST teacher feedback Teacher training	Pre and post test Number of teachers participating in training Teacher interviews	Beginning and end of fall semester Monthly	Program Coord. Trainer Evaluator
Are parents more engaged in their children's schoolwork?	Parent self-reporting Parent workshops PTA participation Parent advisory board	Parent interviews and surveys. Time spent engaged with children on schoolwork Number of parent workshops. Participation in parent workshops PTA participation	Monthly Beginning of program End of fall semester	Program Coord. Trainer Evaluator

Figure 9.4 Sample outline for a process/formative evaluation plan for OurKids AfterSchool

administered at the beginning and end of each semester to determine individual changes. Finally, the last piece to determine is the responsible person for collecting and interpreting the data. In this case, the group leaders are responsible for collecting attendance data, the program coordinator is responsible for collecting data documenting group frequency and administering the pre- and post-tests. The evaluator is responsible for interpreting the data collected.

- *Is the homework help program serving the number of students expected? Are homework helpers feeling confident about their skill level? Are students improving their academic work?* Looking to the activities, outputs, and the short-term outcomes columns provides the information needed to determine how to evaluate progress. The data suggested by the information in these columns includes the number of students registered for the homework help component and rates of attendance. It also directs us to track the number of homework helpers recruited as volunteers. The outcomes column directs the

> evaluator to collect data on the participants' academic improvement and the confidence levels of the homework helpers. The next step is to determine how this data is to be collected. Data collection methods include: reviewing registration materials, student attendance records and homework helper recruitment numbers; attendance records; classroom teacher reports; student grade levels at the beginning, mid-term and end of the program; interviews with homework helpers; and, pre- and post-tests to determine homework helper confidence. The frequency of data collection will be monthly for attendance records, numbers of sessions; beginning, middle and end of program to determine student grade level improvement; and, interviews with homework helpers midway through the program. The responsible persons are the program coordinator collecting attendance records and reaching out to classroom teachers for feedback, homework helpers collecting attendance records, and the evaluator interviewing and interpreting data.

The key to a usable process evaluation is collecting data that can serve to raise red flags if any projections are not being met and provide the opportunity to change course and make improvements as needed. While this type of evaluation is often overlooked, as a social justice planner it is crucial to be prepared to make mid-course corrections to ensure the program is having the desired impacts on the inequity. Waiting until the end of the intervention or program to find out whether or not mistakes were made along the way is too late to go back and improve the program for participants to receive the best possible support. This is one pillar in a social justice intervention, ensuring the program is actually supporting the needs of the participants.

Outcome or Summative Evaluation

A logic model also provides the basis for an outcome evaluation outlining the relationships between program components and changes in behavior in the program hypothesis, highlighting the gaps between program components, assumptions and outcomes. Often program administrators focus on the outcome evaluation and forgo the process evaluation.

> Conducting an outcome evaluation without examining program operation assumes that the program has been conducted consistently according to design and plan. This can lead to what researchers cite as the "Type III error," or making the spurious conclusion that the program was not effective because it did not achieve the expected outcomes. However, it could be that the program was not implemented with fidelity according to the original design.
>
> (Curry, 2008, p. 11)

Operationalizing outcomes – how to measure and define each outcome – allows the outcomes to be tracked and evaluated. "Each outcome to be tracked needs to be translated into one or more outcome indicators. An outcome indicator identifies a specific *numerical measurement* that indicates progress towards achieving an outcome" (Hatry, 1999, p. 55). When developing indicators, it is important clear language is used. For example, stating there will be significant change is too broad. What is meant by significant? How much is significant? Looking at OurKids AfterSchool, the program is predicting an improvement in student reading scores. However, this outcome has been operationalized in the logic model when it is stated 85% of participants will improve reading skills by at least one grade level by the end of the school year. The operationalization of improved reading scores states by how much, when this occurs and how many students achieve the desired outcome. The logic model does not define how this change is measured. In the case of OurKids AfterSchool this change will be determined through the required MCAS (Massachusetts Comprehensive Assessment System) test administered to all elementary and secondary public school students in Massachusetts. This example demonstrates the four necessary indicators needed to operationalize desired outcomes so they can be measured. These include: 1) defining the amount of change sought, 2) specifying the time period by which this change is expected to be achieved, 3) defining who will achieve the desired outcome, and 4) specifying the method of measurement.

It is necessary for social justice planners to become familiar with the basics of outcome evaluation. There is no social justice if the programs do not improve the lives of people and address the social inequities they face. Therefore, it is imperative to demonstrate these interventions are working, and if they are not, information is gathered to help determine why not and what could be done differently. Without measuring the success or failure meeting desired outcomes, there is no way to determine the program is positively impacting the lives of the people it is intended to support. It is also necessary to demonstrate to funders and to the community that the program is working and it is worthy of continued funding and possible replication.

> The hypothesized relationships between program components and outcomes are often used to guide the development of evaluation tools such as a pre/post-survey. In building a survey, items are included to assess changes in knowledge, attitudes and behaviors thought to influence the outcomes.
>
> (Helitzer et al., 2010, p. 224)

For example, hypothesized mechanisms to increase parent involvement in their child's schoolwork would be to provide information and training through a parent newsletter, parent workshops, a parent advisory board and increased participation in the PTA. An evaluation instrument might include questions assessing whether or not parents spent more time engaged with their children's schoolwork and did this result in improved grades for these children. This can be measured through pre- and post-tests with parents self-reporting time spent engaged with their children's schoolwork before, and after the intervention, attendance records for parent workshops, parent evaluations of workshops, and pre- and post-tests of parental knowledge before and after parent workshop participation.

Yuen and Terao (2003) present a nine-step plan for developing an outcome evaluation:

1. Describe the service activity,
2. Briefly describe the target group,
3. List the activities and what will be accomplished through these,
4. Describe the indicators used to determine/measure progress or changes,
5. Describe the methods and tools to be used to determine change,
6. Define the level of success to be achieved,
7. Determine who will complete measurement instruments and frequency of measures,
8. Describe who will collect and analyze data, and
9. Determine who will write report and how will it be used.

(p. 35)

A well-developed logic model providing a comprehensive overview of the program or intervention contains information addressing the first six of these components. Following are two examples of an objective measurement using information from the OurKids AfterSchool logic model:

1. College student volunteer homework helpers will provide one-on-one homework help for up to twenty-five students, five days per week for one-and-a-half hours each day, with 85% of participants achieving a one grade improvement in their reading level by the end of the school year. This will be measured by results in the MCAS test administered at the end of the school year, compared to participant results from the previous school year. The MCAS test is administered by the Massachusetts Department of Elementary and Secondary Education at the end of each school year. The program evaluator is responsible for collecting and interpreting the data and preparing the report to be presented to school administrators and to the parent advisory board.
2. Up to sixty parents will be recruited to participate in a series of six-week parent workshops. Ten parents will be enrolled in each six-week series. A pre- and post-test will be administered at the beginning and end of each workshop series, with 75% of parents completing the

workshop series self-reporting report a 50% increase in the amount of time spent engaged with their child on schoolwork compared to before participating in the workshop series. The workshop leader is responsible for administering the pre- and post-tests. The data is recorded and analyzed by the program evaluator, who will write a report to be presented to the OurKids AfterSchool supervisor, school administrators and to the parent advisory board.

In addition to evaluating progress achieving outcomes, it is also essential to obtain detailed descriptions of how the program is operating, as well as participants' and stakeholders' perceptions and experiences. Qualitative measures, such as participant satisfaction surveys and exit interviews are helpful in gathering this type of information (Patton, 2002). "Qualitative data (informal interviews, for instance) can be as useful in determining the effectiveness of interventions as quantitative data (scores on standardized tests)" (Karsh & Fox, 2009, p. 198). This qualitative data consisting of input from participants about their experience in the program and their level of satisfaction can be obtained through brief interviews, satisfaction surveys or participant evaluations. It is essential for social justice planners to maintain a focus on the participant experience as well as a focus on progress toward the outcomes.

The most recent study of nonprofits to determine the role of program evaluation in accountability was completed by Hoefer (2000). The study found "while it is of critical importance to conduct program evaluations, this is not a universal truism." Hoefer found a number of reasons for programs not engaging in evaluations. There were 48% who reported they had insufficient funds to evaluate the program. Almost half of the programs surveyed reported not enough staff time available to conduct an evaluation. There were 43% who reported they did not conduct an evaluation because the funder did not require one. One-third responded they did not have the proper knowledge to evaluate their program, and a smaller number (14%) responded they felt no need to evaluate the program. While many social sector organizations are run on very tight budgets, and many programs are underfunded, these realities do not absolve organizations from evaluating their programs. Program evaluation is an integral component of any human services intervention. Therefore, when seeking funding for a new program, costs for an evaluation are built into the budget. These costs can be used to cover a portion of a staff person or to retain a consultant versed in program evaluation.

While Hoefer's study referred to above focused on evaluation for accountability, this is only one purpose for conducting a program intervention. "While human service practice improvement is acknowledged as an important outcome of program evaluation, much evaluation is narrowly focused on accountability requirements. This type of evaluation often has limited use and relevance to human service practitioners"

(Herbert, 2015, p. 438). Evaluation for accountability is too often a numbers game. Did the program serve the number of participants projected? How many participants completed the intervention? How many showed some measurable sign of improvement or change? What was the cost per unit of service? Many of these accountability measures ignore the fact the human services is just that – providing services for human beings. One thing we know about human beings, we are all different in our own way. For example, if we are trying to help parents increase the time spent engaged with their children's schoolwork, and we have set the target as a 50% increase in one year, a parent who increases this time with their child by only 25% may be able to provide more support than another parent who met the target and increased their time by 50%. However, the parent providing less time would not be considered a success in an evaluation done solely for accountability. While funders require accountability, just because you are not being required to evaluate effectiveness or satisfaction is not a reason for ignoring these critical issues.

It is the obligation of social justice planners and administrators to be accountable to the communities and people served. The accountability they deserve is not numbers achieved, but how the program has impacted the lives of participants and the community at large. It is the role of social justice program planners and program administrators to evaluate for effectiveness, even when this is not required. This is how we learn what works and what does not work. Where we can work to improve services and outcomes and areas where we have met the mark. A well performed evaluation can help improve services and tell the story of how success was achieved (if that is the case) so more people can be served, or a successful intervention replicated. When the program evaluation is not used to inform these, then the program is not furthering social justice and equity for the community.

Key terms

Process evaluation
Formative evaluation
Outcome evaluation
Summative evaluation
Evaluation plan
Operationalizing outcomes

Main Ideas

1. Program evaluation is a necessary tool for human services program interventions, providing information to determine if the program is achieving what it was designed to.
2. The program evaluation design is based upon the outputs and outcomes detailed in the program logic model.
3. The evaluation is part of a continuous loop providing information for planning and improvement.

4. The process or formative evaluation is engaged in during program implementation providing information to monitor progress and to inform corrections and program improvements.
5. The outcome or summative evaluation provides information to determine if the program has been effective meeting the projected outcomes.

References

Coelho, P. (2017) @paulocoelho, 12/17/2017

Curry, A.M. (2008) Integrating program process and outcome: A program evaluation using the logic model framework. Unpublished doctoral dissertation. New Brunswick, NJ: Rutgers University, https://www-proquest-com.ezproxy.bu.edu/docview/304403591?pq-origsite=primo, retrieved 6/3/2021

Hatry, H. (1999) *Performance measurement*. Washington, DC: The Urban Institute Press

Helitzer, D., Hollis, C., Urquieta de Hernandez, B., Sanders, M., Roybal, S. & Van Deusen, I. (2010) Evaluation for community-based programs: The integration of logic models and factor analysis. *Evaluation and Program Planning*, August, 33(3), 223–233

Herbert, J.L. (2015) Towards program evaluation for practitioner learning: Human services practitioners' perceptions of evaluation. *Australian Social Work*, 68(4), 438–452

Hoefer, R. (2000) Accountability in action? Program evaluation in nonprofit human service agencies. *Nonprofit Management and Leadership*, Winter, 11(2), 167–177

Karsh, E. & Fox, A.S. (2009) *The only grantwriting book you'll ever need, 3rd ed.* Philadelphia, PA: Basic Books

McDavid, J.C., Huse, I., Hawthorne, L.R.L. (2019) *Program evaluation and performance measurement, 3rd ed.* Los Angeles, CA: SAGE Publications

O'Neal-McElrath, T. (2013) *Winning grants step by step*. San Francisco, CA: John Wiley & Sons

Patton, M.Q. (2002). *Qualitative research and evaluation methods, 3rd ed.* Thousand Oaks, CA: Sage Publications

Rossi, P. H., Lipsey, M.W. & Freeman, H.E. (2004) *Evaluation: A systematic approach, 7th ed.* Thousand Oaks, CA: Sage Publications

Royse, D., Thyer, B.A., Padgett, D. K. & Logan, T. K. (2001) *Program evaluation: An introduction, 3rd ed.* Belmont, CA: Brooks/Cole Thomson Learning

W.K. Kellogg Foundation, (2004) Logic model development guide, https://www.wkkf.org/resource-directory/resources/2004/01/logic-model-development-guide, retrieved 5/30/21

Yuen, F.K.O. & Terao, K.L. (2003) *Practical grant writing and program evaluation*. Pacific Grove, CA: Thomson Brooks Cole

Index

Note: **Bold** page numbers refer to tables; *italic* page numbers refer to figures and page numbers followed by "n" denote endnotes.

For Product Safety Concerns and Information please contact our EU representative GPSR@taylorandfrancis.com
Taylor & Francis Verlag GmbH, Kaufingerstraße 24, 80331 München, Germany

www.ingramcontent.com/pod-product-compliance
Lightning Source LLC
Chambersburg PA
CBHW050226280425
25805CB00012B/1411

* 9 7 8 0 3 6 7 7 0 9 7 6 1 *